BUILDING CONSTRUCTION DRAWING

Richard B. Eaton

BUILDING CONSTRUCTION DRAWING

Richard B. Eaton

With an introduction by Jonathan David,
Norman England and John Keenan

DONHEAD

Parts I and II first published in 1914 by E. & F.N. Spon, London and New York
Part III first published in 1917 by E. & F.N. Spon, London and New York
Parts IV and V first published in 1919 by E. & F.N. Spon, London and New York
Part VI first published in 1921 by E. & F.N. Spon, London and New York

Donhead Publishing Ltd
Lower Coombe
Donhead St Mary
Shaftesbury
Dorset SP7 9LY
Tel. 01747 828422
www.donhead.com

ISBN 1 873394 71 3

A CIP catalogue for this book is available from the British Library

Printed in Great Britain by Cromwell Press, Trowbridge

Introduction to the 2004 edition

Published early in the twentieth century, Eaton's book *Building Construction Drawing* was unusual in being prepared for a course for artisans or apprentices. No other publication took his practical approach in providing working drawings, and all were for the technologist rather than the craftsman – even 50 years on McKay and others presented composite drawings, but without specifications and measurements.

Textbooks for students of building construction were first published for architects and engineers, to complement the pattern books for landowners; then in the 1890s came Rivington's series. This was published by Longmans, and written for students at the West Kensington Polytechnic. Four volumes covered a full course (the first three volumes have been reprinted by Donhead). The author was unacknowledged but recent research has shown him to have been Major Percy Smith from the School of Military Engineering at Chatham. Rivingtons was the original publisher.

This was soon followed by 'Mitchell', published by Batsford, for students at the Regent Street Polytechnic. In two volumes it covered the whole of the building technology course. The author was a lecturer at the educational establishment and wrote the books from his course notes to provide their professional trainees with the detail needed for their studies; the level of detail was probably too great for the artisans for whom Eaton was writing. Later came by works by McKay and others which provided more comprehensive drawings.

In his introduction to the recent Donhead reprint of *Rivington's Building Construction*, Lawrance Hurst notes that: 'In pre-Victorian times there were craftsmen main contractors who employed craftsmen sub-contractors for the other trades'. Although this was still the situation when Eaton was writing, within 30 years it had changed radically.

Prior to Eaton, one of the most important folios of working drawings, published in the 1870s, was Busbridge's Portfolio of *Thirty lithographed working drawings of the most important details of building construction*. It contained working drawings but there were no specifications. This practice soon established itself in journals and subsequent compilations of working drawings in book form, the *Architects' Journal* and *Illustrated Carpenter and Builder* being two such publications. They often included notes, but rarely any specifications. The Architectural Press was producing *Specification* by 1903, so the architect was well equipped, but it was not intended for the less educated artisan or apprentice.

Between 1914 and 1921, Eaton's 'Class-book for the elementary student and artisan' was one of the essential texts offering an appropriate level of knowledge for the craftsmen sub-contractors. They all knew what was required by way of detail, but there were few publications providing working drawings, and these were mostly drawings relating to larger engineered construction rather than everyday domestic projects.

It is often bemoaned that modern house builders build identical houses everywhere, differentiating them only by 'stuck on' decoration or a different colour brick. However, this practice pre-dates the major building contractors. Until the middle of the twentieth century the majority of houses were built from 'pattern books', of which there were many. Materials would be local and there would probably be some interpretation by the builder to suit local conditions.

It was volumes such as Eaton's *Building Construction Drawing* which provided many of the 'standard' details that the craftsman would use to supplement the pattern book design.

However, while at first it appears that this book is timeless, in fact the simplicity of its approach makes it very much a product of its time. Before the 1902 Education Act, most apprentices were not sent to secondary school and learnt their skills at work; there were few technical schools of the type where the author taught until 1910. The Technical Instruction Act of 1889 required local authorities to establish Boards and facilities for training in technical subjects.

By the 1930s the larger contractors were building standard house types which incorporated standardized joinery products (often imported), and the range of skills expected of the reader of this book was no longer in demand.

What is reprinted here as one volume appeared originally in six parts written in parallel to the new course as it expanded from elementary to advanced. It appears that after the final part appeared, the volume used to produce this reprint was specially bound by or for the author.

Eaton increased the amount of detail involved as the student proceeded through the course year by year, so that by the end the student was able to undertake a whole building project.

The first Part contained what the author described as 'work which the ordinary student will meet day by day'. Part I contains ten sections consisting of one to four pages of drawings but in most cases only half a page of specification. The drawings are mostly to scale, scales varying between one 48th and one quarter. The only 'textbook' material is the section on the bonding of brickwork.

The next part included more advanced work – bay and dormer windows, staircases and porches, including some quite 'up market' designs – and the final design, for an elaborate staircase, occupies eight pages.

With Part III Eaton changed his approach to a whole-project composite set of drawings and specifications, referring back to the previous Parts.

Parts IV and V appeared with the subtitle 'Joinery Drawings, Specifications and Measurements'. The examples were more extensive and detailed and introduced the 'taking off' of materials.

The final Part again provided more advanced examples, with the specifications on the left facing the drawings.

Richard Barnes Eaton was born in 1864 and attended the British School in Poole. He trained as a joiner and in 1901 joined Poole Borough Council as a Clerk of Works. He retired in 1924 as an assistant Borough Engineer and died in 1946. He and his family appear to have lived in Poole all his life.

He joined the part time teaching staff at Poole School of Art and Technology, teaching building construction. His philosophy was to pass on his expertise to his pupils in a way that could be understood by all members of the building team – by using specifications and drawings for each project, rather than descriptive text.

Even after the foundation of technical schools such as that at Poole, many apprentices were following in the paths of their fathers and were more likely to be selected for their skills rather than their academic achievements. The training was therefore designed to be familiar to them, using the documents they found in their workplace.

Eaton's volumes received good reviews as they appeared. The author's own copy, used for this reprint and held in the CIRCA Trust's (Construction Industry Resource Centre Archive) archives, includes pasted into the front and endpapers various reviews by the technical press of the day (including *Architects' Journal, Illustrated Carpenter and Builder, The Surveyor* and *The Librarian*; a report and photograph from a local paper on the occasion of Eaton's retirement; letters from London County Council and Derby College on their listing of these books; a design, apparently by Eaton, for a rising pivot for doors to open over carpets; and various other documents linked to the author. Some of these are reproduced at the end of this publication.

It might be argued that the practices described in these pages are obsolete. True, the modern housebuilder would have little call for a craftsman trained by Eaton. However, even though they are in imperial units, the details and specifications are as useful today as when they were written.

Eaton's drawings and specifications fall happily between the specific detailing of the early and late Victorian periods found in Rivington and Mitchell respectively, and the more general approach and influence of the Arts and Crafts movement of McKay in the 1930s. The drawings and specifications can still be used to provide authentic joinery even if required to incorporate energy efficient glazing. The details are relevant to the maintenance of most domestic and much commercial property built between 1900 and 1939, though not perhaps for the period after 1945. The end of this practice is confirmed in a memo found in the CIRCA Trust archive in which Godfrey Way Mitchell, chairman of George Wimpey, wrote in 1943 that the end of war would bring a new style of architecture which would involve economic use of scarce labour and materials, a greater level of factory production and more use of the new materials of concrete and steel.

The reprinting of this work in one volume will provide designers and craftsmen with a unique library of details offering a valuable complement to the better known publications of the nineteenth and early twentieth centuries.

Jonathan David
Trustee of the CIRCA Trust and technical journalist

Norman England
Trustee of the CIRCA Trust and architectural ironmongery consultant

John Keenan
Curator to the CIRCA Trust, retired chartered builder

The CIRCA Trust (Construction Industry Resource Centre Archive) was founded to create an archive to serve the construction industry. At a time when many organizations are disposing of their technical libraries, but there is increased interest in building conservation and repair of traditional buildings, the information and expertise is being lost to the profession. Books are not the greatest problem, as in most cases copies can be found in the British Library.

However, there is regular demand for information about how buildings were constructed, covering the standards, techniques, materials and products.

The CIRCA Trust's archive contains a great many publications in all these categories: standards, technical documents from trade and professional associations, journals and magazines (including their advertisements which can be crucial in dating changes to product specifications), reports and technical advice from government departments and organizations such as the Building Research Station/Establishment – the list is almost endless.

The Trust is run by volunteers and has no guaranteed income. Its archive is housed in a listed former flour mill in Stroud which, although appropriate, requires constant dehumidification and considerable maintenance and improvement. Much of the collection has arrived in less than pristine condition, and often needs conservation to a greater or lesser degree. Members and Friends help to provide income, as do search fees. In addition, the mill is used as a base by several local societies with an interest in building conservation and local history.

The archives are used by many people: construction history experts; lawyers and expert witnesses seeking information on building failures; television companies seeking material for programmes; individuals and architectural and engineering practices seeking information needed to carry out appropriate repairs and maintenance to buildings; conservation and building control officers; students of construction and industrial archaeology. They may need design information, but often what is needed is the exact specification used on a particular date. This is where the collections of standards, technical literature and magazines that are unique in the UK really come into their own.

The CIRCA Trust can be contacted at:
Kimmins Mill
Meadow Lane
Dudbridge
Stroud GL5 5JP
UK

BUILDING CONSTRUCTION DRAWING

A CLASS-BOOK FOR THE ELEMENTARY STUDENT AND ARTISAN

BY

RICHARD B. EATON
LECTURER ON BUILDING CONSTRUCTION

IN SIX PARTS

Comprising over 400 pages of Specifications of Details
of Building Construction and Joinery Work. With
157 Full-paged Dimensioned Drawings

London

E. & F. N. SPON, LTD., 57 HAYMARKET, S.W. 1

1921

PART I

CONTENTS

PART II

CONTENTS

PART III
CONTENTS

PART IV

CONTENTS

xiv

PART V

CONTENTS

BUILDING CONSTRUCTION DRAWING

PART VI
CONTENTS

BUILDING CONSTRUCTION DRAWING

A CLASS-BOOK FOR THE ELEMENTARY STUDENT AND ARTISAN

BY

RICHARD B. EATON

LECTURER ON BUILDING CONSTRUCTION, POOLE SCHOOL OF
ART AND TECHNOLOGY

Part I

26 PLATES

London

E. & F. N. SPON, LTD., 57 HAYMARKET

New York

SPON & CHAMBERLAIN, 123 LIBERTY STREET

1914

PREFACE

THE object of this work is to provide the Building Construction student and those connected with the Building Trade with a graduated set of drawings which will help them to acquire a knowledge of drawing and also of the simpler forms of Building Construction.

The drawings are chiefly those of work which the ordinary student will meet day by day.

Short specifications have been appended to many of the drawings. The practical utility of the association of a specification with its corresponding drawing at the outset of a student's training will be recognized at once.

As a Building Construction teacher, I feel that in compiling this series of drawings I am meeting a long-felt need. I have endeavoured to make the drawings as clear and practical as possible, and hope many students will profit by the use of them.

A second series of drawings dealing with more advanced work will be issued shortly.

RICHARD B. EATON.

POOLE, *January* 7, 1914.

SPECIFICATION

BRICKWORK

THE brickwork throughout to be executed with hard, well-burnt bricks of approved quality.

The facings to be of the best red brick of an approved manufacture.

All mortar shall be composed of one part of Portland cement or grey stone lime, as the case may be, and two parts of clean sharp sand.

The brickwork, where possible, to be executed in English bond; all other, stretcher bond. The hollow work to be built in stretcher bond and to have 2″ to 3″ cavity (as the case may be), bonded together with galvanized wrought-iron wall ties placed 3′ 0″ apart horizontally and 12″ vertically, with additional ties around door and window openings.

The brickwork to be built on proper footing courses and to rise not more than four courses to the foot.

The outside face of brickwork to have joints raked out and pointed down at finish with a neat weather struck-joint. The inside face to be left rough for plastering.

Turn fair axed segmental arches over door and window openings. See Plate No. 15.

Turn relieving arches over door and window openings.

Build in 4-lb. lead trays over door and window openings, to be 9″ longer than opening. See Plate No. 15.

Bed and point all window and door frames in hair mortar.

Do all beam-filling to roofs. See Plate No. 10.

The chimneys above the roof to be built in cement mortar.

Build 4½″ or 9″ sleeper and fender walls in cement mortar. See Plate No. 5.

The damp course to be of two courses of slate bedded and pointed in cement with lapped joints. See Plate No. 5.

Brickwork.

Plate 1

English Bond

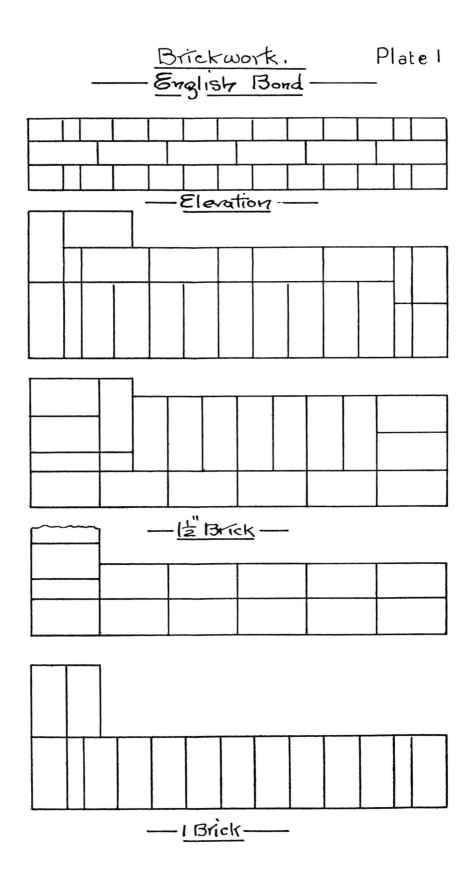

— Elevation —

— 1½" Brick —

— 1 Brick —

Brickwork.   Plate 2.

Double Flemish Bond

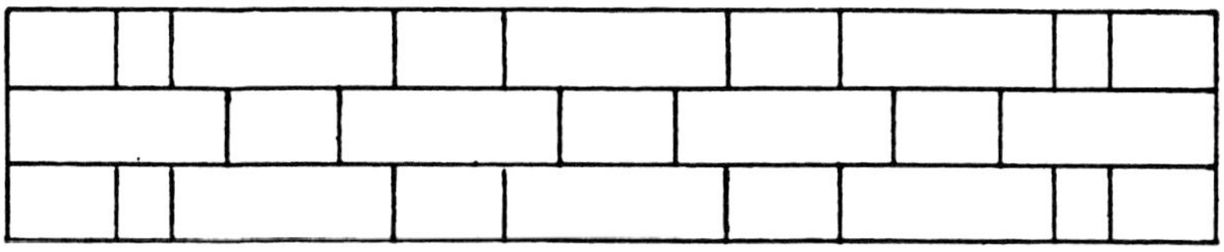

Elevation

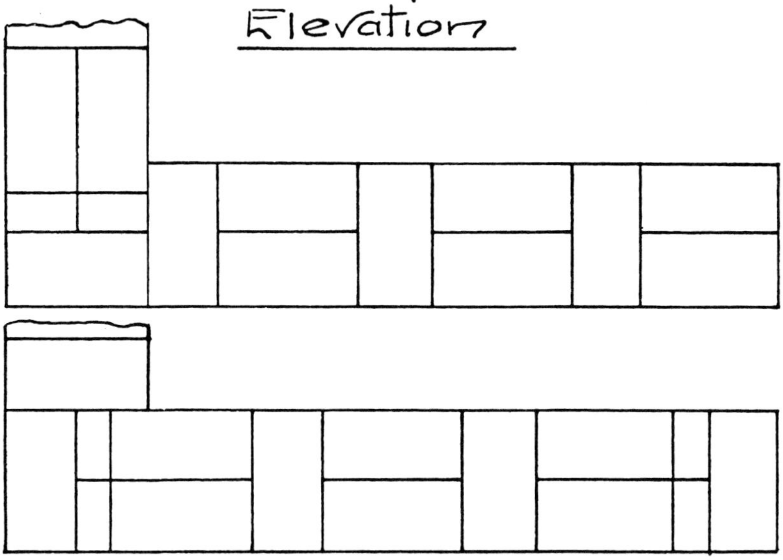

1 Brick

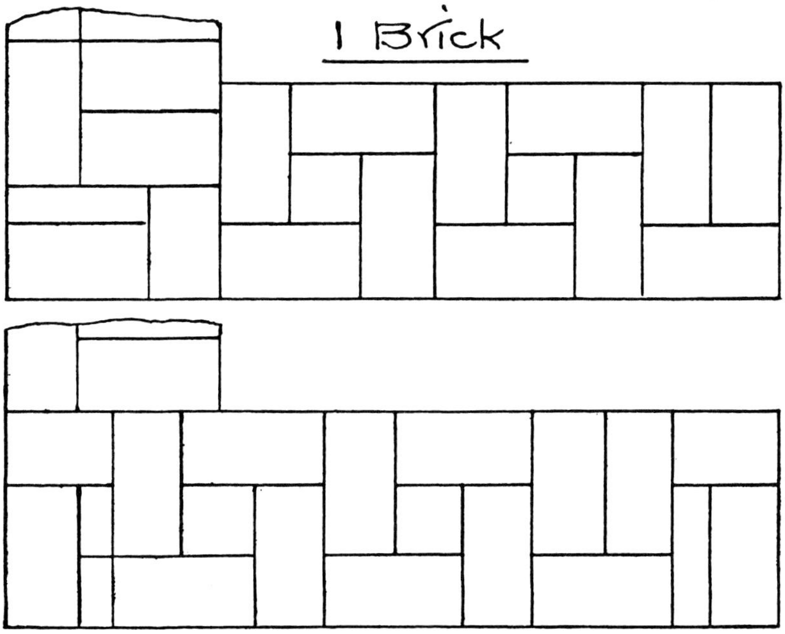

1½ Brick

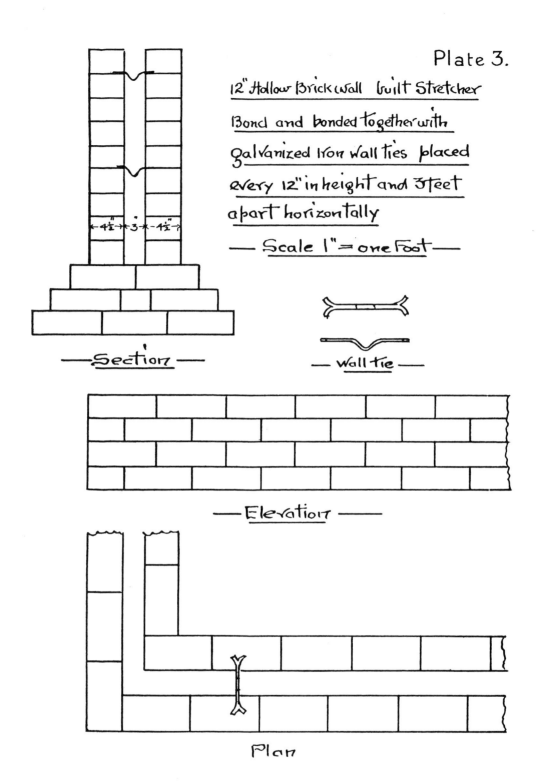

Plate 3.

12" Hollow Brickwall built Stretcher Bond and bonded together with galvanized Iron wall ties placed every 12" in height and 3 feet apart horizontally

— Scale 1" = one Foot —

— Section —

— Wall tie —

— Elevation —

Plan

4½" 3" 4½"

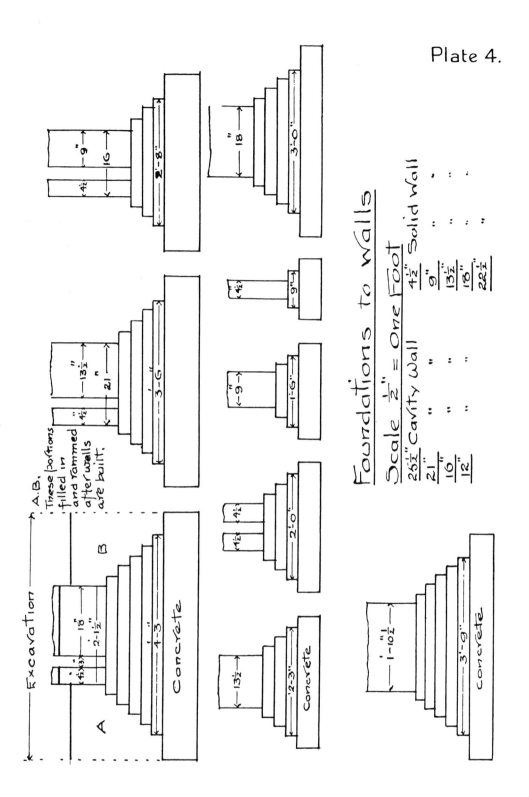

Plate 4.

Foundations to Walls

Scale $\frac{1}{2}$" = One Foot

25½" Cavity Wall   4½" Solid Wall

21"	9"
16"	13½"
12"	18"
	22½"

A.B.

These bottoms filled in and rammed after walls are built.

Excavation

B

A

Concrete

Concrete

Concrete

Concrete

5

SPECIFICATION

GROUND FLOOR

EXCAVATE to the depth shown, and put cement concrete bed 4″ thick under floor. The concrete to be composed of four parts of clean gravel, two parts clean, sharp, washed sand, and one part of Portland cement, to be turned twice dry and twice wet on proper stages provided by the contractor.

The sleeper and fender walls to be half-brick thick on one course of footings built in cement mortar.

Put damp-proof course of two courses of slate bedded in cement with joints lapped.

Plates and joists to be 4″ × 2″; flooring 6″ × 1″, best red, with splayed heading joints properly cramped up and nailed with $2\frac{1}{2}$″ floorbrads and cleaned off flush at finish.

Fill in hearth space with dry brick rubble; on the top of this put 4″ cement concrete with $\frac{3}{4}$″ floated cement face, and lay 3″ × 3″ encaustic tiles square pattern, with border tiles 2″ wide to match, laid and grouted in cement, and cleaned off at finish.

The plates, joists, and underside of floorboard to have one coat of creosote before fixing.

Plate 5.

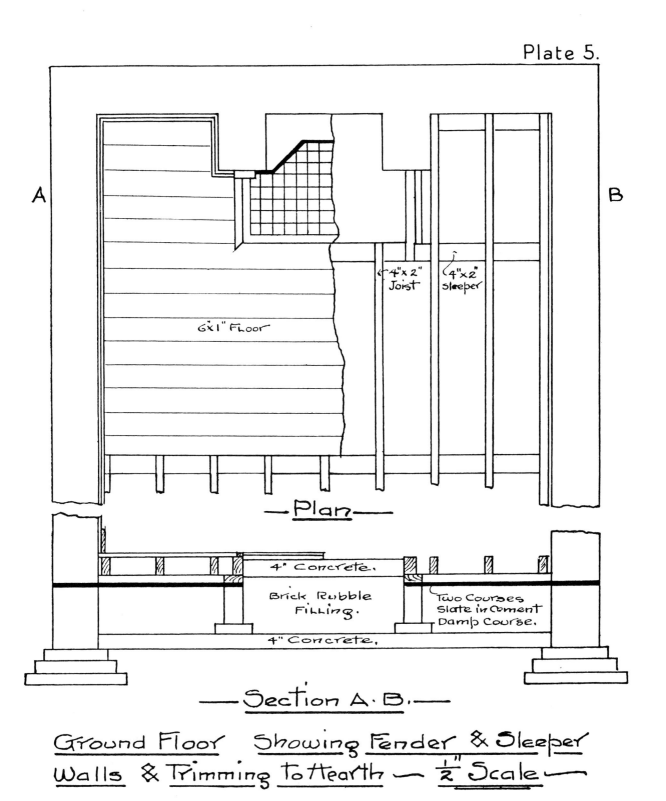

A | B

4"x 2" Joist

4"x 2" sleeper

6"x1" Floor

— Plan —

4" Concrete.

Brick Rubble Filling.

Two Courses Slate in Cement Damp Course.

4" Concrete.

— Section A. B. —

Ground Floor Showing Fender & Sleeper Walls & Trimming to Hearth — $\frac{1}{2}$" Scale —

7

SPECIFICATION

First Floor

WALL plates to be $4\frac{1}{2}''\times 3''$ bedded in lime mortar.

Ordinary joists $2''\times 9''$, trimmer joists $3''\times 9''$, all properly framed and spiked together. The short trimmer joist to have long tenons morticed for wedge and wedged up tight to shoulder. The joints to be as shown on drawing.

Put two rows of $2''\times 1\frac{1}{2}''$ herring-bone struts with blocking pieces between joist and wall at ends.

The floor to be $6''\times 1''$, best red deal, with splayed heading joints properly cramped up and nailed with $2\frac{1}{2}''$ floorbrads and cleaned off flush at finish.

Turn half-brick trimmer arch set in cement mortar to hearth and fill in above with cement concrete to the requisite level. Float the face of concrete in cement $\frac{3}{4}''$ thick and lay tile hearth with $3''\times 3''$ encaustic tiles in cement grouted in and cleaned off at finish.

Floors ~ Detail of Trimming To Fireplace. Plate 6.
½" Scale.

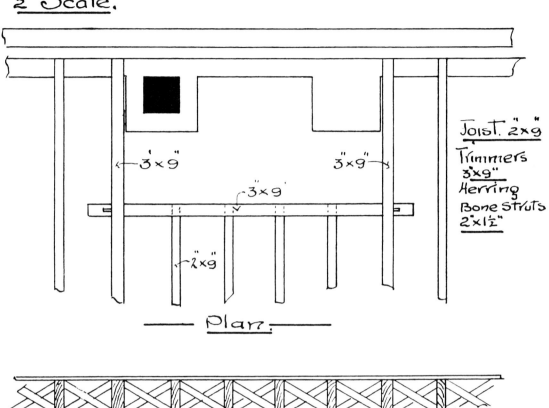

Joist. 2"x9"
Trimmers 3"x9"
Herring Bone Struts 2"x1½"

3"x9"   3"x9"

3"x9"

2"x9"

——— Plan. ———

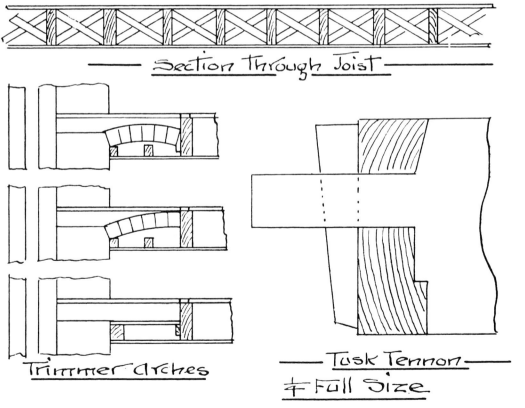

——— Section Through Joist ———

Trimmer Arches

——— Tusk Tennon ———
¼ Full Size

Plate 7

Brick & Tile Floors. — $\frac{3}{4}$" Scale,—
on 4" Concrete Bed, Laid & grouted in Cement

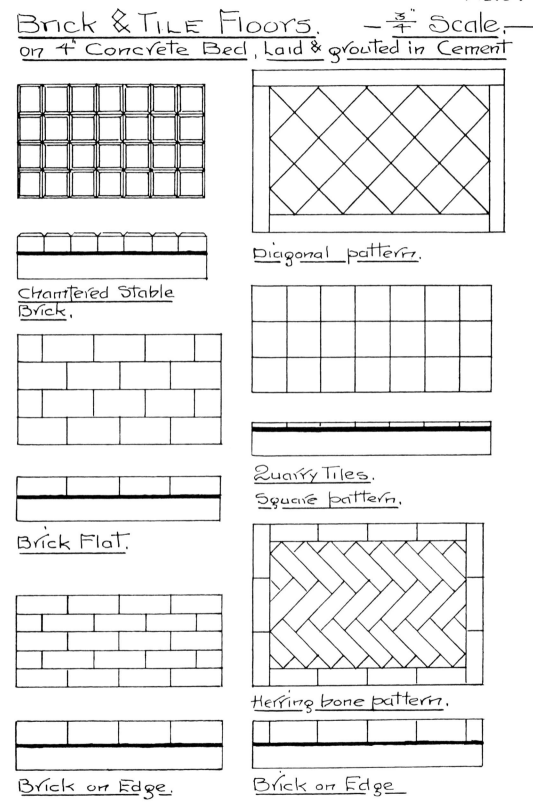

Chamfered Stable Brick.

Diagonal pattern.

Brick Flat.

Quarry Tiles.
Square pattern.

Brick on Edge.

Herring bone pattern.

Brick on Edge

SPECIFICATION

TIMBER

THE timber to be good and approved quality Baltic red fir, free from sap, shakes, large, loose, or decayed knots and other defects.

The joinery to be made from the best selected Christiania deals, or deals of equal quality.

ROOF

The sizes of timber for roof to be as follows: Plates $4\frac{1}{2}'' \times 3''$, ceiling joists $4'' \times 2''$, ties $4\frac{1}{2}'' \times 3''$, rafters $4'' \times 2''$, ridge $8'' \times 1''$, purlins $5'' \times 4''$, struts $5'' \times 3''$, all framed and spiked together; no rafters to be more than $12''$ apart; trimmer rafters to be $1''$ thicker than ordinary rafters; fascia board $1'' \times 7''$, eaves board $1'' \times 6''$. Cover the roof with $5'' \times \frac{3}{4}''$ rough boarding, and on this lay approved sarking felt in horizontal courses lapped $3''$. Put $1'' \times \frac{1}{4}''$ sawn strips on felt over rafters as counter battens; slating battens to be $2'' \times \frac{3}{4}''$. Provide all requisite tilting fillets.

The roof to be covered with best Bangor purple Countess slates laid to a $3''$ lap. The horizontal and vertical joints to be true to line and nailed with compo nails.

Do all requisite cutting to hips, valleys, verges, and ridge.

Put to ridge plain crested ridge tile bedded and pointed in cement.

Provide and fix to eaves $5''$ ogee cast-iron eaves gutter-jointed with red lead and fixed with galvanized bolts and screws. Provide the requisite angles, stopped ends, and outlets.

Provide and fix strong $2\frac{1}{2}''$ cast-iron rain-water pipes jointed with red lead and fixed with galvanized rose-head nails, to have all requisite swan necks and shoes.

The eaves gutters to have two coats of approved oxide paint before being fixed.

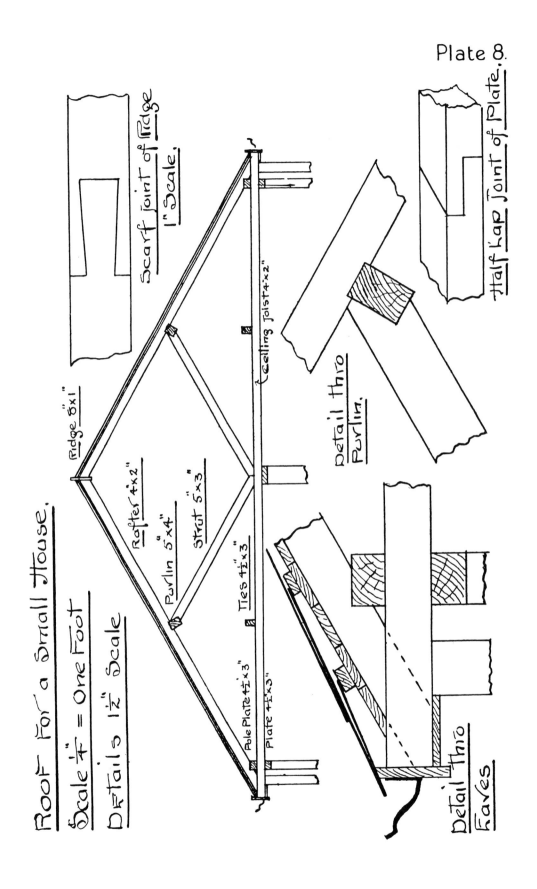

Plate 8.

Scarf Joint of Ridge
1" Scale.

Half Lap Joint of Plate.

Roof for a Small House.
Scale 1/4" = One Foot
Details 1½" Scale

Ridge 5x1"
Rafter 4"x2"
Purlin 5"x4"
Strut 5"x3"
Ceiling Joist 4"x2"
Ties 4½"x3"
Pole Plate 4½"x3"
Plate 4½"x3"

Detail thro
Purlin.

Detail thro
Eaves.

12

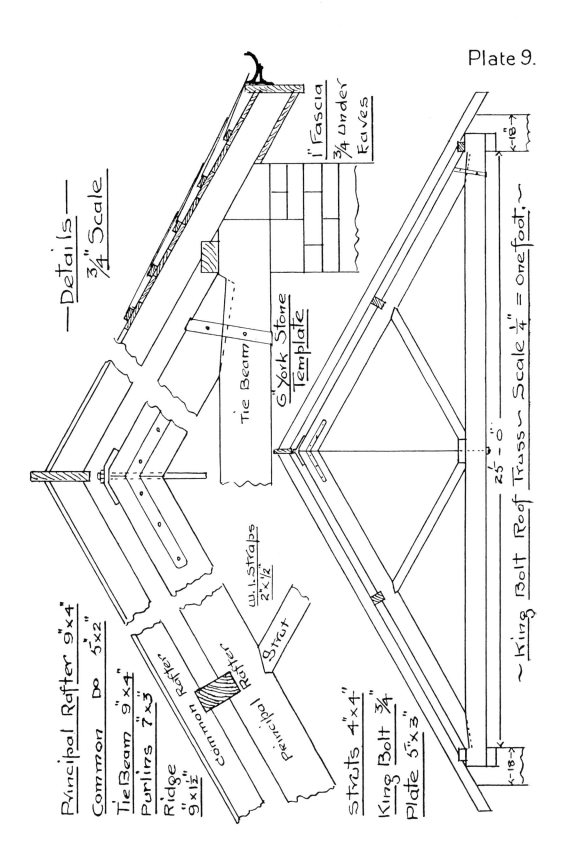

Plate 9.

— Details —
3/4" Scale

1" Fascia
3/4 Under
Eaves

6" York Stone
Template

Tie Beam

W.I. Straps
2"×1/2"

Strut

Common Rafter

Principal Rafter

Principal Rafter 9"×4"
Common Do 5"×2"
Tie Beam 9"×4"
Purlins 7"×3"
Ridge 9"×1½"

Struts 4"×4"
King Bolt 3/4"
Plate 5"×3"

25'-0"

←18"→

←18"→

— King Bolt Roof Truss — Scale 1/4" = one foot. —

13

Details of Eaves
1" Scale

Plate 10.

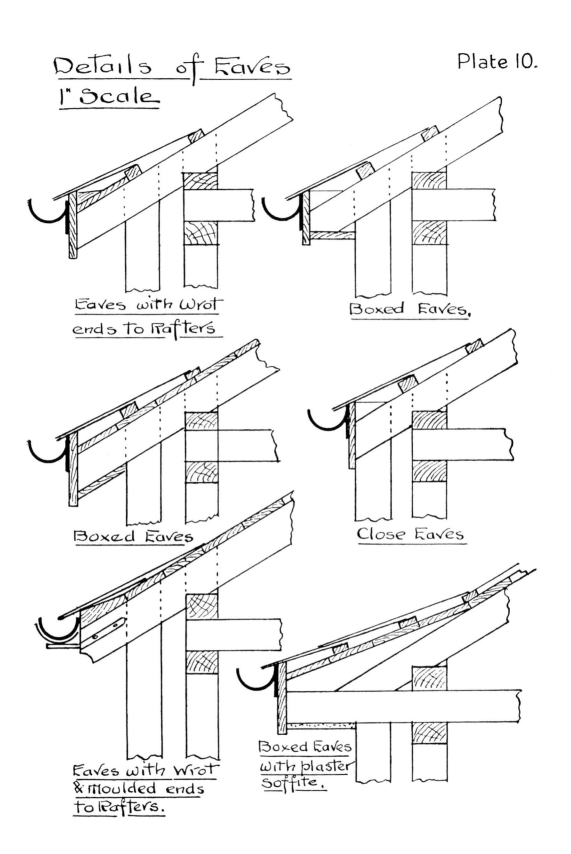

Eaves with Wrot ends to Rafters

Boxed Eaves.

Boxed Eaves

Close Eaves

Eaves with Wrot & moulded ends to Rafters.

Boxed Eaves with plaster Soffite.

SPECIFICATION

ENTRANCE DOORWAY

THE entrance door-jambs to be 5″ × 4″, with 6″ × 5″ head, wrot, rebated, and rounded, grooved for linings and dowelled to step with ¾″ iron dowels. The sidelight to have 11½″ × 3″ wrot, rebated, weathered, throated, and grooved cill; 2″ ovolo-moulded sash with 1⅛″ bars.

The door to be 2″ framed and ovolo-moulded on solid, the bottom part in six small panels, top with marginal bars and segmental head prepared for glass. Put on rail of door 2½″ × 2¼″ bevelled moulding with returned ends, the rail of door to be bevel-rebated to receive same. The window board to sidelight to be 1¼″ thick tongued to frame, and with rounded and returned nosing. Linings to be 1″ thick, tongued to frame.

Put 3″ × 1″ plain architraves around jambs. The door to be hung with 4″ bright steel butts and fitted with two-bolt mortice lock and strong brass furniture.

Glaze the door and sidelight with best arctic glass properly bedded, sprigged, and back-puttied.

The steps to be 12″ × 6″ finely tooled Purbeck stone, 6″ longer than opening.

For Brickwork, see Specification of Brickwork.

Plate II.

Entrance Doorway ~ $\frac{3}{4}$" Scale ~

Elevation

Section

Plan

16

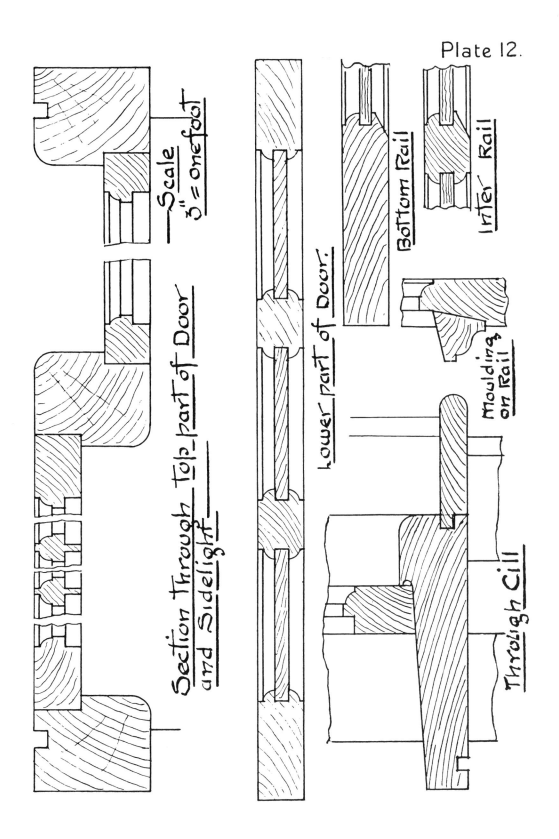

Plate 12.

Scale
3" = one foot

Section through Top part of Door
and Sidelight

Lower part of Door.

Bottom Rail

Inter Rail

Moulding
on Rail

Through Cill

17

Plate 13

Section through Front Wall of Cottage

12" Hollow Walls, Outside Face Finished with Rough Cast.

½" Scale

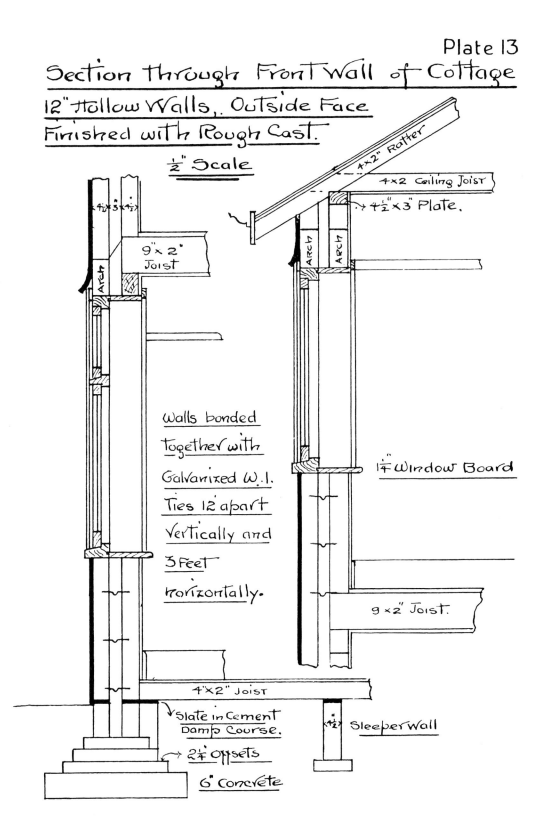

4½"×3"×4½"

4×2" Rafter

4×2 Ceiling Joist

4½"×3" Plate.

Arch

Arch

Arch

9"×2" Joist

Arch

1¼" Window Board

Walls bonded
together with
Galvanized W.I.
Ties 12" apart
Vertically and
3 feet
horizontally.

9×2" Joist.

4"×2" Joist

Slate in Cement
Damp Course.

2¼" Offsets

4½" Sleeper Wall

6" Concrete

Plate 14.

Details of Sash Frame
1½" Scale.

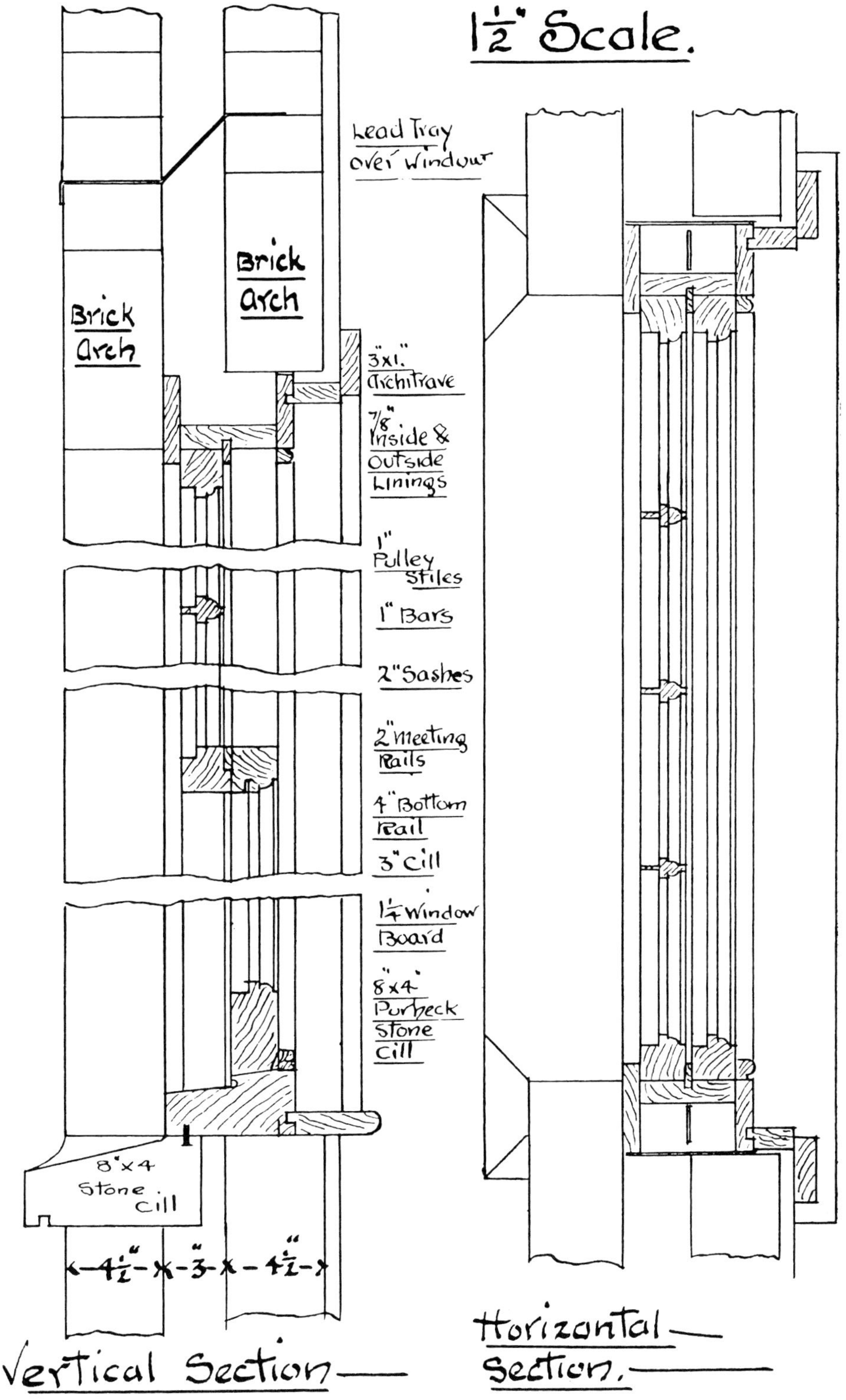

Lead Tray over Window

Brick Arch

Brick Arch

Brick Arch

3"x1." Architrave

7/8" Inside & Outside Linings

1" Pulley Stiles

1" Bars

2" Sashes

2" Meeting Rails

4" Bottom Rail

3" Cill

1¼" Window Board

8"x4" Purbeck Stone Cill

8"x4" Stone Cill

$\leftarrow 4\frac{1}{2}" \rightarrow \times \rightarrow 3" \times \rightarrow 4\frac{1}{2}" \rightarrow$

Vertical Section

Horizontal Section.

SPECIFICATION

Windows

PROVIDE and fix to window openings deal cased frames with $6\frac{1}{2}'' \times 3''$ weathered, throated, and grooved cills, $1''$ pulley stiles grooved for parting bead and tongued to linings, $\frac{3}{4}''$ outside linings, $\frac{7}{8}''$ inside linings grooved for pulley stiles, $\frac{3}{8}''$ parting bead, $\frac{3}{4}''$ stopbead, $1\frac{1}{2}''$ bottom bead tongued to cill, $\frac{1}{4}''$ back and division linings; axle pulleys to be $1\frac{3}{4}''$, with brass face and wheel, of an approved make; sashes $2''$ ovolo-moulded, with $1\frac{1}{8}''$ bars in top sash and with moulded horns. Sashes to be hung with best flax cord and cast-iron weights, and to have approved brass sash fastener.

Window boards to be $1\frac{1}{4}''$ thick, with rounded nosing and returned ends and tongued to frame, $1''$ linings tongued to frames, and $3'' \times 1''$ plain architraves with heads framed to uprights.

Glaze the sashes with best 21 oz. British sheet glass properly bedded, sprigged, and back-puttied.

Provide and fix $8\frac{1}{2}'' \times 4''$ Purbeck stone cill, finely tooled, weathered, and throated, and grooved for water bar and with stooled ends.

Provide $1'' \times \frac{1}{4}''$ galvanized water bar and bed frame in white lead on stone cill.

For Brickwork, see Specification of Brickwork.

Detail of Window ¾" Scale. Plate 15.

Elevation.

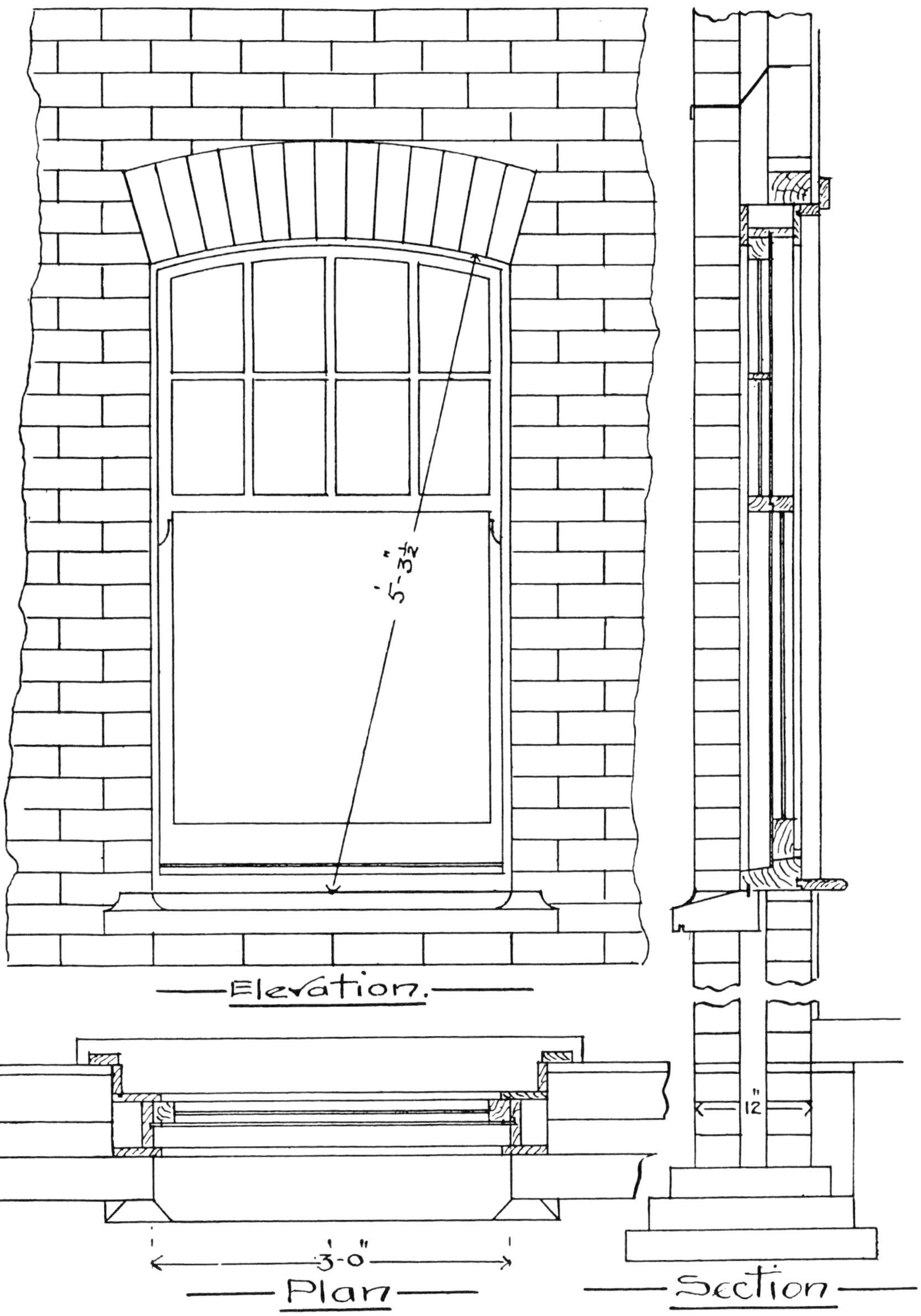

5'-3½"

Plan

3'-0"

Section

12"

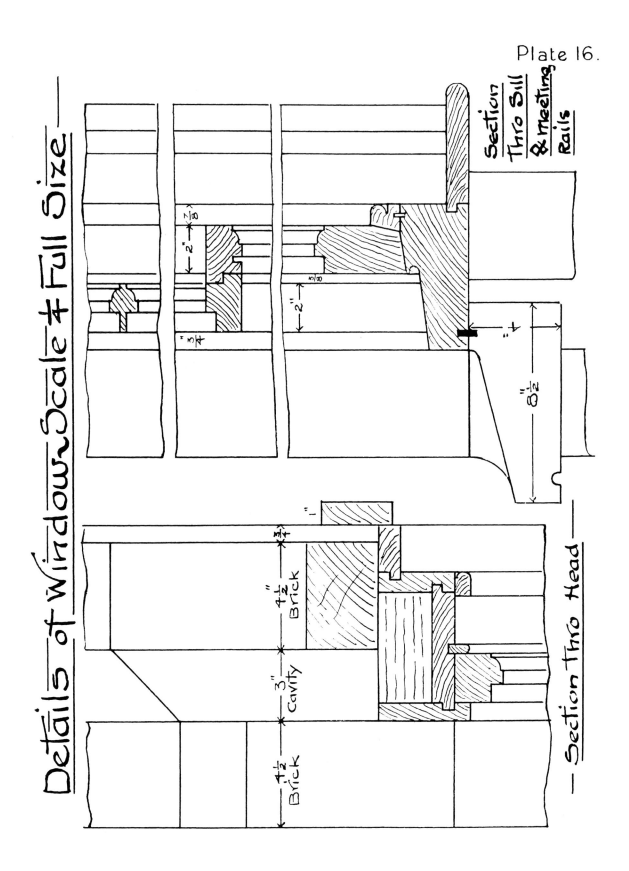

Plate 16.

Details of Windows—Scale ¾ Full Size—

Section Thro Sill & meeting Rails

— Section thro Head —

22

Details of Window

Scale ¼ Full Size

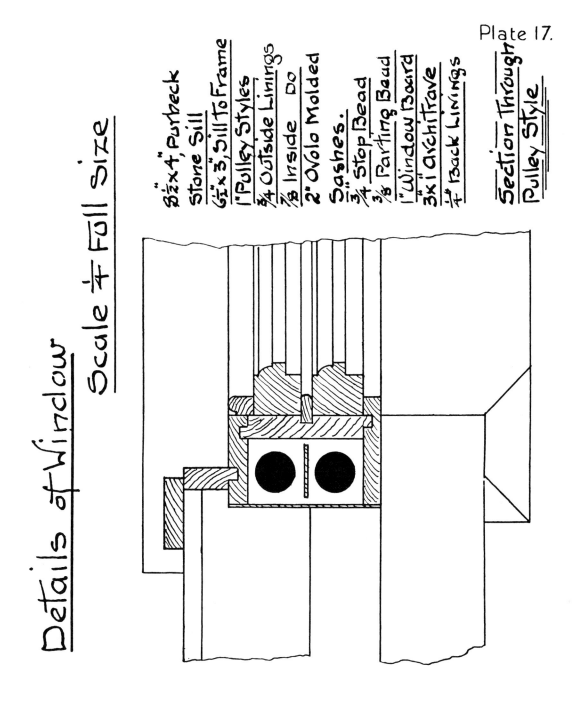

Plate 17.

8½"x4" Purbeck Stone Sill
6½"x3", Sill to Frame
1" Pulley Styles
¾" Outside Linings
⅞" Inside   Do
2" Ovolo Molded

Sashes.
¾" Stop Bead
⅜" Parting Bead
1" Window Board
3"x1" Architrave
¼" Back Linings

Section Through
Pulley Style

SPECIFICATION

WINDOWS

THE stone dressings around windows to be of Bath stone from an approved quarry, and finished with a finely dragged face. The cills to be $8\frac{1}{2}'' \times 6''$, grooved, weathered, throated, and stooled. Jambs $4\frac{1}{2}''$ thick, with moulded edge and bonded as drawing. Heads $12'' \times 4\frac{1}{2}''$, with moulded edge. Label $6\frac{1}{2}'' \times 3''$, moulded, and with returned ends.

Provide $1'' \times \frac{1}{4}''$ galvanized water bar and bed frame in white lead on stone cill.

Provide and fix to window openings casements and frames with $5'' \times 3\frac{1}{2}''$ grooved, rebated, weathered, and rounded cills, $5'' \times 3''$ transoms, $5'' \times 4''$ jambs and heads rebated, rounded, and throated.

Sashes to be $2''$ ovolo-moulded, bottom sash hung at side to open outwards, top sash hung at top to open outwards. Sashes to be hung with $3\frac{1}{2}''$ strong brass butts, and to have brass fanlight opener to top sash, and brass stay bar fitting and fastener to bottom sash.

Put $1\frac{1}{4}''$ tongued and nosed window board with returned ends. Linings to be $1''$, tongued to frames. Architraves $3'' \times 1''$, plain, with head framed to uprights.

Glaze the top sash with leaded lights filled in with 21 oz. best British sheet glass. The bottom sash to be glazed with best selected 32 oz. British sheet glass.

For Brickwork, see Specification of Brickwork.

Casement Window with — Plate 18.
Stone Dressings ¾" Scale

Elevation

Plan

Section

25

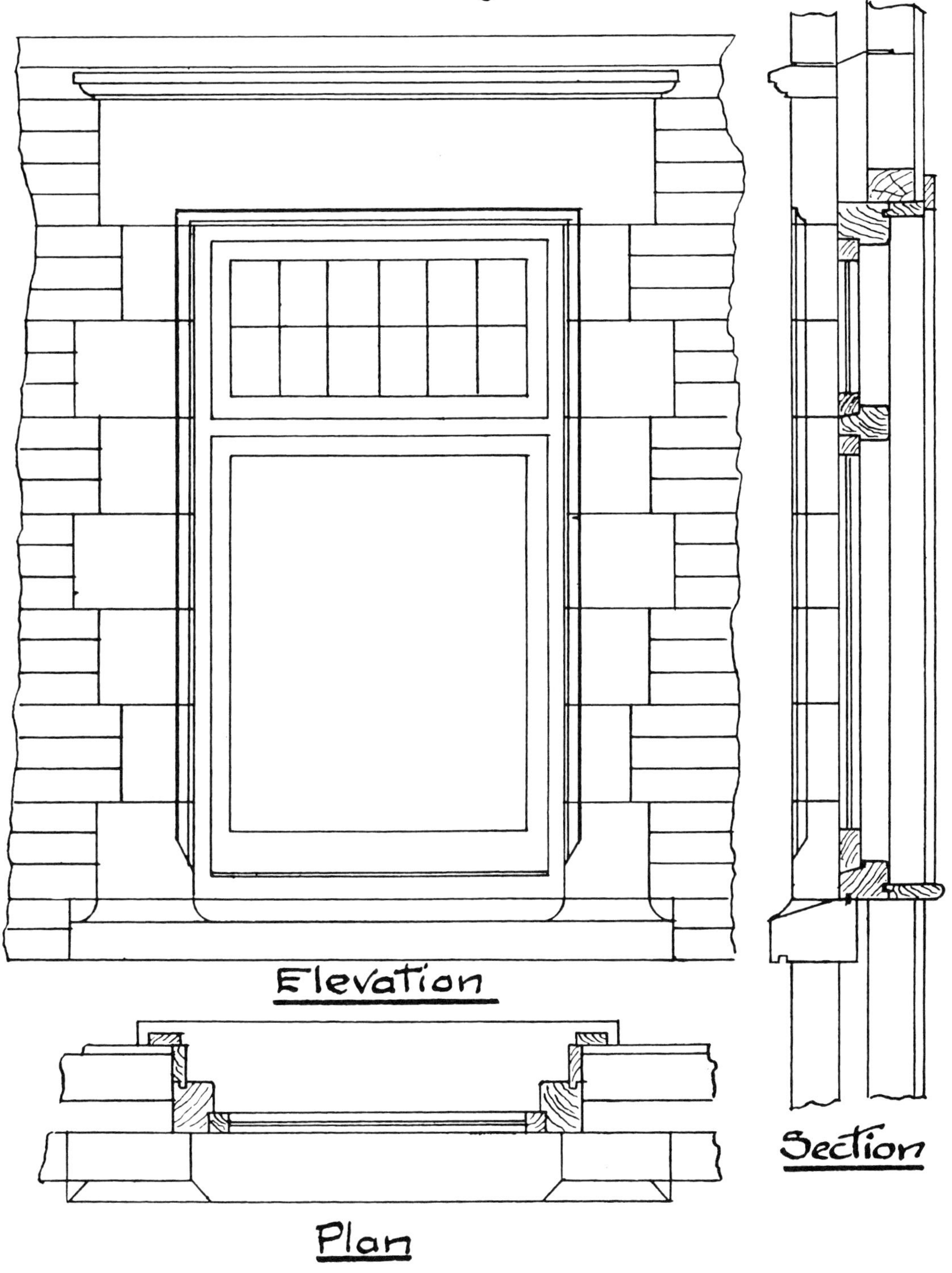

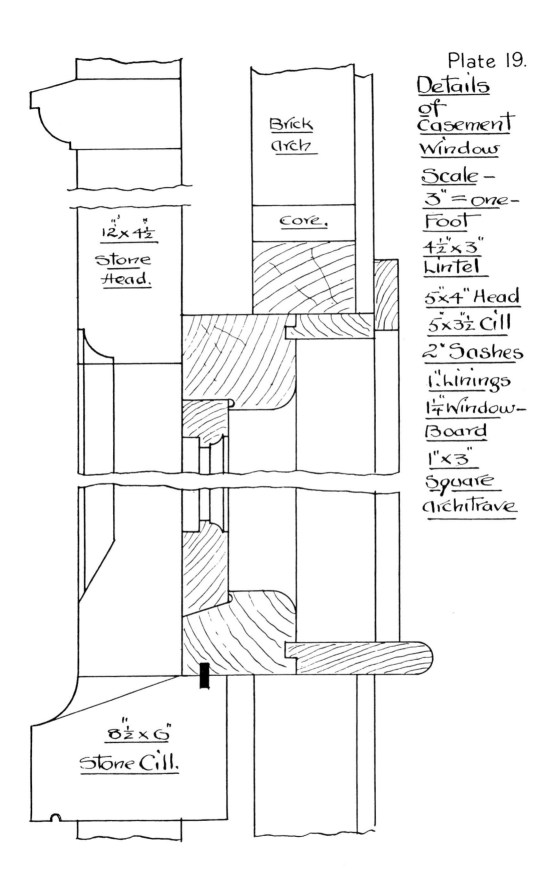

Plate 19.

Details of Casement Window

Scale – 3" = one-Foot

$4\frac{1}{2}$" × 3" Lintel

5" × 4" Head

5" × $3\frac{1}{2}$" Cill

2" Sashes

1" Linings

$1\frac{1}{4}$" Window-Board

1" × 3" Square Architrave

Brick Arch

Core.

12" × $4\frac{1}{2}$" Stone Head.

$8\frac{1}{2}$" × 6" Stone Cill.

Details of Casement Window
Scale 3" = one Foot.

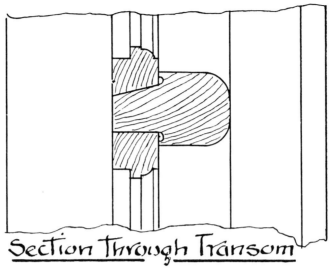

Section Through Transom

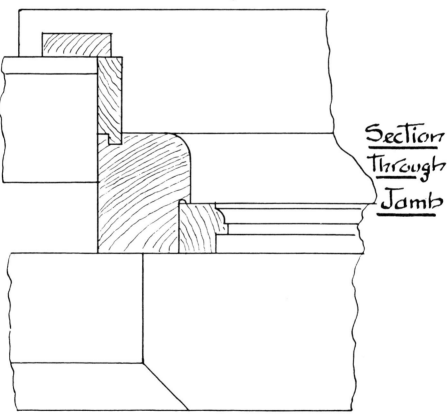

Section Through Jamb

Plate 20.

SPECIFICATION

Internal Doors and Linings

Put to door openings 1½″ solid rebated linings full width of walls and plaster, fixed to proper grounds.

The architraves to be 4″ × 1″, plain, framed together at head, and with 4″ × 2″ moulded top, with returned and mitred ends; the architraves to be dovetailed into back of moulded top and fastened with screws.

Doors to be 2″, six-panelled, square-framed, and hung to linings with 3½″ bright steel butts and fitted with two-bolt mortice lock and strong brass furniture.

The doors throughout to be framed together and stacked in a dry place and glued up when directed.

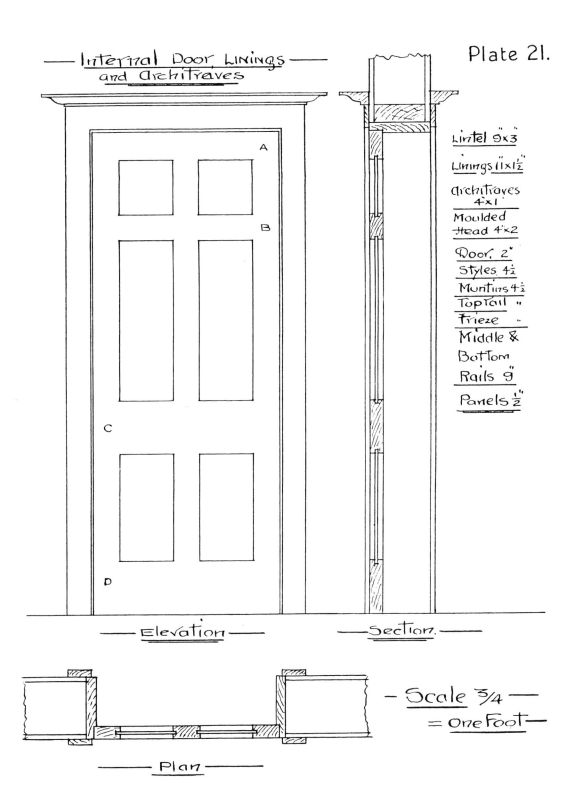

Plate 21.

Internal Door Linings and Architraves

A

B

C

D

— Elevation —

— Section. —

Lintel 9"x3"

Linings 11"x1½"

Architraves 4"x1"

Moulded Head 4"x2"

Door. 2"

Styles. 4½"

Muntins 4½"

Top rail "

Frieze "

Middle & Bottom Rails 9"

Panels ½"

— Plan —

— Scale ¾ —

= One Foot —

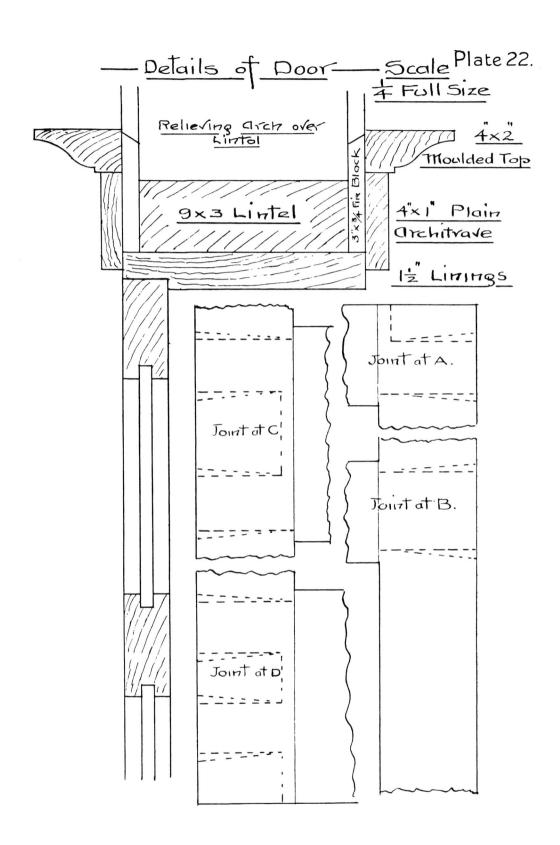

— Details of Door — Scale Plate 22.
$\frac{1}{4}$ Full Size

Relieving Arch over Lintel

4×2″ Moulded Top

9×3 Lintel

3″×¾″ Fir Block

4″×1″ Plain Architrave

1½″ Linings

Joint at A.

Joint at C

Joint at B.

Joint at D

SPECIFICATION

Stairs

The stairs to be constructed of best selected red deal, with $1\frac{1}{4}''$ treads, $\frac{7}{8}''$ risers, $1\frac{1}{4}''$ winders, with cross-tongued and glued joints, $1\frac{1}{2}'' \times 11''$ moulded wall string, $1\frac{1}{2}'' \times 11''$ outer string, with $3\frac{1}{2}'' \times 1\frac{1}{2}''$ bevelled and moulded capping grooved for string and morticed for balusters, $4\frac{1}{2}'' \times 4\frac{1}{2}''$ square newels, with $7'' \times 2''$ moulded cap dowelled to same. Balusters to be $1\frac{1}{4}''$ thick, cut and tapered $1\frac{1}{2}''$ to $2\frac{1}{2}''$. $3\frac{1}{2}'' \times 3\frac{1}{2}''$ moulded mahogany handrail tenoned to newels. Form ramped strings as shown on drawing. The whole to be properly framed, housed, wedged, blocked, and glued together.

The spandril to be $1\frac{1}{4}''$ thick, square-framed, and panelled, and with $1\frac{1}{2}''$ half round cover mould over joint with string. Form door in end under landing to match spandril, hung with $3\frac{1}{2}''$ bright steel butts, and fitted with two-bolt mortice lock and brass furniture.

Put No. 3, $4'' \times 3''$ fir carriage pieces under stairs properly fitted to floor and trimmer joist and fastened with spike nails. The soffit to be covered with $\frac{3}{4}''$ V-jointed matchboard in narrow widths.

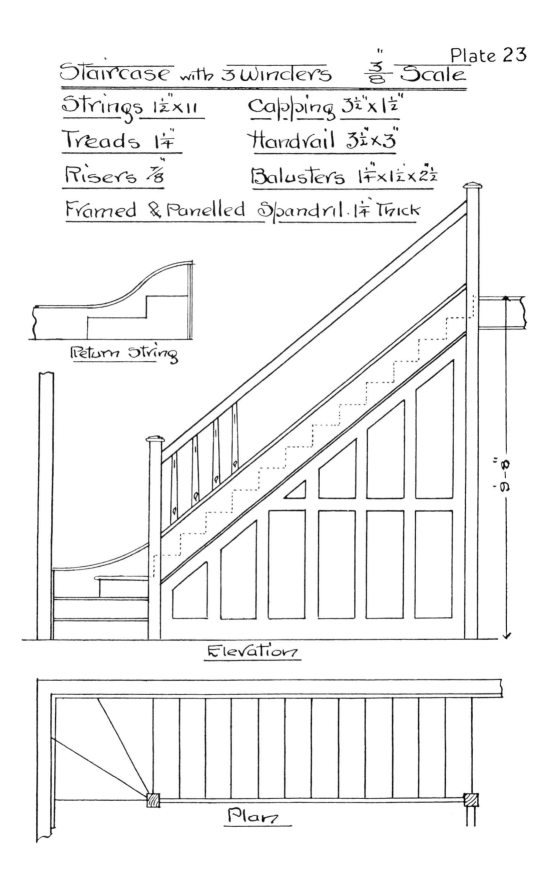

Staircase with 3 Winders $\frac{3}{8}$" Scale

Plate 23

Strings 1½"×11   Capping 3¼"×1½"

Treads 1¼"   Handrail 3¼"×3"

Risers ⅞"   Balusters 1¼"×1½"×2½"

Framed & Panelled Spandril. 1¼" Thick

Return String

Elevation

Plan

9'-8"

Plate 24.

Details of Staircase
1" Scale & ¼ Full Size

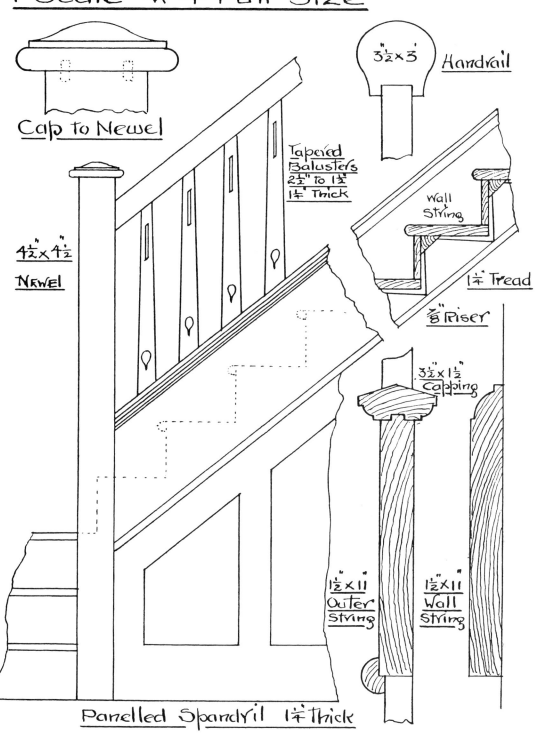

Cap to Newel

$3\frac{1}{2}" \times 3'$ Handrail

Tapered Balusters $2\frac{1}{2}"$ to $1\frac{1}{4}"$ $1\frac{1}{4}"$ Thick

Wall String

$4\frac{1}{2}" \times 4\frac{1}{2}"$ Newel

$1\frac{1}{4}"$ Tread

$\frac{7}{8}"$ Riser

$3\frac{1}{2}" \times 1\frac{1}{2}"$ Capping

$1\frac{1}{2}" \times 11"$ Outer String

$1\frac{1}{2}" \times 11"$ Wall String

Panelled Spandril $1\frac{1}{4}"$ Thick

SPECIFICATION

Entrance Doorway

The entrance doorway to be built in Bath stone from an approved quarry, and finished with a finely dragged face; to have 15″ moulded plinth course, 3″ string courses, and 9″ blocking course, all worked true to line. The piers to be bonded to inside brickwork with No. 2 galvanized wrought-iron ties to each joint. The joints of arch to be joggled and run with cement.

Put 12″ × 6″ rubbed and nosed Portland stone steps.

Turn semi-arch over doorway to carry inside brickwork in two half-brick rings set in cement.

Put 5-lb. lead tray over doorway, brought out over blocking course, and turned down ¼″ and neatly dressed to stone.

The jambs to be 5″ × 4″, wrot, rebated, and moulded and dowelled to step with ¾″ iron dowels; to have semicircular head and 3″ rebated and moulded transom. Put 2″ ovolo-moulded fanlight over.

The door to be 2″, six-panelled, square-framed, and moulded on solid, hung to jambs with 4″ bright steel butts and fitted with approved Yale night-latch with No. 4 keys. Put 3½″ approved bronze metal centre knob on door.

The fanlight to be glazed with best 26 oz. British sheet glass, properly bedded, sprigged, and back-puttied.

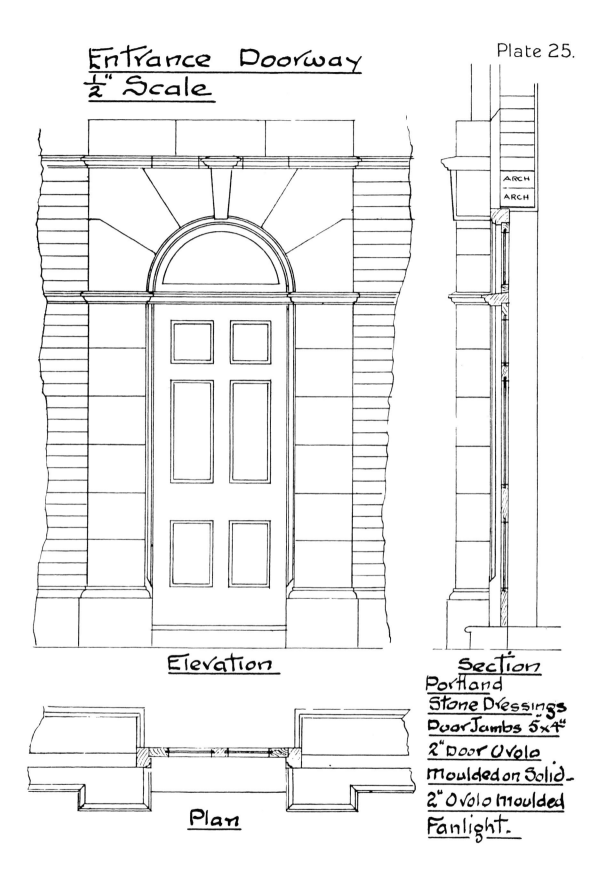

Entrance Doorway
½" Scale

Plate 25.

ARCH
ARCH

Elevation

Plan

Section
Portland
Stone Dressings
Door Jambs 5x4"
2" Door Ovolo
Moulded on Solid
2" Ovolo Moulded
Fanlight.

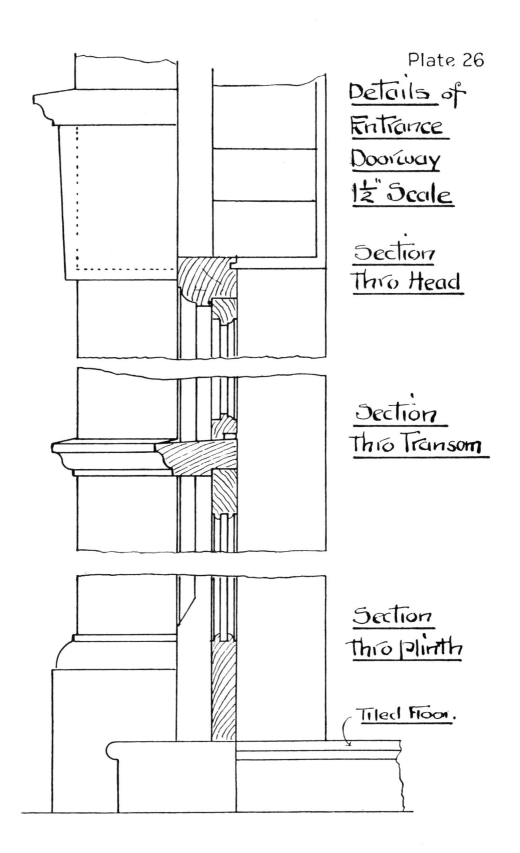

Plate 26

Details of
Entrance
Doorway
$1\frac{1}{2}''$ Scale

Section
Thro Head

Section
Thro Transom

Section
Thro Plinth

Tiled Floor.

BUILDING CONSTRUCTION DRAWING

A CLASS-BOOK FOR THE ELEMENTARY STUDENT AND ARTISAN

BY

RICHARD B. EATON

LECTURER ON BUILDING CONSTRUCTION, POOLE SCHOOL OF
ART AND TECHNOLOGY

Part II

26 PLATES

London
E. & F. N. SPON, Ltd., 57 HAYMARKET
New York
SPON & CHAMBERLAIN, 123 LIBERTY STREET
1914

PREFACE

In presenting Part II. of *Building Construction Drawing* to the student, I have endeavoured to give examples of more advanced work. No attempt has been made to figure the drawings throughout, as a full specification of sizes is given to each set.

My aim has been to make the drawings practical and instructive, and I hope the student will gain knowledge by the study of them.

RICHARD B. EATON.

Poole, *February* 21, 1914.

SPECIFICATION

Bay Window

THE bay windows to be constructed as shown on the drawings.

The interior brickwork to be executed with good, hard, sound, well-burnt bricks and left rough for plaster.

The exterior facings to be the best selected red bricks and pointed in at finish with a neat weather-struck joint in cement.

Provide all requisite splays for external angles and birds'-mouth splays for internal angles.

The external walls to be built hollow and bonded together with galvanized wrought-iron ties placed 3′ 0″ apart horizontally and 12″ vertically, with additional ties around openings.

The mortar to be composed of one part of grey stone lime and two parts of clean sharp pit sand.

Put a damp-proof course of two courses of slate bedded and pointed in cement, with lapped joints.

The window heads to be $12'' \times 4\frac{1}{2}''$ Purbeck stone finely tooled and stop chamfered.

Put $8'' \times 4''$ finely tooled, weathered, and throated Purbeck stone cills, grooved for water bar, and with stooled and returned ends.

Put 4-lb. lead trays over windows, 11″ wide and 9″ longer than opening.

Bay Window

Plate 27

For a Small House ~ $\frac{3}{8}$" Scale

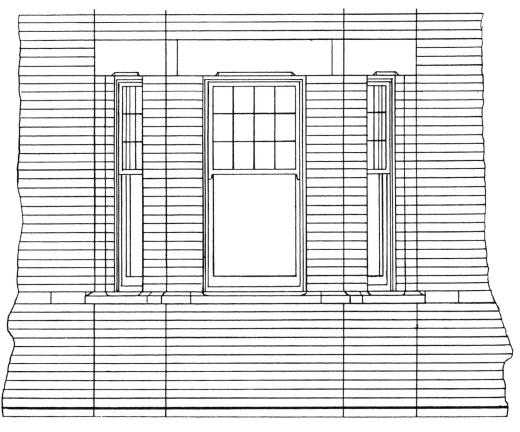

— Elevation —

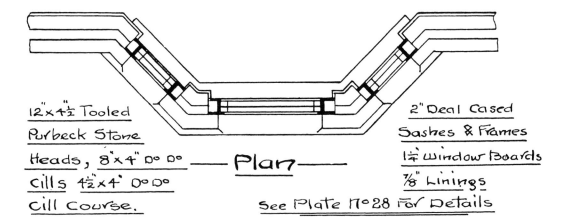

12"x4½" Tooled
Purbeck Stone
Heads, 8"x4" Do Do   — Plan —
Cills 4½"x4" Do Do
Cill Course.

2" Deal Cased
Sashes & Frames
1¼ Window Boards
⅞" Linings

See Plate No 28 For Details

SPECIFICATION

SASHES AND FRAMES FOR BAY WINDOW

THE sashes and frames to be made from the best selected Christiania deals, and to have $6'' \times 3''$ weathered, throated, and grooved cills, $1\frac{1}{4}''$ heads and pulley stiles, grooved for parting bead and tongued to linings, $\frac{7}{8}''$ inside and outside linings, grooved for pulley stiles and heads, $\frac{3}{4}''$ stop bead, $\frac{3}{8}''$ parting bead, $2'' \times 1\frac{1}{4}''$ splayed and tongued bottom bead, $\frac{1}{4}''$ back and division linings, $2''$ ovolo-moulded sashes, with $1\frac{1}{8}''$ bars in top sash only, double hung on approved $1\frac{3}{4}''$ secret axle pulleys with brass face and wheel, with best flax cords.

Put around outside of frames $1\frac{1}{4}'' \times 1\frac{1}{4}''$ cove moulding to cover joint with brickwork.

Put strong approved brass sash fasteners.

The cills to have $1'' \times \frac{1}{4}''$ galvanized water bar and to be bedded in white lead.

The sashes to be glazed with best selected 21-oz. glass, properly bedded, sprigged, and puttied in.

Put $1\frac{1}{4}''$ tongued and rounded window boards with returned ends and tongued to frames, and $\frac{7}{8}''$ linings tongued to frames.

Put $3'' \times 1''$ plain architraves around windows.

Put $11'' \times 4''$ cambered beam across opening.

Lintels to be $6'' \times 4''$, properly halved and spiked together.

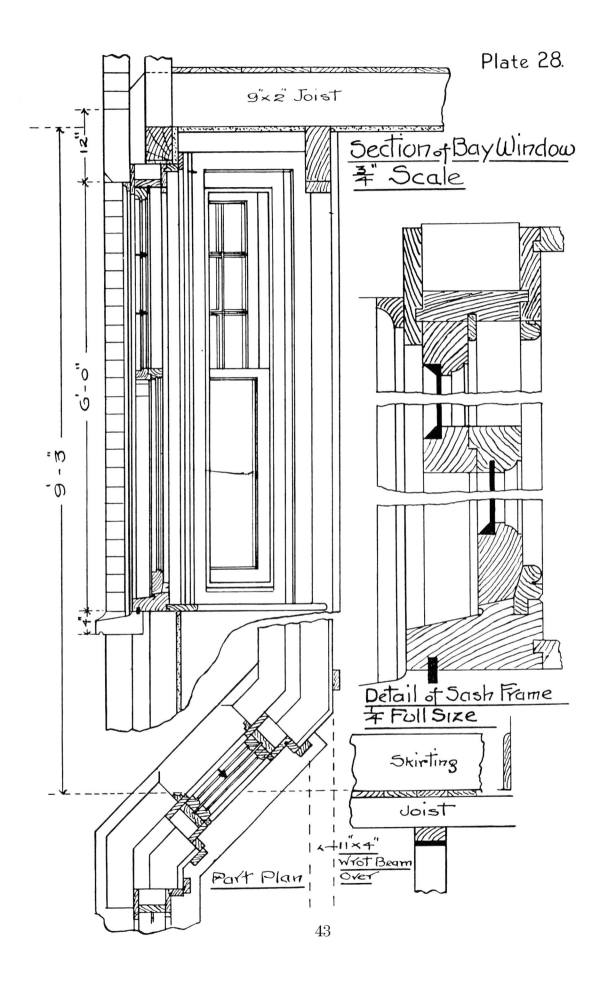

Plate 28.

9"x2" Joist

Section of Bay Window
$\frac{3}{4}$" Scale

12"

6'-0"

9'-3"

4"

Detail of Sash Frame
$\frac{1}{4}$ Full Size

Skirting

Joist

Part Plan

11"x4"
Wrot Beam
Over

43

SPECIFICATION

GABLE OVER BAY WINDOW

PUT on the top of stone heads to carry brickwork above, $9'' \times 4''$ wrot. beam with returns tenoned to main beam over brackets, the ends of beam to be supported on framed wood brackets with $4'' \times 3''$ posts and head and $4\frac{1}{2}'' \times 4''$ shaped bracket filled in with $1\frac{1}{2}''$ square bars placed diagonally, and resting on corbel courses as shown.

The lead tray on top of beam to be of 4-lb. lead $11''$ wide, and to run the whole length of beam.

The cover mouldings to beam to be $2'' \times 2\frac{1}{2}''$ and $2'' \times 1\frac{1}{2}''$.

Barge boards to be $11'' \times 2''$ ovolo-moulded, with shaped bottom and returned mouldings; put $4'' \times 1\frac{3}{4}''$ moulding under slates.

The sizes of roof timbers to be as follows:—$4\frac{1}{2}'' \times 3''$ plates, $6'' \times 4''$ purlins, $4'' \times 2''$ rafters, $9'' \times 1\frac{1}{2}''$ ridge; $\frac{3}{4}''$ roof boarding, $2'' \times \frac{3}{4}''$ battens, $9'' \times 1\frac{1}{2}''$ valleys. The roof to be covered with Delabole Countess slates, each slate nailed with two compo nails. Do all requisite cutting to valleys and verges. The ridge tile to be plain crested, bedded and pointed in cement.

Lay 5-lb. lead valleys properly dressed down to roof.

Put $5'' \times 4''$ cast-iron O.G. eaves gutters with all requisite stop ends, outlets, and angles, jointed with red lead and fastened with galvanized screws and bolts and nuts.

The rain-water pipes to be $3''$ cast-iron, with all requisite swan necks, shoes, etc., and fastened with rose-head nails.

Put small casement window, for light under roof, to have $7'' \times 4''$ weathered, grooved, and throated cill, $5'' \times 4''$ rebated head and jambs, $2''$ ovolo-moulded sashes with $1\frac{1}{8}''$ bars.

Put $4\frac{1}{2}'' \times 3''$ lintel over window.

The front of brickwork to be rendered in cement, trowelled smooth and panelled as shown.

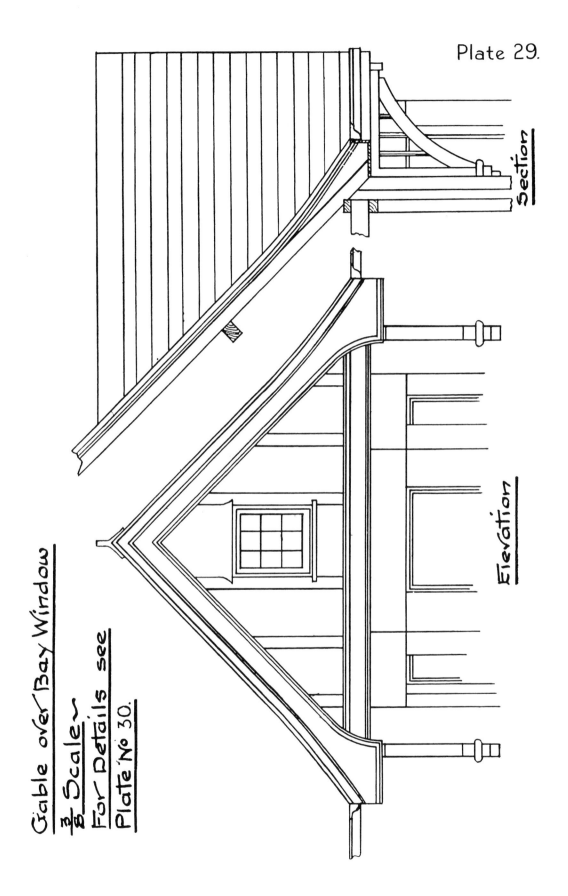

Plate 29.

Gable over Bay Window

⅜ Scale~

For Details see

Plate No 30.

Section

Elevation

45

Plate 30.

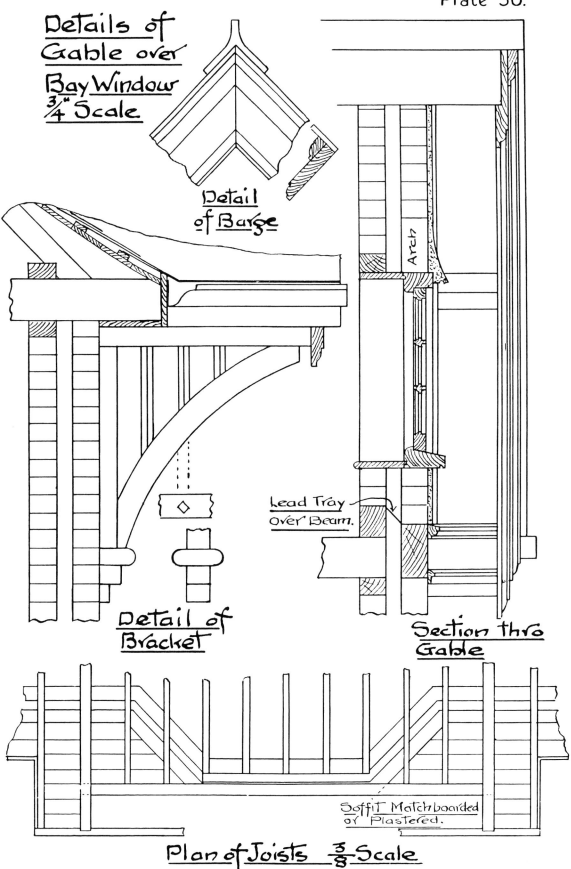

Details of
Gable over
Bay Window
¾" Scale

Detail
of Barge

Arch

Lead Tray
Over Beam.

Detail of
Bracket

Section thro
Gable

Soffit Matchboarded
or Plastered.

Plan of Joists ⅜ Scale

SPECIFICATION

ROOF OVER BAY WINDOW

BRICKWORK and stonework as specified for Plate 27.

Roof timbers   ,,   ,,   ,,   ,,   29.

,,   covering   ,,   ,,   ,,   ,,   29.

Gutters and rain-water pipe   ,,   ,,   ,,   29.

The brick gable above bay window to be carried on tooled and moulded Purbeck stone corbels 9″ thick and bonded as shown on drawing.

The lintels over windows to be formed of concrete composed of four parts of clean washed gravel, two parts of clean sharp washed sand, and one part of Portland cement.

Put to carry side walls of gable 11″ × 4″ deal properly framed to plate and bolted to purlin and between rafters with $\frac{1}{2}$″ bolts and nuts; put 5″ × 4″ strut under beam. The floor joists to be 9″ × 2″, trimmer joists 1″ thicker than ordinary joist. Ceiling joists 4″ × 2″. Ashlars 4″ × 2″ tenoned to 4″ × 2″ plates.

Put 4-lb. lead tray on beam under brickwork. Form sunk gutters with 5-lb. lead and with 5-lb. lead flashing stepped to brickwork and secured with lead wedges and pointed in cement at finish.

Plate 31.

Roof over Bay Window $\frac{3}{8}$". Scale.

Elevation

Part Plan of Joists & Bonding of Corbel Stones

Plate 32

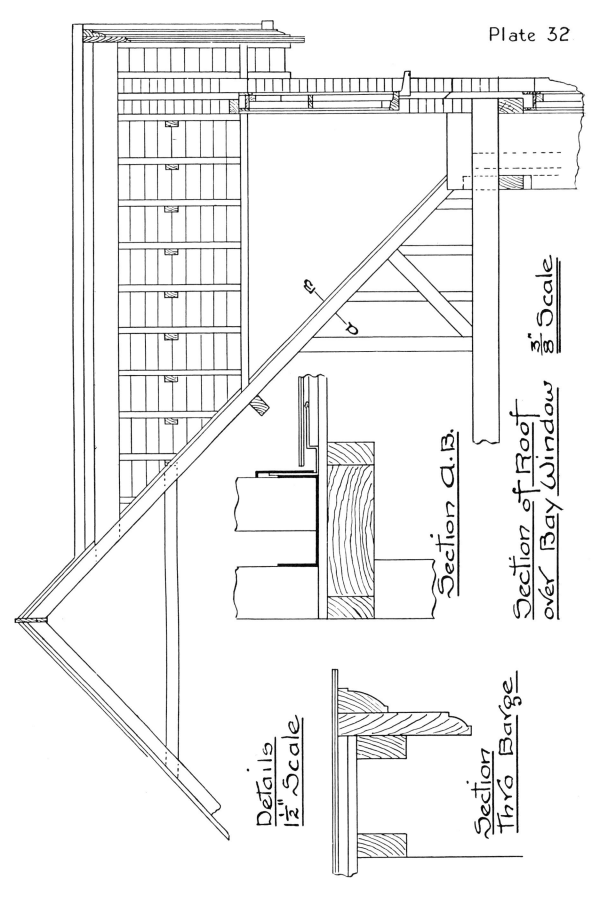

Section A.B.

Details
1½" Scale

Section of Roof
over Bay Window   3"/8 Scale

Section
Thro Barge

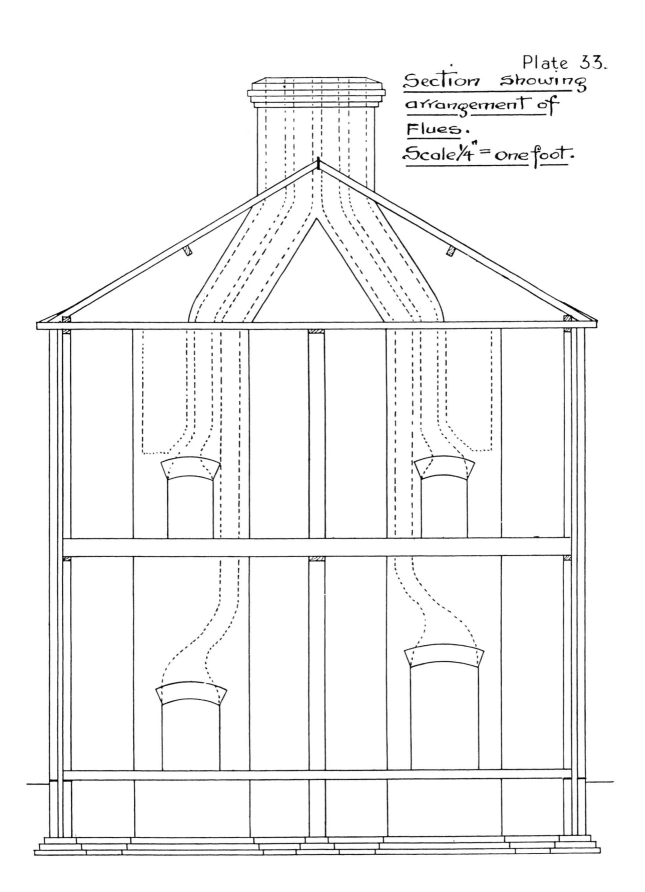

Plate 33.
Section showing
arrangement of
Flues.
Scale 1/4" = one foot.

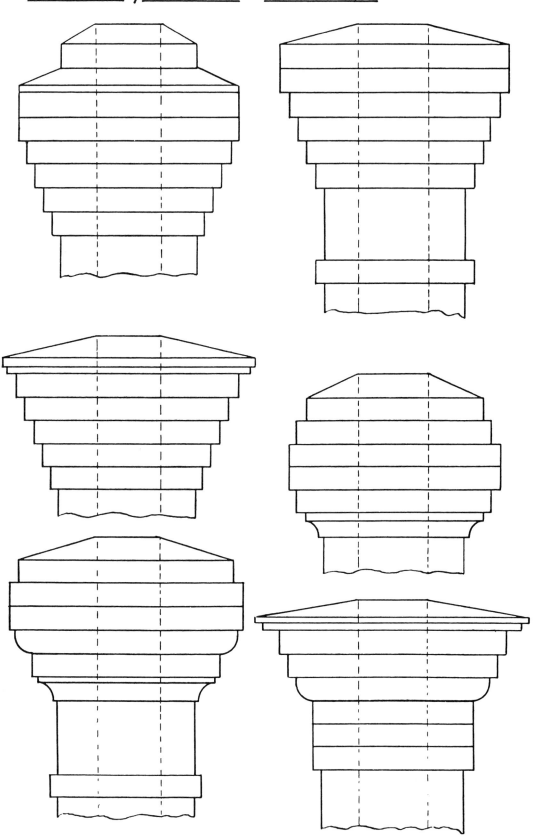

SPECIFICATION

Dormer Window

The dormer window to have 10″ × 4″ rebated, weathered, throated, and grooved cill; 6″ × 5″ rebated, moulded, throated, and grooved corner-posts; 5″ × 3″ rebated, moulded, and throated head and muntins; 2″ ovolo-moulded sashes, with plain leaded lights glazed with best selected 21-oz. glass. The sashes to be side hung with 3½″ bright steel butts and fitted with brass stay bars with two pins to each, and strong brass casement fasteners.

Ceiling joist 4″ × 2″ firred to falls and covered with 1″ rough board and with 2″ rolls for lead. Put 3″ half-round nosing with 3″ × 1½″ bevelled and throated fillet under.

Studding to cheeks to be 4″ × 2″ covered with 1″ rough board.

Cover the flat with 6-lb. milled lead properly dressed over rolls and nosing, the bottom edge to be secured to fillet with 8-lb. lead tacks 12″ apart.

The cheeks of dormer to be covered with 6-lb. lead dressed around corner-post and into groove of frame; put 1½″ half-round cover strip bedded in white lead and nailed to frame. The top edge of cheek to be copper nailed 2″ apart. Put No. 3 soldered dots to each cheek. The bottom edge to be fastened with 8-lb. lead tacks. Put 4-lb. lead soakers one to each slate. The lead apron where flat abuts against roof to be 6-lb. lead.

The apron under cill to be of 6-lb. lead, carried up under cill, turned into groove, and properly dressed down to slating.

Put 1¼″ tongued and rounded window board to cill.

Lath, plaster, float and set to cheeks and ceiling of dormer.

The angles to be rounded and finished in Parian cement.

Plate 35

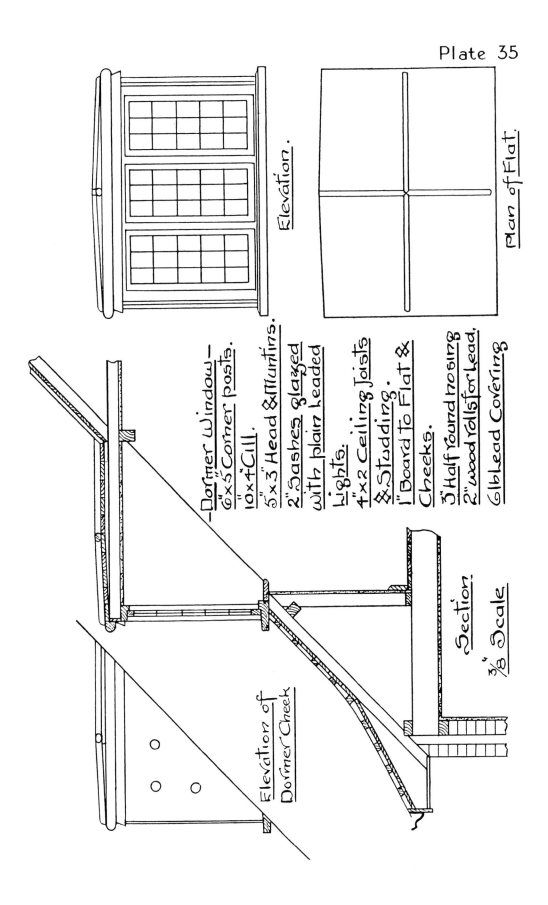

Elevation.

Plan of Flat.

Dormer Window —
6"×5"Corner posts.
10×4"Cill.
5"×3" Head & Muntins.
2"Sashes glazed
with plain leaded
lights.
4"×2 Ceiling Joists
& Studding.
1"Board to Flat &
Cheeks.
3"Half round nosing
2"wood rolls for lead.
6lb Lead Covering

Elevation of
Dormer Cheek

Section.
⅜" Scale

Details of Dormer Window ~

Plate 36.
Scale
3 inches
= One
Foot.

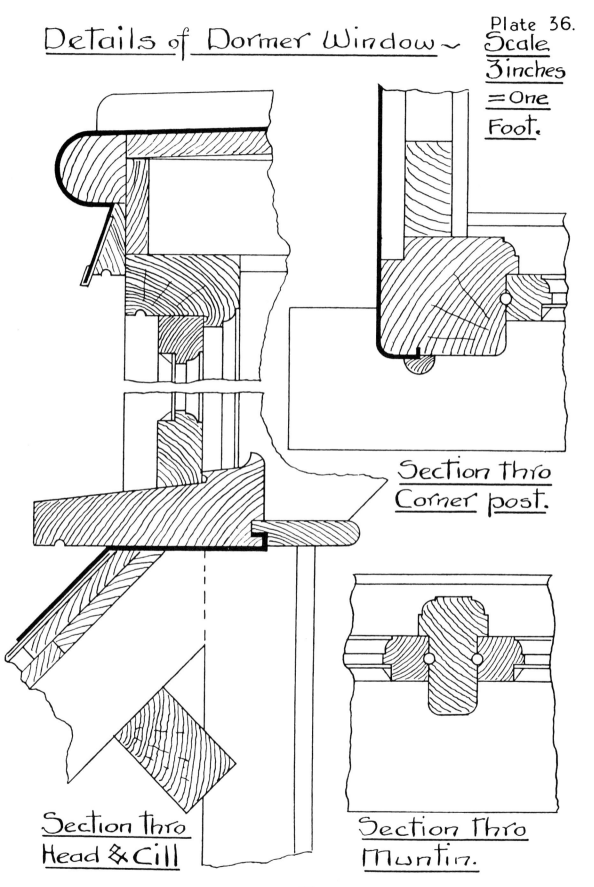

Section thro
Corner post.

Section thro
Head & Cill

Section Thro
Muntin.

55

SPECIFICATION

Dormer Window with Curved Top

Construct dormer window as shown on drawing with $10'' \times 4''$ rebated, weathered, and throated cill; $6'' \times 5''$ rebated, rounded, and grooved corner-posts; $5'' \times 3\frac{1}{4}''$ rebated, rounded, and throated head; $5'' \times 3''$ rebated, rounded, and throated muntins; $2''$ ovolo-moulded sashes with plain leaded lights glazed with best selected 21-oz. glass. The sashes to be side hung on $3\frac{1}{2}''$ bright steel butts, and fitted with brass stay bars with two pins to each, and strong brass casement fasteners.

Put $5\frac{3}{4}'' \times 4\frac{1}{2}''$ weathered moulding across head; the side plates to be $9\frac{1}{4}'' \times 4''$, rebated, moulded, and mortised for studding. The curved moulding to be $5\frac{3}{4}'' \times 4''$, rebated for boarding.

Studding to dormer cheeks $3'' \times 2''$, curved ceiling ribs $3'' \times 2''$.

Cover the top and cheeks with $1''$ rough boarding; put $2''$ wood rolls for lead. The plates to have $2\frac{1}{4}'' \times 1\frac{1}{2}''$ bevelled fillet nailed on to form gutter. On the boarding lay 6-lb. milled lead properly dressed over rolls, the front edge to be copper nailed $3''$ apart. Form gutters at side as shown, with outlet on each side, discharging on to roof. Provide for outlets of gutter two short pieces of $2''$ lead pipe brought up through moulding and jointed to gutter.

The cheeks of dormer to be covered with 6-lb. lead dressed around corner-posts and into groove; put $1\frac{1}{2}''$ half-round cover strip bedded in white lead and nailed to post.

Put 5-lb. lead covering to head moulding, turned up at back edge under cement and over front edge of moulding.

The top edge of cheek to be carried up over top of boarding and copper nailed $3''$ apart; put No. 3 soldered dots to each cheek. The bottom edges to be fastened with 8-lb. lead tacks.

Put 4-lb. lead soakers one to each slate.

The apron under cill to be 6-lb. lead carried up under cill, turned into groove and properly dressed down to slating.

Put $1\frac{1}{4}''$ tongued and rounded window board to cill.

Lath, plaster, float and set to ceiling and cheeks of dormer.

The panel above head moulding to be covered with $\frac{3}{4}''$ mesh expanded metal and rendered in cement trowelled smooth.

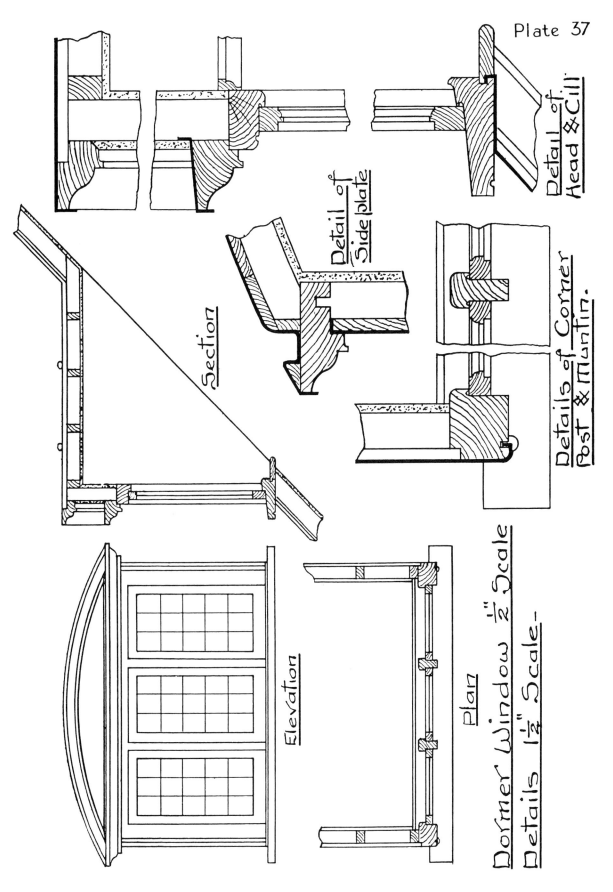

Plate 37

Detail of Head & Cill

Detail of Side plate

Details of Corner Post & Muntin.

Section

Elevation

Plan

Dormer Window ½" Scale
Details 1½" Scale-

SPECIFICATION

Porch to Entrance Doorway

THE porch to be executed with Bath stone from an approved quarry, and finished with a finely dragged face, built in coursed ashlar 12″ thick, both faces finished fair.

The stonework to be bonded as shown, and laid with joints not more than $\frac{1}{8}$″ thick and bedded with stone-dust putty, $\frac{3}{4}$″ from face; joints to be raked out and neatly pointed in cement.

Put 18″ moulded plinth and $4\frac{1}{2}$″ moulded string-course.

The jambs of doorway and windows to be moulded on both faces and stopped as shown.

Put moulded cills to windows.

The arches over porch entrance and doorway to be joggled and run with cement.

Put blocking course as shown, with groove cut in same to receive asphalte.

Provide all requisite shoring and planking for temporary supports for concrete, the planking to be covered with oiled paper before concrete is laid.

Cover down the porch with cement concrete $4\frac{1}{2}$″ thick, re-inforced with $1\frac{1}{2}$″ mesh expanded metal.

Lay Limmer asphalte $\frac{3}{4}$″ thick in two layers with joints lapped and carried up side walls and into groove of stonework.

Put rubbed and nosed Portland stone steps 6″ thick to porch and entrance doorway, the step to porch to have circular front edge as plan.

The floor of porch to have 4″ cement concrete bed, with floated cement face $\frac{3}{4}$″ thick; on this lay best selected encaustic tiles, square pattern, with narrow tiles around margins.

The windows to have 5″ × 4″ rebated, weathered, and throated cills; 5″ × 3″ rebated, weathered, and throated heads and jambs; 2″ ovolo-moulded sashes with leaded lights glazed with best selected 21-oz. glass.

The ceiling of porch to be finished in cement trowelled smooth.

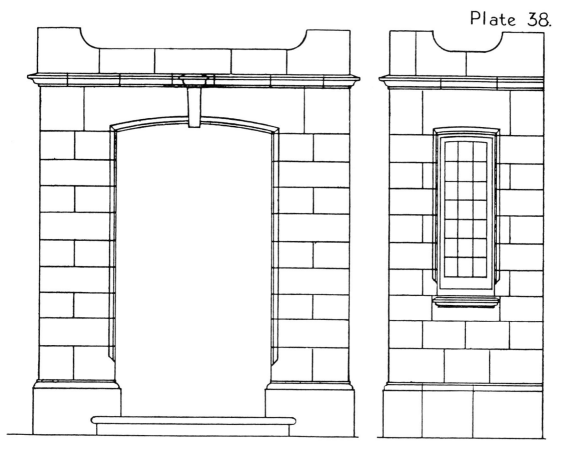

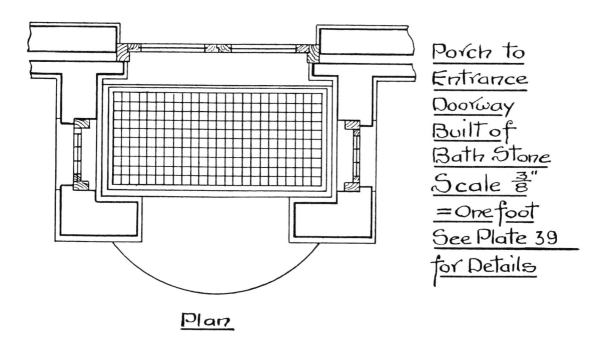

Plate 38.

Front Elevation   Side Elevation

Plan

Porch to
Entrance
Doorway
Built of
Bath Stone
Scale $\frac{3}{8}$″
= One foot
See Plate 39
for Details

59

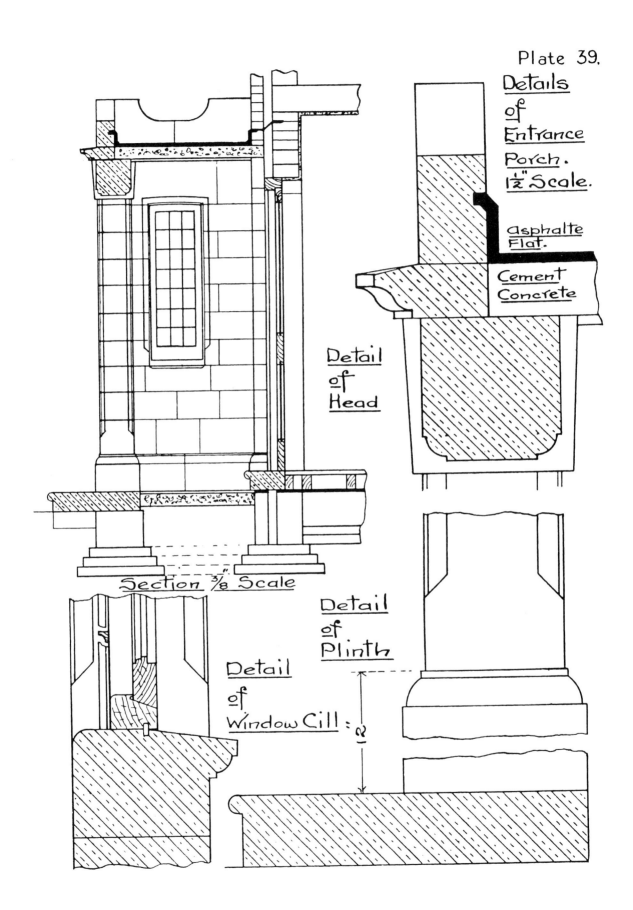

Plate 39.

Details
of
Entrance
Porch.
1½" Scale.

Asphalte
Flat.

Cement
Concrete

Detail
of
Head

Section ⅜" Scale

Detail
of
Window Cill

Detail
of
Plinth

1:2

SPECIFICATION

ENTRANCE DOORWAY

THE entrance door frame to be $6'' \times 4''$ rebated, stop moulded, and grooved, with segmental head.

Doors to be $2\frac{1}{2}''$ thick, framed, panelled, and ovolo-moulded on solid, with segmental head.

Bottom panels to be $1\frac{1}{4}''$ thick, flat on inside, raised and splayed on outside; the top panels to be prepared for leaded lights.

The shutting stiles to be bevel rebated and beaded. Hang doors with $4\frac{1}{2}''$ strong brass butts, No. 3 to each door. Put to doors No. 2, 10'' strong brass barrel bolts and 6'' two-bolt full rebated mortice lock with 4 keys and strong approved bronze metal furniture.

The top panels to be filled in with leaded lights, p.c., 4s. per foot sup., and secured to framing with $\frac{1}{4}''$ wrought-iron saddle bars, No. 3 to each door. Put slip moulding around framing, mitred at angles and fastened with round-headed brass screws.

Put to inside of door frame 1'' linings tongued to frame, and $3'' \times 1\frac{1}{2}''$ moulded architrave.

Asphalte Flat

4" Cement Concrete

4" Cement Concrete

—Elevation—

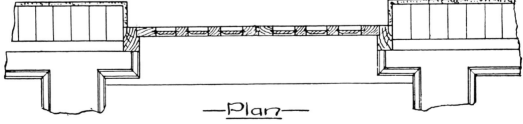

—Plan—

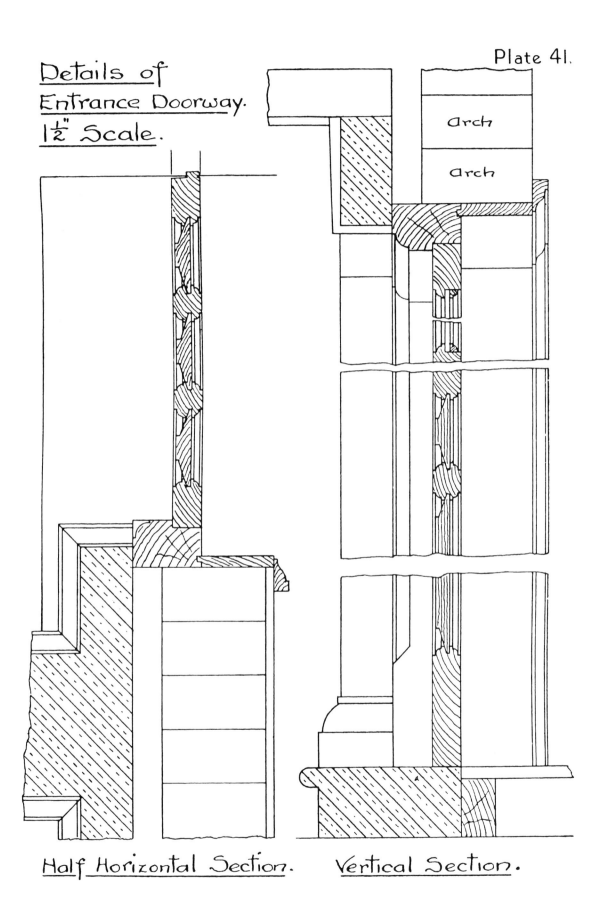

Plate 41.

Details of
Entrance Doorway.
1½" Scale.

arch

arch

Half Horizontal Section.

Vertical Section.

SPECIFICATION

Bay Window

FOR specification of brickwork, see page 40
,,   ,,   ,,   concrete,   ,,   48

Provide and fix No. 3 8' × 4" rolled steel joists 11' 0" long, 18 lbs. to the foot run, to carry brickwork over opening.

Put 16" × 9" × 4" Purbeck stone templates under ends of same.

Fill in spaces between rolled steel joists with cement concrete.

A proper centre to be made for arch, with side boxings to receive concrete. Put No. 4 $\frac{1}{2}$" diameter wrought-iron rods shaped to arch and turned into brickwork 6" at springing line; underneath these rods put a sheet of $\frac{3}{4}$-mesh expanded metal and fasten to rods with stout wire. Put No. 6 pairs of hangers of $\frac{3}{8}$" wrought-iron rod crossed under rolled steel joists, fastened to arch rods and clipped over flange of rolled steel joists. The arch to be filled in with cement concrete. Finish the arch and piers in Keen's cement; run necking moulding as shown, returned and mitred on face of wall and returned back to side posts of bay.

The bay window to have rebated, weathered, throated, and grooved frame as details, with 10" × 4" cill, 7" × 4$\frac{1}{2}$" transom, 5" × 4" head, 11" × 5" side posts. The angle posts to be 5" thick and show 5$\frac{1}{2}$" on each face, mitred together at angles as detail and fastened with long screws. The joint at angles of cill to be as detail, with slip tongues and No. 2 8" handrail screws to each.

Sashes to be 2" ovolo-moulded; top sashes to have leaded lights glazed with 21-oz. best selected glass; bottom sashes glazed with 26-oz. best selected glass. No. 4 top sashes to be hung at top with 3" brass butts, and to have strong brass stay bars with two pins to each. No. 4 bottom sashes to be side hung with 3$\frac{1}{2}$" brass butts, and to have strong brass stay bars and approved brass casement fasteners.

The joists to overhang bays 6" and cut to fall to guttering. Put 6" × 1" eaves board and 6$\frac{1}{2}$" × 1" fascia board.

The flat to be covered with 1" rough board, and on this lay Limmer asphalte in two thicknesses with lapped joints. The asphalte to be carried up wall 5" and well worked into joint of brickwork. The bottom edge to be brought down over edge of gutter 1". Put 5" × 4" moulded eaves gutter to eaves, with splay angles, outlet and stopped ends, fastened with galvanized screws and bolts and jointed with red lead.

Put 2$\frac{1}{2}$" cast-iron rain-water pipe with swan neck and shoe complete.

Put over opening 4-lb. lead tray 12" wide, and to overhang vertical flashing 6" on each side of window.

The lead soaker to side posts to be of 4-lb. lead, turned into groove of post and turned on inner edge 2" to back face of outer wall.

Put 5-lb. lead flashing turned into groove and properly stepped to brickwork, fastened with lead wedges and neatly stopped in with cement.

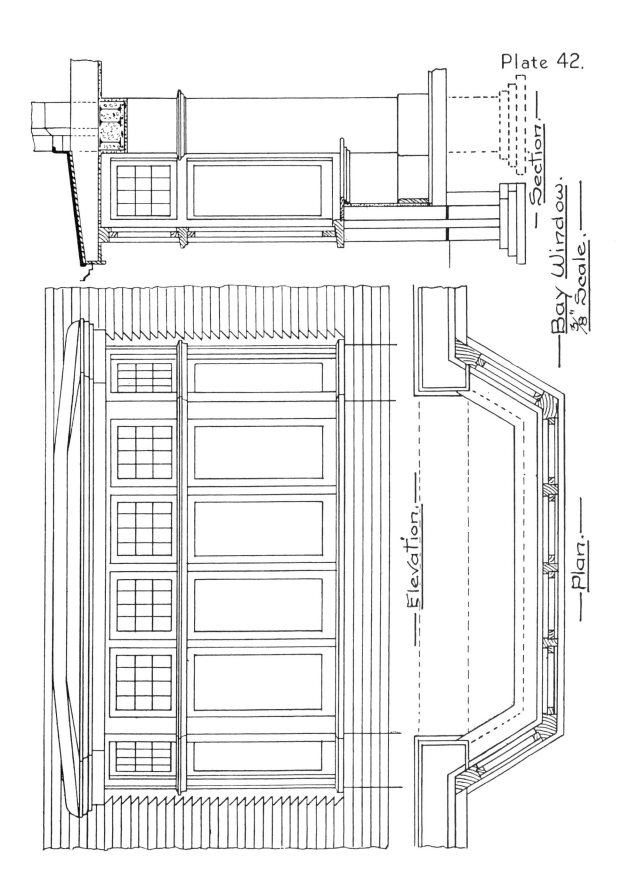

Plate 42.

— Section. —

— Bay Window. —
⅝" Scale.

— Elevation. —

— Plan. —

Plate 43

Details of Bay Window, $\frac{1}{2}$ Scale.
Elevation of Arch, under Rolled steel joists

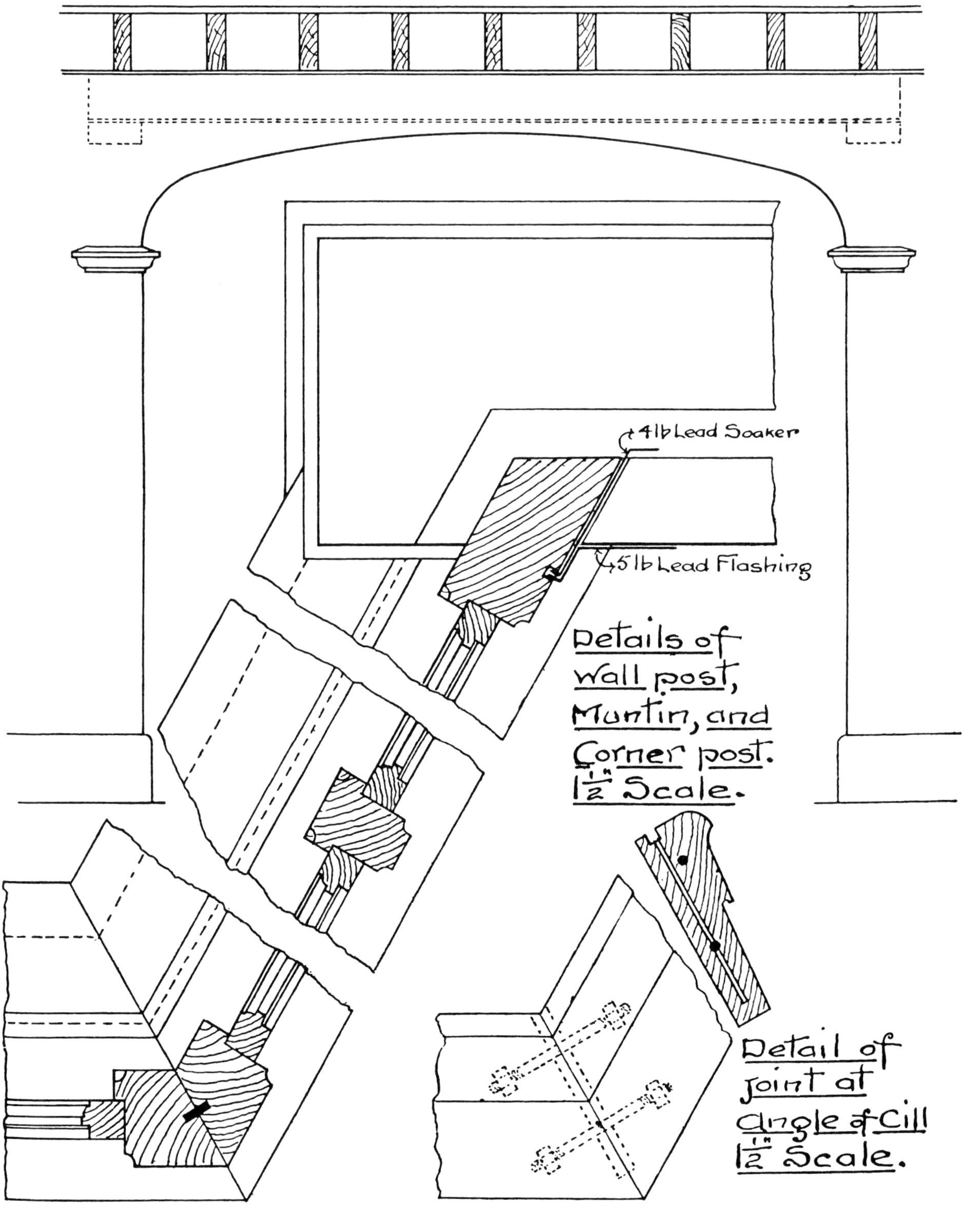

4 lb Lead Soaker

4 5 lb Lead Flashing

Details of Wall post, Muntin, and Corner post. $1\frac{1}{2}$ Scale.

Detail of Joint at Angle of Cill $1\frac{1}{2}$ Scale.

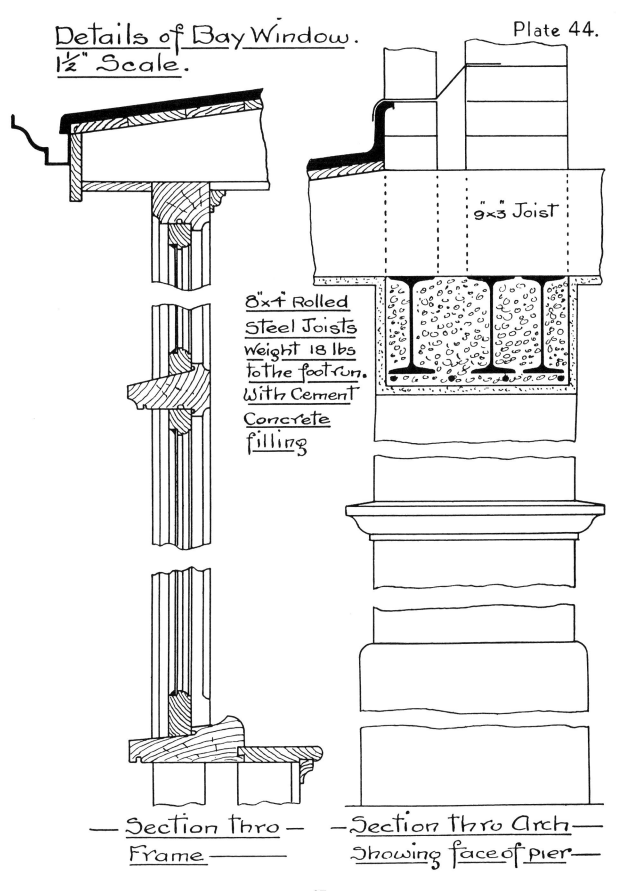

Details of Bay Window.
1½" Scale.

Plate 44.

9"x3" Joist

8"x4" Rolled
Steel Joists
Weight 18 lbs
to the foot run.
With Cement
Concrete
filling

— Section thro —
Frame

— Section thro Arch —
Showing face of pier

SPECIFICATION

STAIRCASE

THE staircase to be constructed out of best selected Memel deals and to have 11″ × 2″ housed and moulded strings, 13″ × 1½″ nosed and grooved treads, 4¾″ × 1¼″ risers tongued to treads, 6″ × 6″ newels tapered to 5″ at cap, 10″ × 5″ moulded caps to newels, and with moulded drops as shown, 4½″ × 4″ mahogany rail ramped as shown housed and tenoned to newels, joints to be dowelled and fastened with proper handrail screws, 1¾″ plain round balusters, 4″ × 2″ moulded capping to outside string and 2¼″ × 1¾″ moulding tongued to under edge of string; put 1¼″ × ½″ cover fillet over joint of string with plaster. The stairs to have proper fir carriage pieces properly splayed to floor and trimmers and securely fixed. The joists of landings to be 5″ × 3″, mortised and tenoned together and securely fixed and wedged in walls. The landings to be 1½″ thick, with glued and tongued joints, and carefully fitted to stairs.

The screen between newels to be 1¼″ square, framed and panelled up to dado height; put 2″ door at end hung to wall newel with 3½″ brass butts. The mouldings to screen to be as follows: capping on dado over stairs and second landing 6″ × 2½″, and 5″ × 2″ on door, 11″ × 3½″ grooved frieze moulding, 7″ × 4″ ceiling moulding; put 3″ × 2″ grooved rail under frieze moulding and 2″ × 1¼″ rail above frieze. The muntins to be 3″ × 2″. The shaped ribs to be 1⅜″ thick.

Put 1¼″ panelled spandril above string on first flight at back of panelled dado.

The spandril framing under outside string of first flight to be 1½″ thick; put similar panelling in end between newels of first flight, and form door in same hung with 3½″ brass butts.

The lining board on trimmer joists to be ¾″ thick, with 3¾″ × 1¾″ moulding and 2¾″ × 1¼″ nosings. Put 7″ × 3″ rebated and moulded capping at top of landing between newels mortised for balusters. The skirting to be 9″ × 1″ with hollow worked on edge.

The whole of the mouldings and skirting to be properly mitred around newels.

Lath, plaster, float and set soffit of stairs and landings.

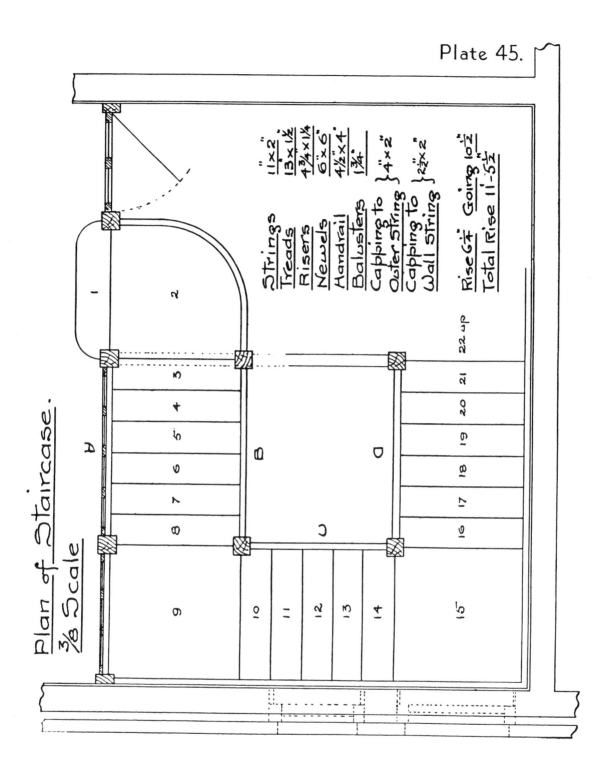

Plate 45.

Plan of Staircase.
⅜ Scale

Strings — 11" × 2"
Treads — 13 × 1½
Risers — 1¾ × 1¼"
Newels — 6" × 6"
Handrail — 4½" × 4"
Balusters — 1¾"
Capping to } 4" × 2"
Outer String
Capping to } 2½" × 2
Wall String

Rise 6⅛" Going 10½"
Total Rise 11'-5½"

Plate 46.

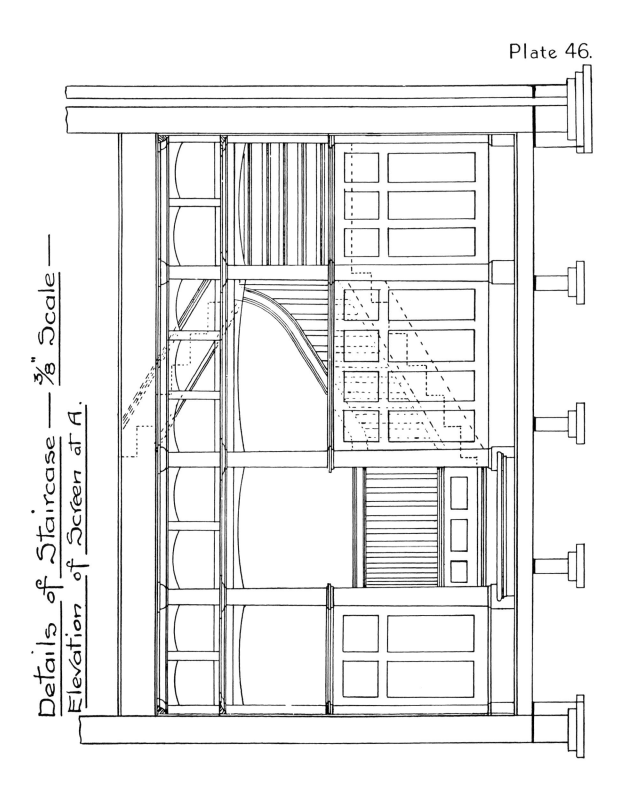

Details of Staircase — ⅜" Scale —

Elevation of Screen at A.

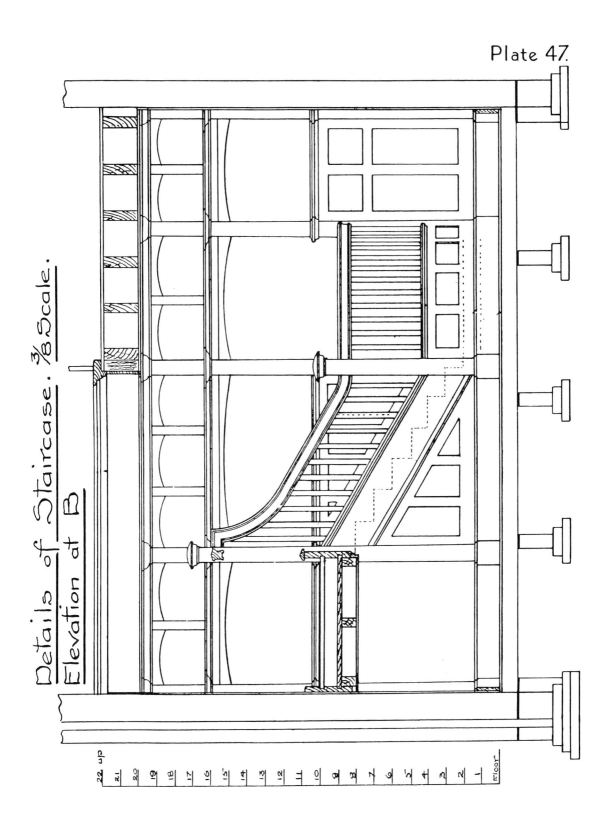

Plate 47.

Details of Staircase. ⅜ Scale.

Elevation at B

71

Plate 48.

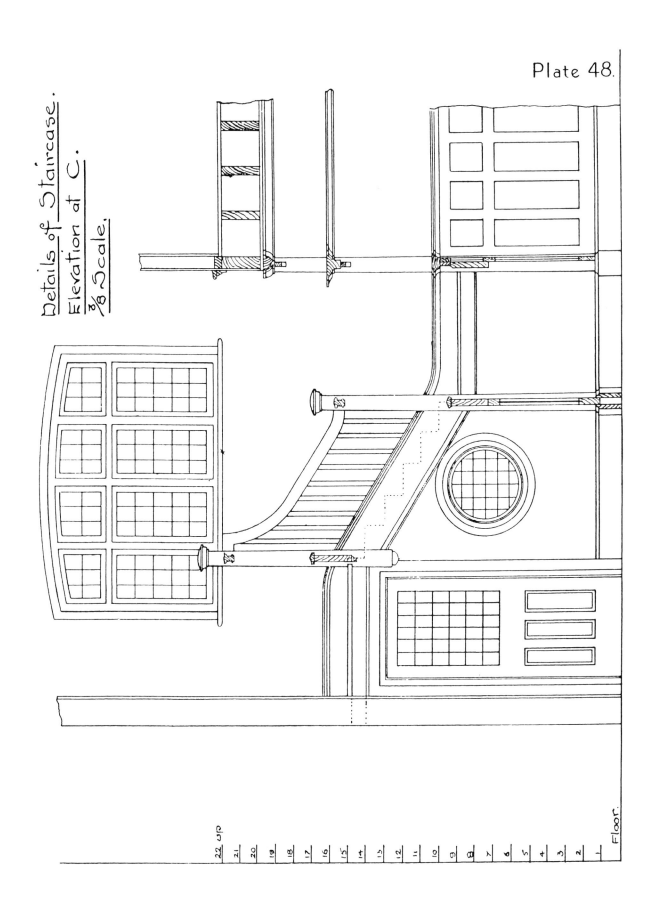

Details of Staircase.
Elevation at C.
⅜ Scale.

Details of Staircase. ⅜ Scale Plate 49.
Elevation at D.

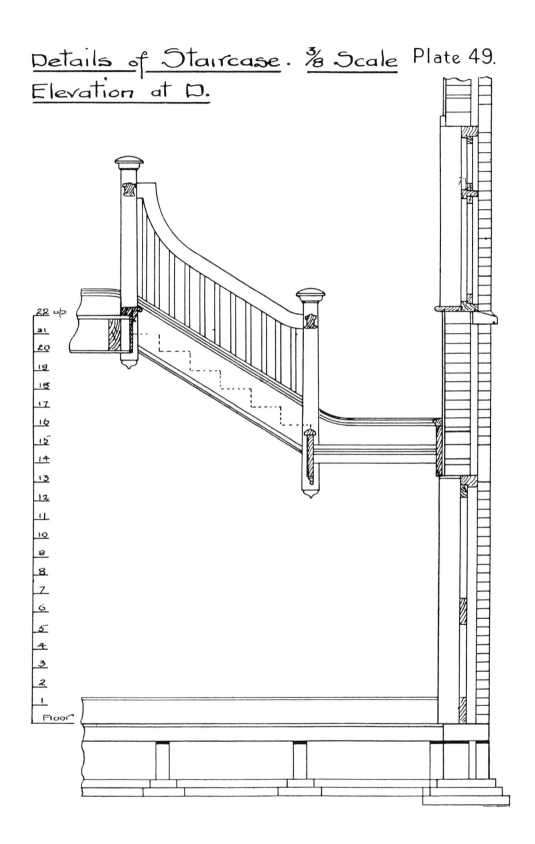

22 u/o
21
20
19
18
17
16
15
14
13
12
11
10
9
8
7
6
5
4
3
2
1
Floor

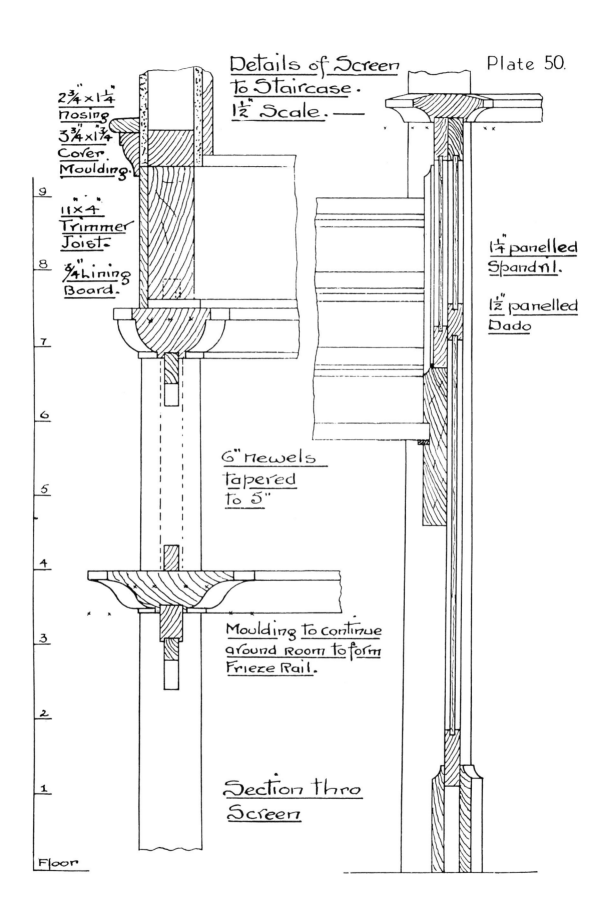

Details of Screen
to Staircase.
1½" Scale. —

Plate 50.

2¾"×1¼"
nosing
3¾"×1¾"
Cover.
Moulding.

9

11"×4"
Trimmer
Joist.

8

¾" Lining
Board.

7

6

5

4

3

2

1

Floor

6" newels
tapered
to 5"

Moulding to continue
around Room to form
Frieze Rail.

Section thro
Screen

1¼" panelled
Spandrl.

1½" panelled
Dado

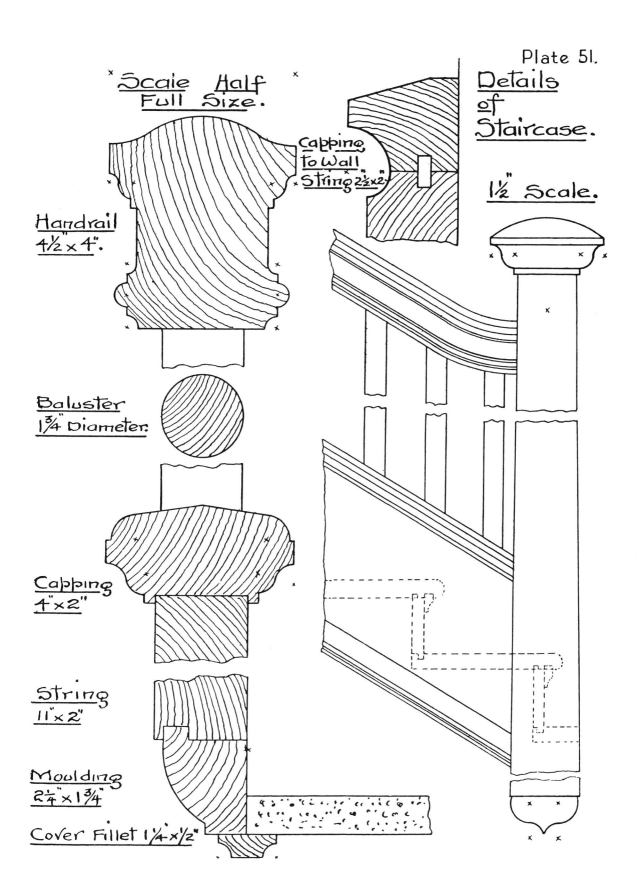

Scale Half Full Size.

Plate 51.

Details of Staircase.

Capping To Wall String 2½×2″

1½″ Scale.

Handrail 4½×4″.

Baluster 1¾″ Diameter.

Capping 4″×2″

String 11″×2″

Moulding 2¼″×1¾″

Cover Fillet 1¼″×½″

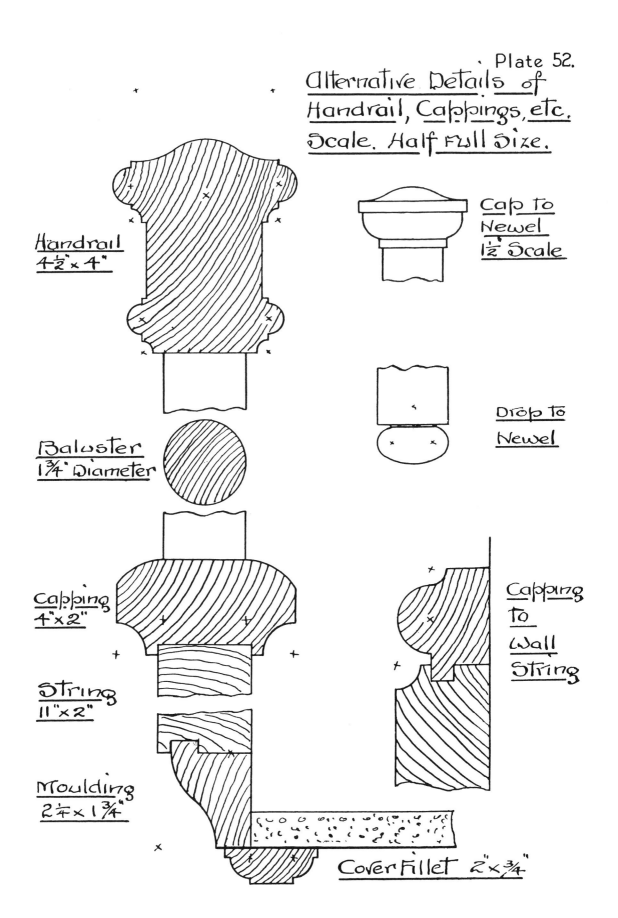

Plate 52.
Alternative Details of
Handrail, Cappings, etc.
Scale. Half Full Size.

Handrail
4½" x 4"

Cap to
Newel
1½ Scale

Baluster
1¾" Diameter

Drop to
Newel

Capping
4" x 2"

Capping
to
Wall
String

String
11" x 2"

Moulding
2¼" x 1¾"

Cover Fillet 2" x ¾"

BUILDING CONSTRUCTION DRAWING

A CLASS-BOOK FOR THE ELEMENTARY STUDENT AND ARTISAN

BY

RICHARD B. EATON

LECTURER ON BUILDING CONSTRUCTION, POOLE SCHOOL OF
ART AND TECHNOLOGY

Part III

25 PLATES

London

E. & F. N. SPON, Ltd., 57 HAYMARKET, S.W. 1

New York

SPON & CHAMBERLAIN, 120 LIBERTY STREET

1917

PREFACE

In Part III. of *Building Construction Drawing* full specifications have not been given to Plates 53 to 69 inclusive; the specifications for the various trades being similar to those contained in Parts I. and II.

Plates 70 to 77 inclusive, comprise plans, elevations, and sections of a small villa residence. A short specification for these drawings is appended.

The early difficulties of the young student in working with plan and specification together are familiar to me, and I hope these difficulties will be lessened in some degree by the study of this small work.

RICHARD B. EATON.

"Lakeside," Seldown,
      Poole.

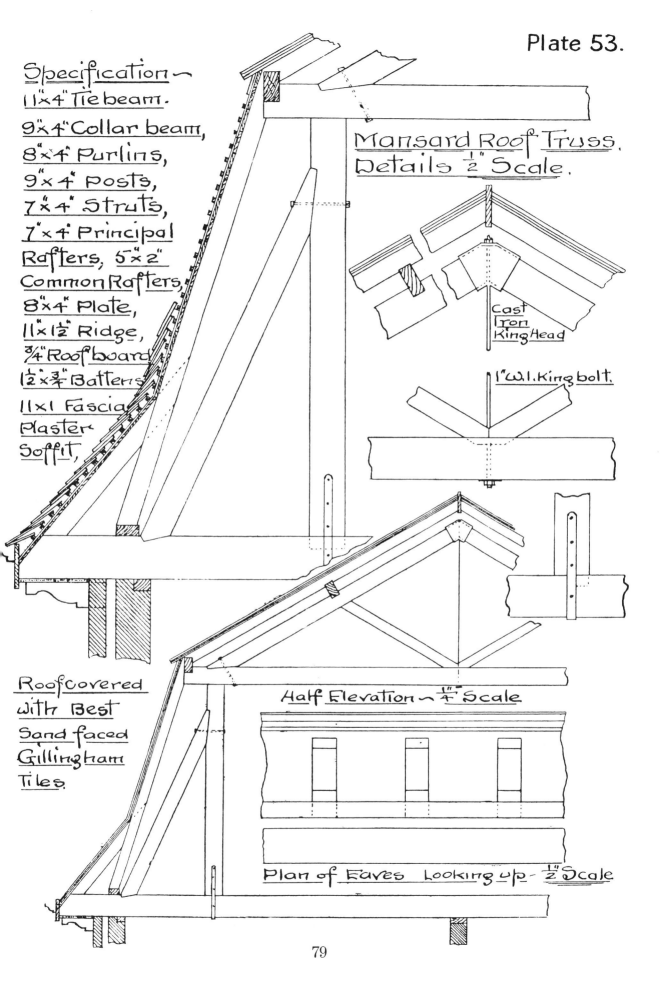

Plate 53.

Specification ~
11"×4" Tie beam.
9"×4" Collar beam,
8"×4" Purlins,
9"×4" Posts,
7"×4" Struts,
7"×4" Principal
Rafters, 5"×2"
Common Rafters,
8"×4" Plate,
11"×1½" Ridge,
¾" Roof board
1½"×¾" Battens,
11"×1 Fascia
Plaster
Soffit,

Roof covered
with Best
Sand faced
Gillingham
Tiles

Mansard Roof Truss.
Details ½" Scale.

Cast
Iron
King Head

1" W.I. King bolt.

Half Elevation ~ ¼" Scale

Plan of Eaves Looking up - ½" Scale

Plate **54.**

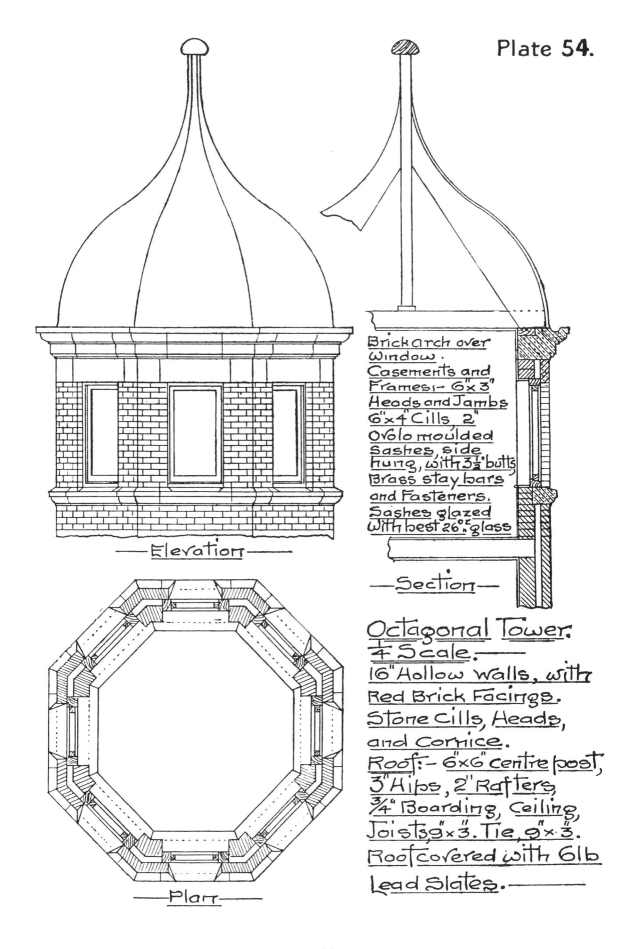

— Elevation —

Brick arch over
Window.
Casements and
Frames:- 6"x 3"
Heads and Jambs
6"x 4" Cills, 2"
Ovolo moulded
Sashes, side
hung, with 3½"butts
Brass stay bars
and Fasteners.
Sashes glazed
With best 26°˙ glass

— Section —

Octagonal Tower.
¼ Scale.—
16" Hollow walls, with
Red Brick Facings.
Stone Cills, Heads,
and Cornice.
Roof:- 6"x 6" centre post,
3" Hips, 2" Rafters,
¾" Boarding, Ceiling,
Joists, 9"x 3". Tie, 9"x 3".
Roof covered with 6lb
Lead Slates.—

— Plan —

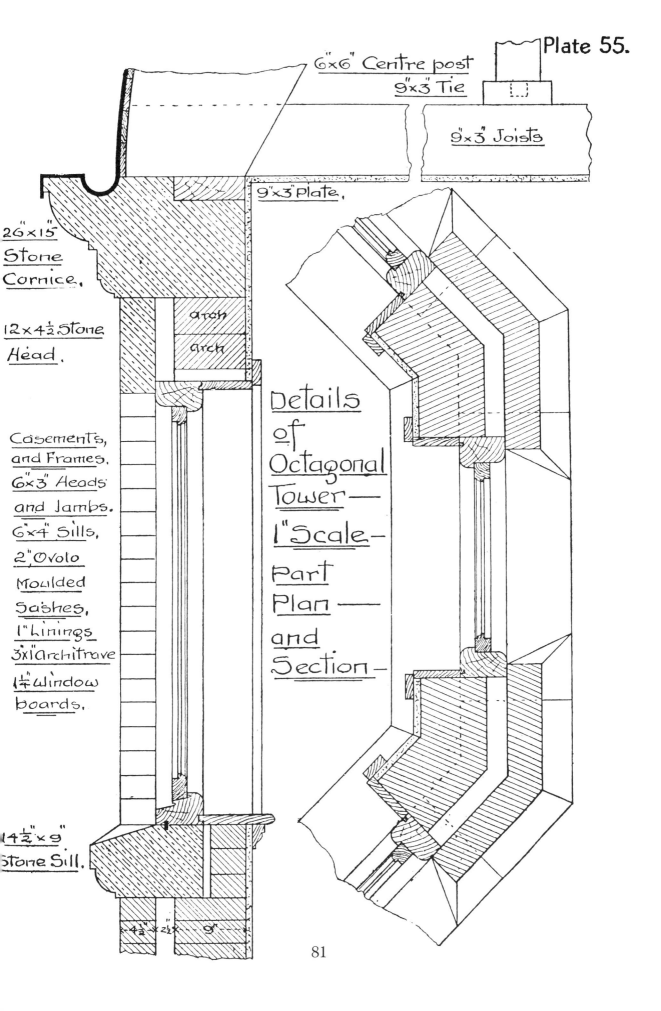

Plate 55.

6"x6" Centre post

9"x3" Tie

9"x3" Joists

9"x3" Plate.

26"x15" Stone Cornice.

12"x4½" Stone Head.

arch

arch

Casements, and Frames. 6"x3" Heads and Jambs. 6"x4" Sills, 2" Ovolo Moulded Sashes, 1" Linings 3"x1" Architrave 1¼" Window boards.

Details of Octagonal Tower— 1" Scale— Part Plan — and Section—

14½"x9" Stone Sill.

4½" 2½" 9"

81

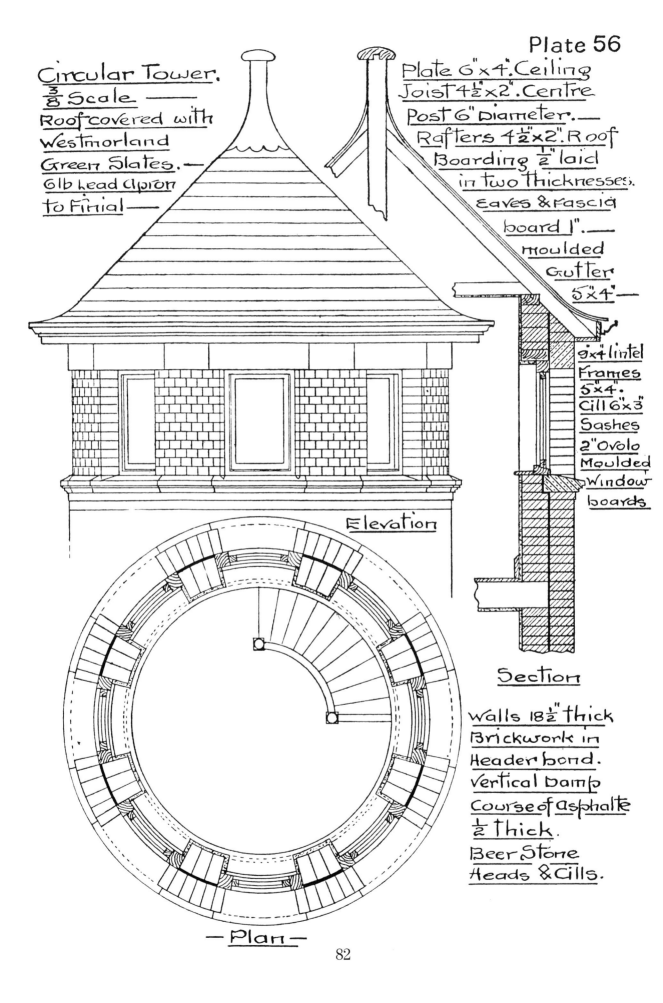

Plate 56

Circular Tower.
$\frac{3}{8}$ Scale ——
Roof covered with
Westmorland
Green Slates.——
6 lb Lead Apron
to Finial ——

Plate 6"×4". Ceiling
Joist 4½"×2". Centre
Post 6" Diameter.——
Rafters 4½"×2". Roof
Boarding ½" laid
in two thicknesses.
Eaves & Fascia
board 1".——
Moulded
Gutter
5"×4"——

9"×4" lintel
Frames
5"×4".
Cill 6"×3"
Sashes
2" Ovolo
Moulded
Window
boards

Elevation

Section

Walls 18½" thick
Brickwork in
Header bond.
Vertical Damp
Course of Asphalte
½ thick.
Beer Stone
Heads & Cills.

—Plan—

Bay Window.— ⅜" Scale — Plate 57.

12" hollow wall under frame,
Casements & Frame:— 8×3 Sill, 5"×3' Head
Jambs & muntins, 2" ovolo moulded sashes
Two bottom sashes side hung, fanlights
hung at top. opening out.
Transom 8"×4".

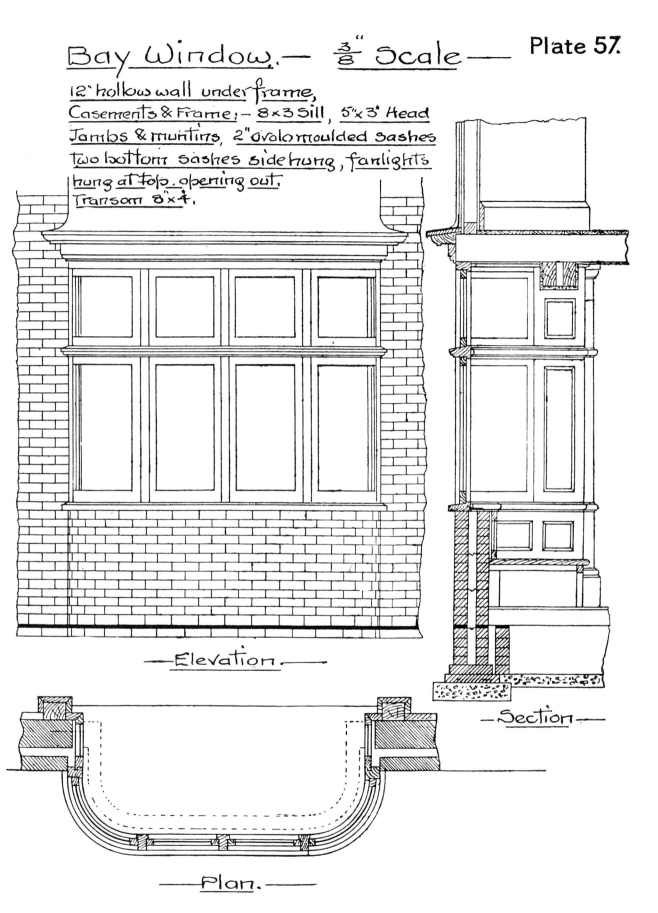

—Elevation.—

—Section—

—Plan.—

83

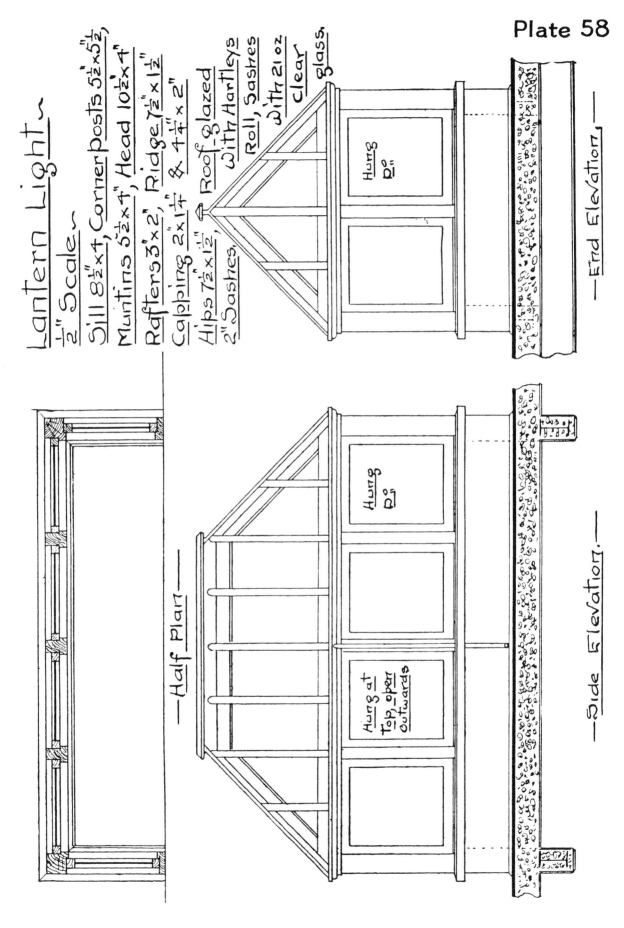

Plate 58

Lantern Light.

½" Scale.

Sill 8½×4, Corner posts 5½×5½, Muntins 5½×4", Head 10½×4" Rafters 3×2", Ridge 7½×1½" Capping 2×1¼" & 4¼×2" Hips 7½×1½", Sashes 2" Sashes. Roof glazed with Hartleys Roll, Sashes with 21oz clear glass.

Hung Do.

Hung Do.

Hung at Top, open Outwards

— Half Plan —

— Side Elevation. —

— End Elevation. —

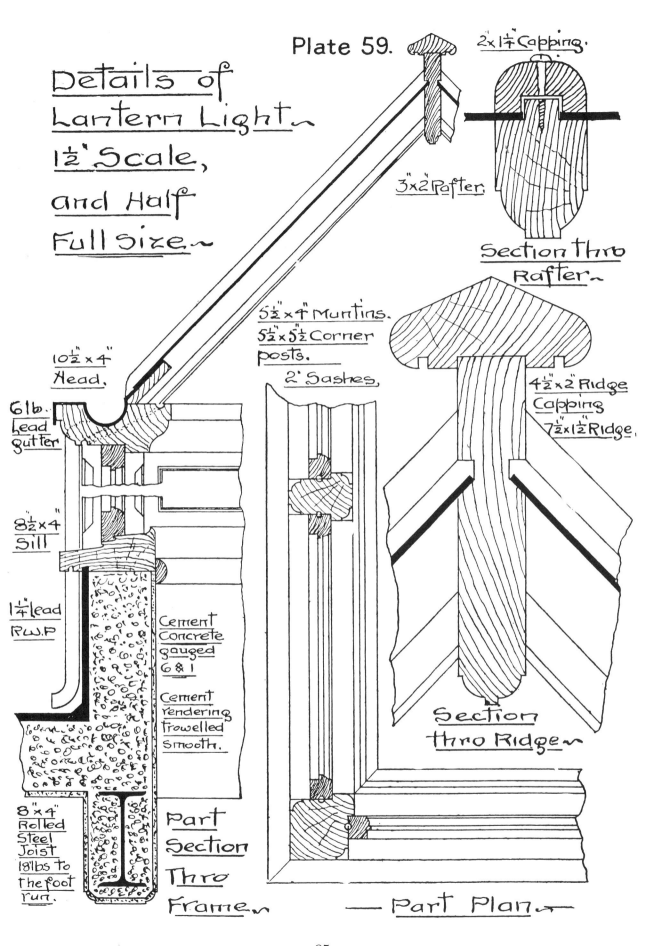

Plate 59.

Details of
Lantern Light.
1½" Scale,
and Half
Full Size.

2×1¼" Capping.

3"×2" Rafter.

Section thro Rafter.

10½"×4" Head.

6 lb. Lead gutter

8½"×4" Sill

1¼" lead R.W.P

Cement Concrete gauged 6 & 1

Cement rendering Trowelled smooth.

8"×4" Rolled Steel Joist 18 lbs to the foot run.

Part Section Thro Frame.

5½"×4" Muntins.
5½"×5½" Corner posts.
2" Sashes,

4½"×2" Ridge Capping
7½"×1½" Ridge.

Section thro Ridge.

— Part Plan.

85

Plate 60

Window with Stone Dressings ~ ½" Scale ~

— Elevation — B

— Section —

A.B.

— Plan —

Plan for a Small House.

Scale ⅛ = One Foot. — Specification — of Principal Items.

6" Cement Concrete Foundations, 11½" Hollow Walls, Red Brick Facings, Gauged Arches, Tooled Purbeck Stone Steps, Tiled floor to verandah on 6"C Concrete bed, Similar floors to Larder & W.C. Brick on edge to floor of Coals, Tiled hearths, Walls of Kitchen to have Tiled Dado of 6"x3" White glazed Tiles 3'-6" high, Build Copper in Kitchen 9" brick in cement Roof covered with Gillingham Sand faced Tiles, 6lb Lead Hips & Ridge, Asphalte Flat to Verandah, Ground Joists & Sleepers 4"x2", 1st Floor Joists 9"x2", Ceiling Joists 5"x2" Plates 4"x3" Ties 4"x2" Rafters 4"x2", Hips & Ridge 9"x1½", Purlins 5"x3, Roof board 3"x¼, Batters 2"x¾, Counter Batters 2"x2, Fascia 7"x1, Soffit 9"x1, 4"x3" C.I. moulded Eaves Gutter

Flashings, 6lb
Lead, Gutters
6lb Soakers
4lb, Trays 4lb
Floors 7"x1" best
Red Windows
5"x3" Frames 2
Sashes, Doors
2"5 panel,
Entrance door
5"x3" Frame 2
Door, Top glass,
Skirtings 8"x1"
Architraves 3"x1
Stairs, 12 Treads
1"Risers, 1.25 Strings
3½"x3" Handrail
2"x1 Balusters 3
4lc8 P.C & 5 Each
Bath P.C £6|10|-
Sink P.C. £3.

Sashes Glazed with 21oz glass
Wood & Ironwork painted 4 coats in 2 tints.

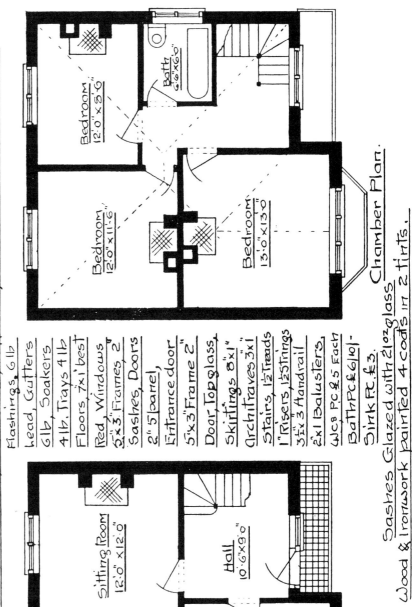

Ground Plan

Sitting Room 12'·0" x 12'·0"

Larder

Coal

Kitchen 11'·6" x 9'·3"

Hall 10'·6" x 9'·0"

Parlour 13'·0" x 13'·0"

No 2, 8"x4" RSJ 14' over

Chamber Plan

Bedroom 12'·0" x 5'·9"

Bath 6'·6" x 6'·0

Bedroom 12'·0" x 11'·6"

Bedroom 13'·0" x 13'·0

Plate 61.

87

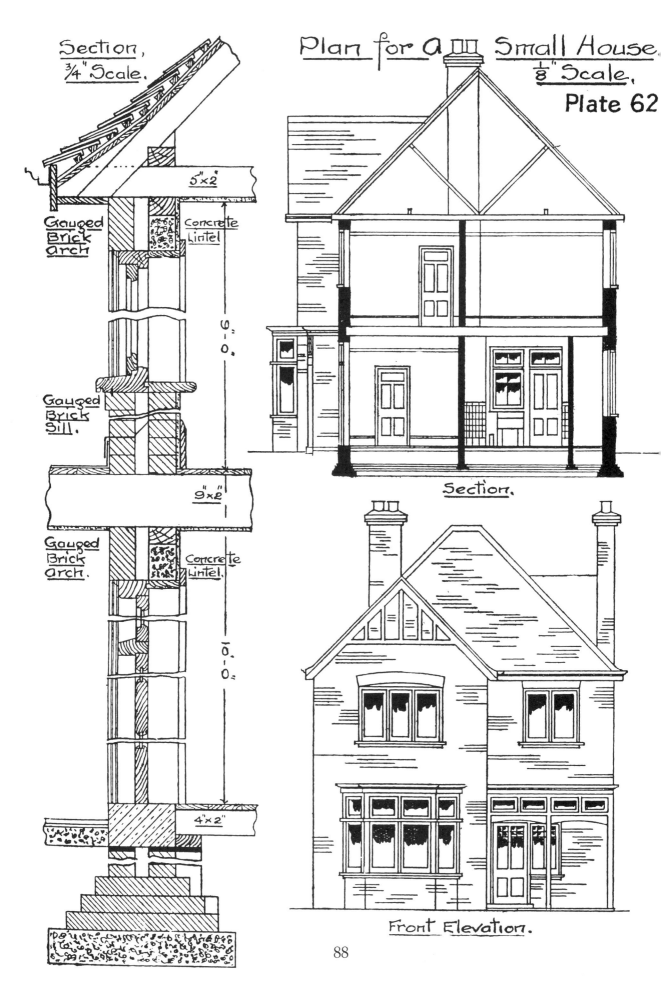

Section,
3/4" Scale.

Plan for a Small House.
1/8" Scale.

Plate 62

5"×2"

Gauged Brick arch

Concrete Lintel

9'·0"

Gauged Brick Sill.

9"×2"

Gauged Brick Arch.

Concrete Lintel.

9'·0"

4"×2"

Section.

Front Elevation.

88

Plate 63.

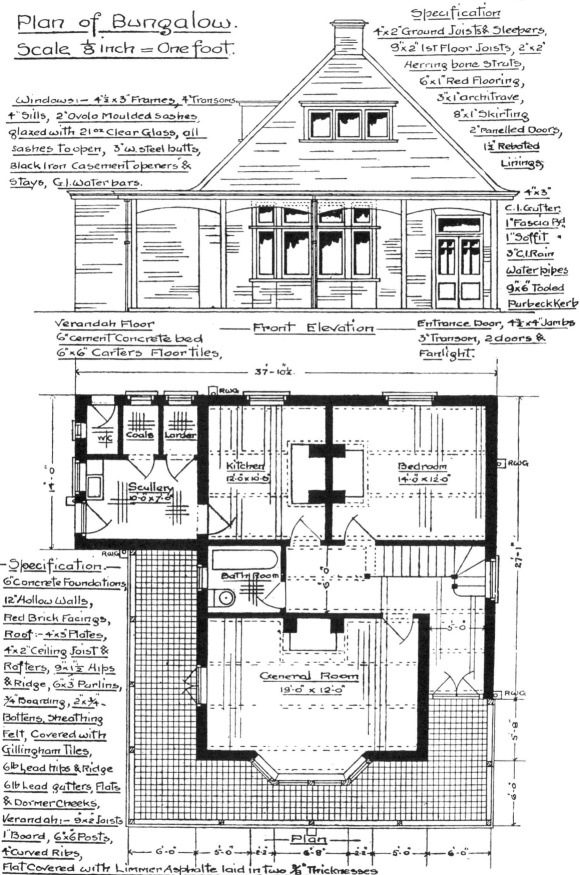

Plan of Bungalow.
Scale ⅛ inch = One foot.

Specification
4"x2" Ground Joists & Sleepers,
9"x2" 1st Floor Joists, 2"x2"
Herring bone Struts,
6"x1" Red Flooring,
3"x1" architrave,
8"x1" Skirting
2" Panelled Doors,
1½" Rebated
Linings

Windows:— 4½x3" Frames, 4" Transoms,
4" Sills, 2" Ovolo Moulded sashes,
glazed with 21oz Clear Glass, all
sashes To open, 3" W. steel butts,
Black Iron Casement openers &
Stays, G.I.Water bars.

4"x3"
C.I.Gutter,
1" Fascia Bd.
1" Soffit
3" C.I.Rain
Water pipes
9"x6" Tooled
Purbeck Kerb

Front Elevation

Verandah Floor
6" cement Concrete bed
6"x6" Carters Floor tiles,

Entrance Door, 4½x4" Jambs
3" Transom, 2 doors &
Fanlight.

—Specification.—
6" Concrete Foundations,
12" Hollow Walls,
Red Brick Facings,
Roof :— 4"x3" Plates,
4"x2" Ceiling Joist &
Rafters, 9"x1½" Hips
& Ridge, 6"x3" Purlins,
¾" Boarding, 2"x¾"
Battens, Sheathing
Felt, Covered with
Gillingham Tiles,
6lb Lead Hips & Ridge
6lb Lead gutters, Flats
& Dormer Cheeks,
Verandah:— 9"x2" Joists
1" Board, 6"x6" Posts,
4" Curved Ribs,
Flat Covered with Limmer Asphalte laid in Two ⅜" Thicknesses

W.C
Coals
Larder
Scullery
10·0" x 7·0"
Kitchen
12·0" x 10·0"
Bedroom
14·0" x 12·0"
Bath Room
General Room
19·0" x 12·0"

Plan

37'-10½"
27'-1"

6·0"   5·0"   2·2"   6·8"   2·2"   5·0"   6·0"

Plate 64.

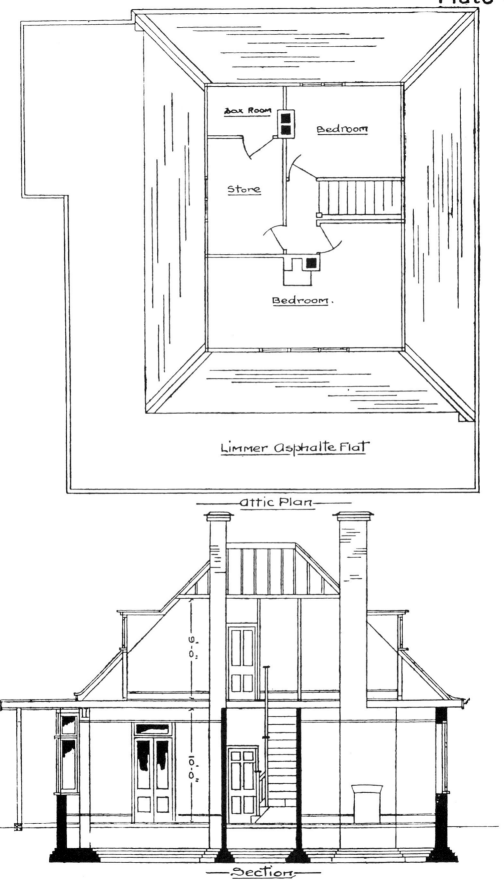

Box Room

Bedroom

Store

Bedroom.

Limmer Asphalte Flat

Attic Plan

Section

9'-0"

10'-0"

90

Porch to Entrance
¼" Scale. Plate 65.

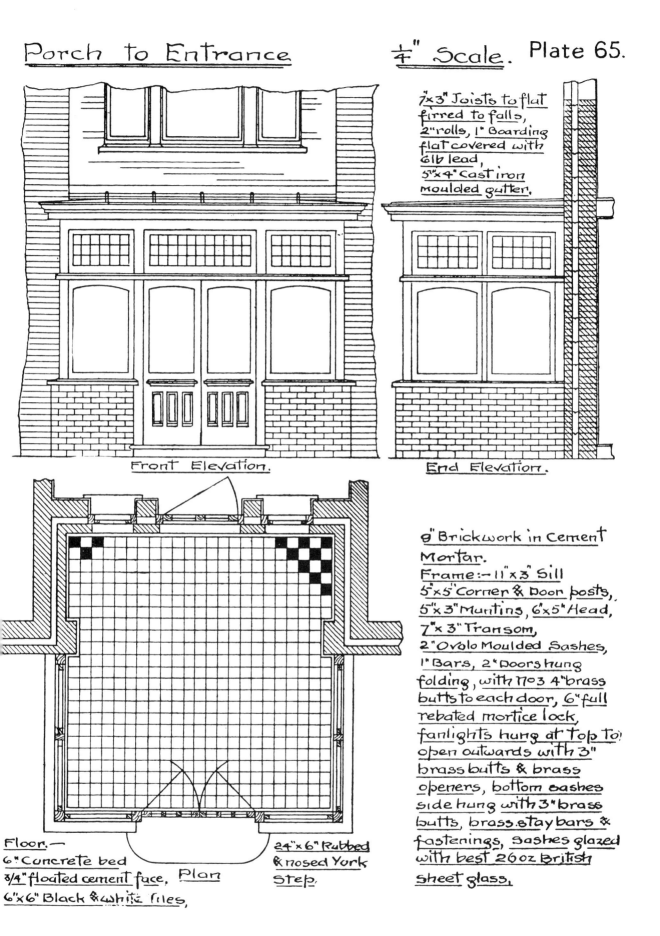

7"x3" Joists to flat
firred to falls,
2"rolls, 1" Boarding
flat covered with
6lb lead,
5"x4" Cast iron
moulded gutter.

Front Elevation.

End Elevation.

9" Brickwork in Cement
Mortar.
Frame:— 11"x3" Sill
5"x5" Corner & Door posts,
5"x3" Muntins, 6"x5" Head,
7"x3" Transom,
2" Ovolo Moulded Sashes,
1" Bars, 2" Doors hung
folding, with Nº 3 4" brass
butts to each door, 6" full
rebated mortice lock,
fanlights hung at top to
open outwards with 3"
brass butts & brass
openers, bottom sashes
side hung with 3" brass
butts, brass stay bars &
fastenings, sashes glazed
with best 26 oz British
sheet glass,

Floor.—
6" Concrete bed
¾" floated cement face,
6"x6" Black & white tiles,

Plan

24"x 6" Rubbed
& nosed York
Step.

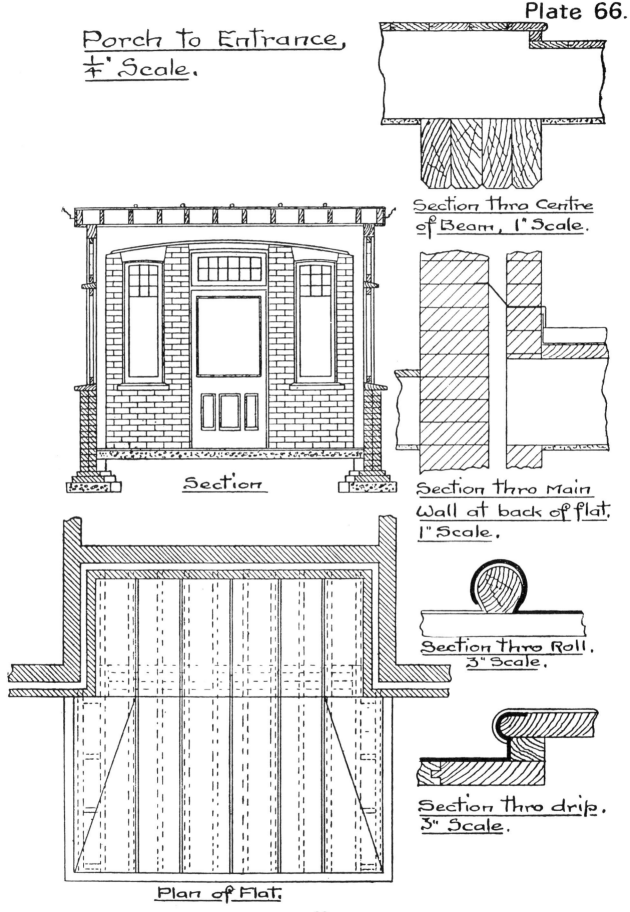

Plate 66.

Porch to Entrance,
¼" Scale.

Section thro Centre
of Beam, 1" Scale.

Section

Section thro Main
Wall at back of flat.
1" Scale.

Section thro Roll.
3" Scale.

Section thro drip.
3" Scale.

Plan of Flat.

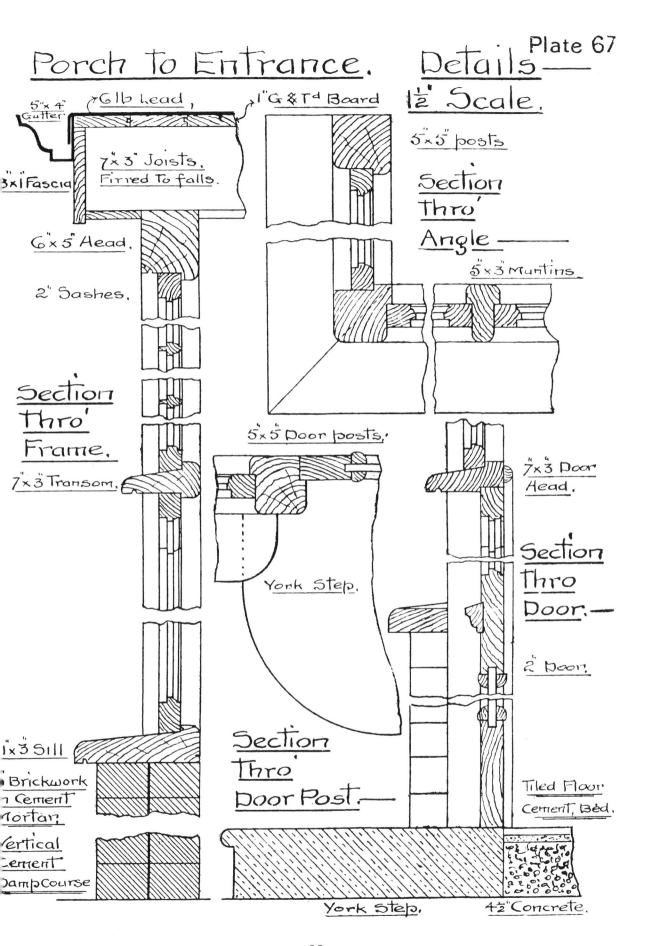

Porch to Entrance. Details—

Plate 67

1½" Scale.

5"x4" Gutter

6 lb Lead

1" G & T'd Board

3"x1" Fascia

7"x3" Joists, Firred To falls.

6"x5" Head.

2" Sashes.

5"x5" posts

Section Thro' Angle —

5"x3" Muntins

Section Thro' Frame.

7"x3" Transom.

5"x5" Door posts.

7"x3" Door Head.

Section Thro Door.—

2" Door.

York Step.

Section Thro' Door Post.—

1"x3" Sill

Brickwork in Cement Mortar.

Vertical Cement Damp Course

York Step.

Tiled Floor Cement Bed.

4½" Concrete.

Plate 68.

Details of Sewer Manhole.
$\frac{1}{2}"$ Scale.

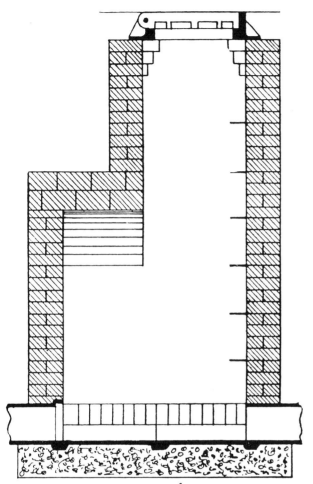
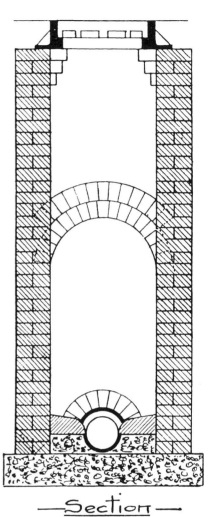

— Section —   — Section —

Cement Concrete
bottom 8"thick,
Walls 9" Brick in
Cement Inside lined
with Saltglazed bricks,
Saltglazed bull nosed
brick benchings,
Saltglazed stoneware
Channel, Galvanized
W.I. step irons
Cast Iron Manhole
Cover.

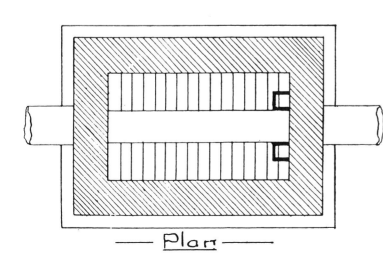

— Plan —

Plate 69.

Details of Manhole at Bend of Sewer.
½" Scale.

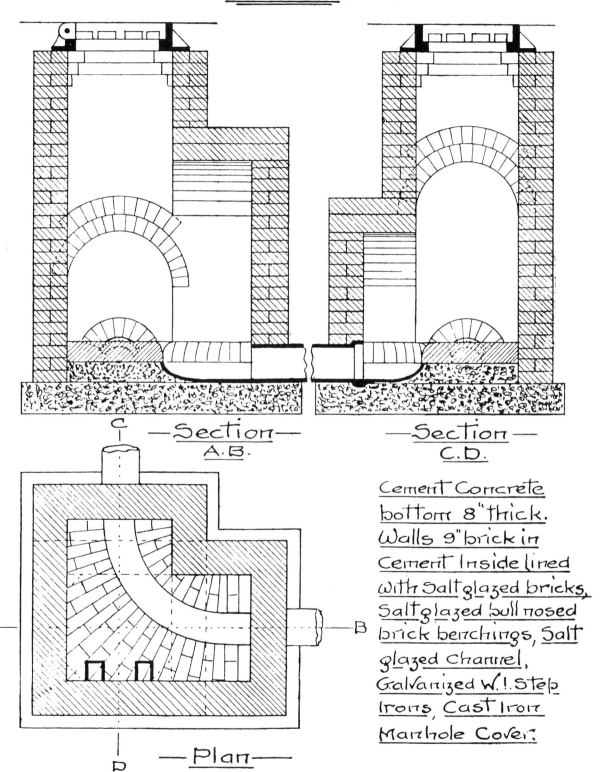

—Section—
A.B.

—Section—
C.D.

—Plan—

Cement Concrete
bottom 8" thick.
Walls 9" brick in
Cement Inside lined
with salt glazed bricks,
Salt glazed bull nosed
brick benchings, Salt
glazed channel,
Galvanized W.I. Step
Irons, Cast Iron
Manhole Cover.

Plate 70.

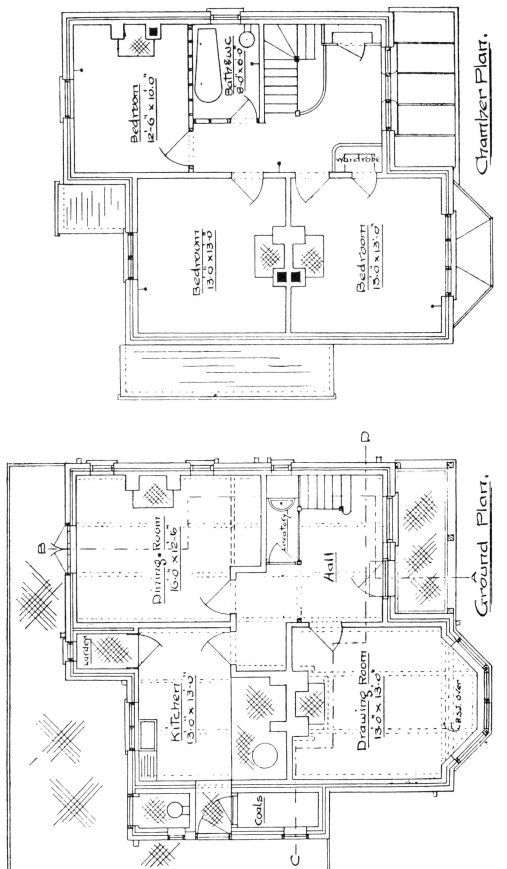

Plan of Villa Residence
⅛" Scale

Chamber Plan.

Bedroom
12'-6" × 10'-0"

Bath & w.c.
8'-0" × 6'-0"

wardrobe

Bedroom
13'-0 × 13'-0

Bedroom
13'-0 × 13'-0

Ground Plan.

Dining Room
16'-0 × 12'-6

larder

Kitchen
13'-0 × 13'-0

Coals

Lavatory

Hall

Drawing Room
13'-0 × 13'-0

R.S.J. over

96

Plate 71.

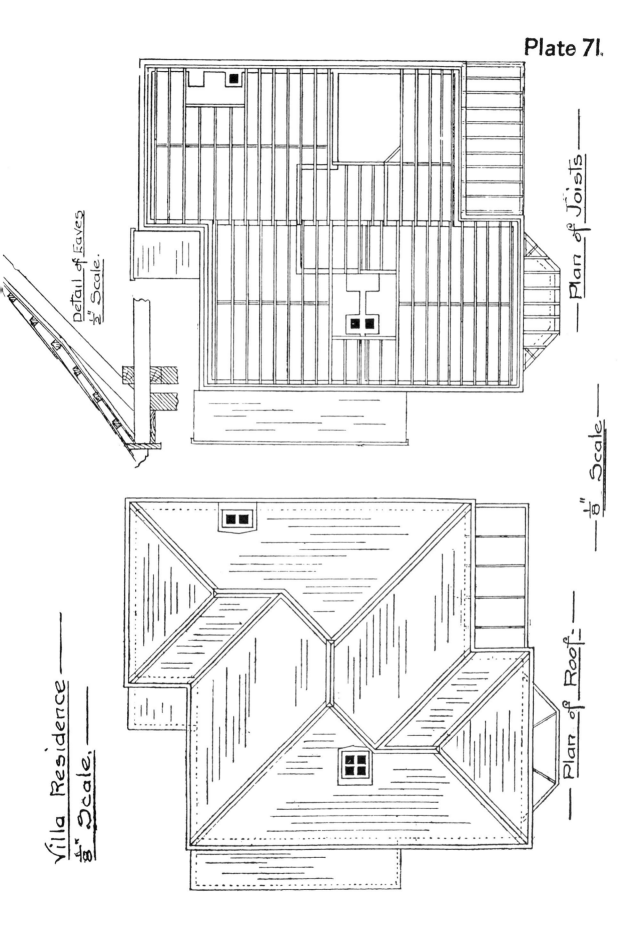

Detail of Eaves
½" Scale.

Plan of Joists

Villa Residence
⅛" Scale.

Plan of Roof.

⅛" Scale

Plate 72.

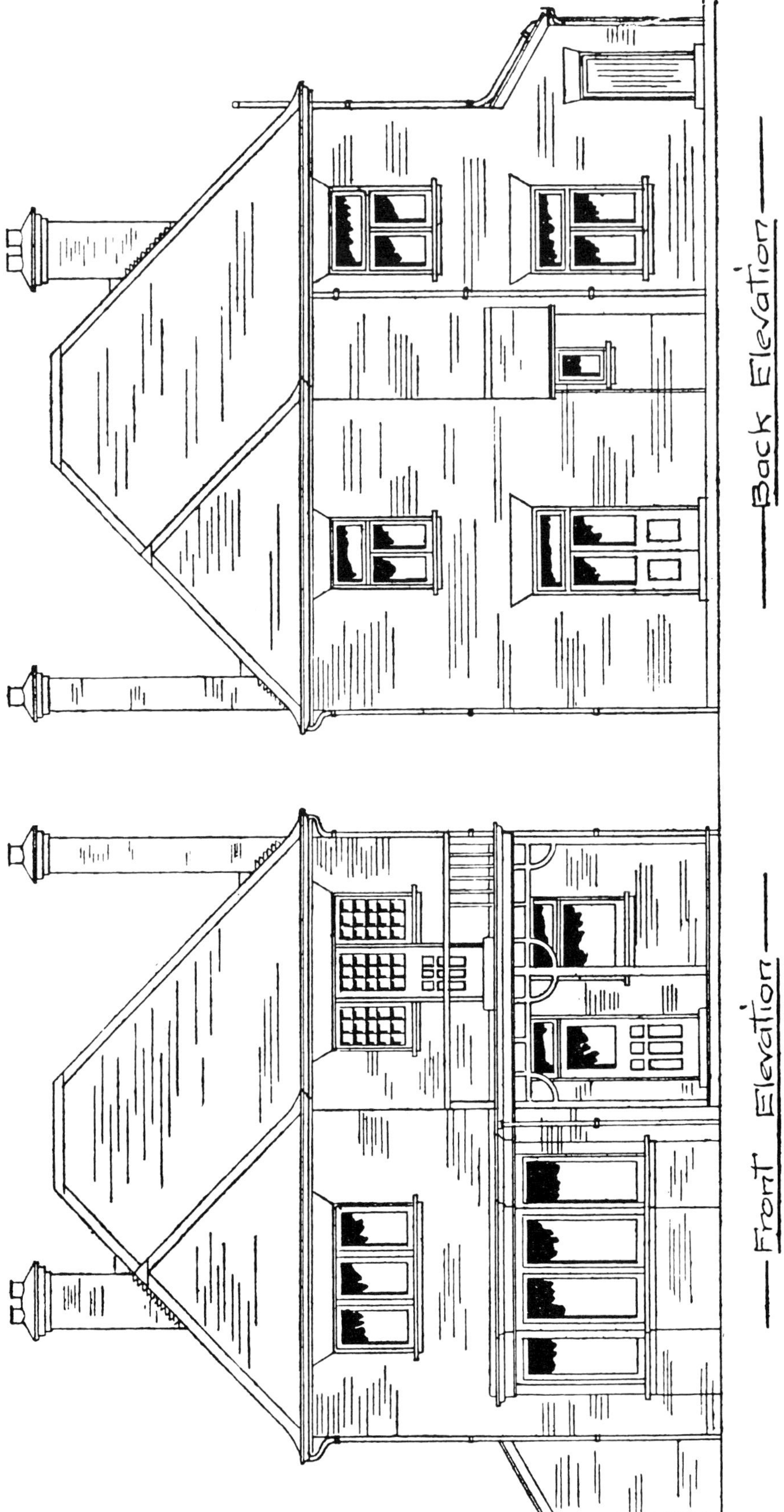

Villa Residence.

⅛" Scale

Back Elevation

Front Elevation

Plate 73.

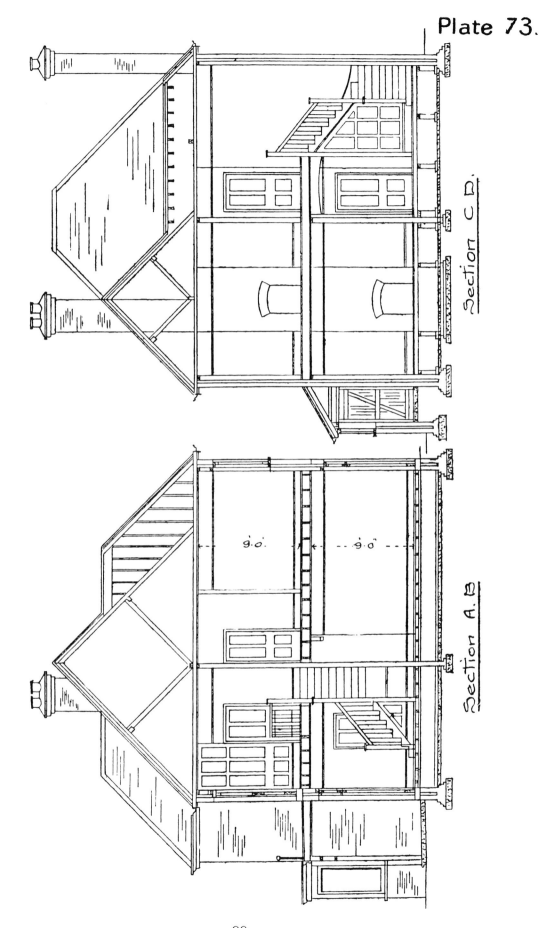

Villa Residence

⅛" Scale.

Section C D.

Section A B.

9.0"   9.0"

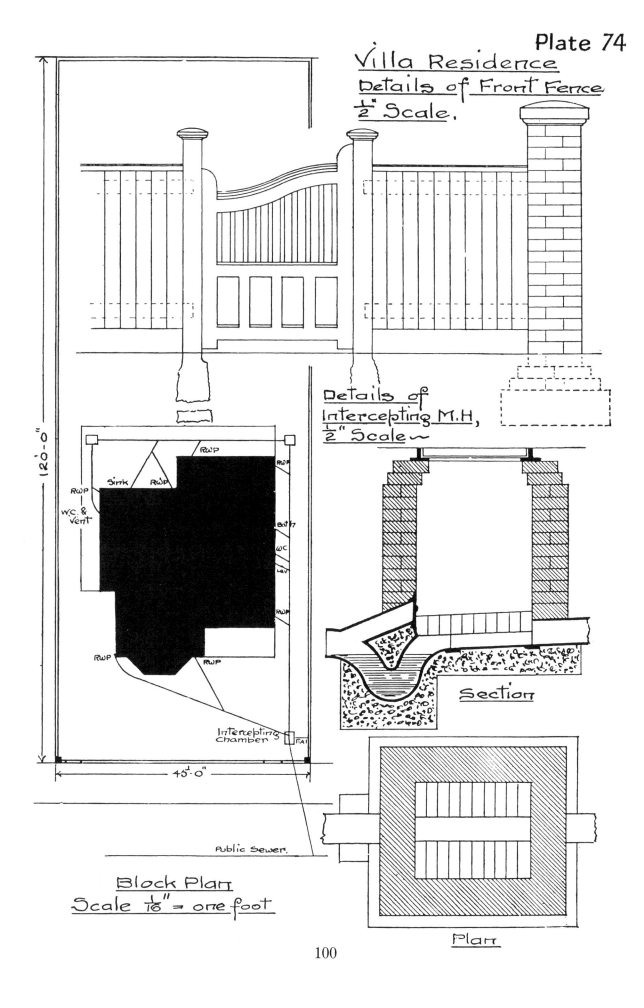

Plate 74

Villa Residence
Details of Front Fence
½" Scale.

Details of
Intercepting M.H.
½" Scale

Section

Plan

12'-0"

RWP

Sink   RWP

W.C. &
Vent

RWP   RWP

Bath

WC

Lav

RWP

RWP   RWP

Intercepting
Chamber   FAI

45'-0"

Public Sewer.

Block Plan
Scale 1/16" = one foot

Details of Windows. "Scale. Plate 75.

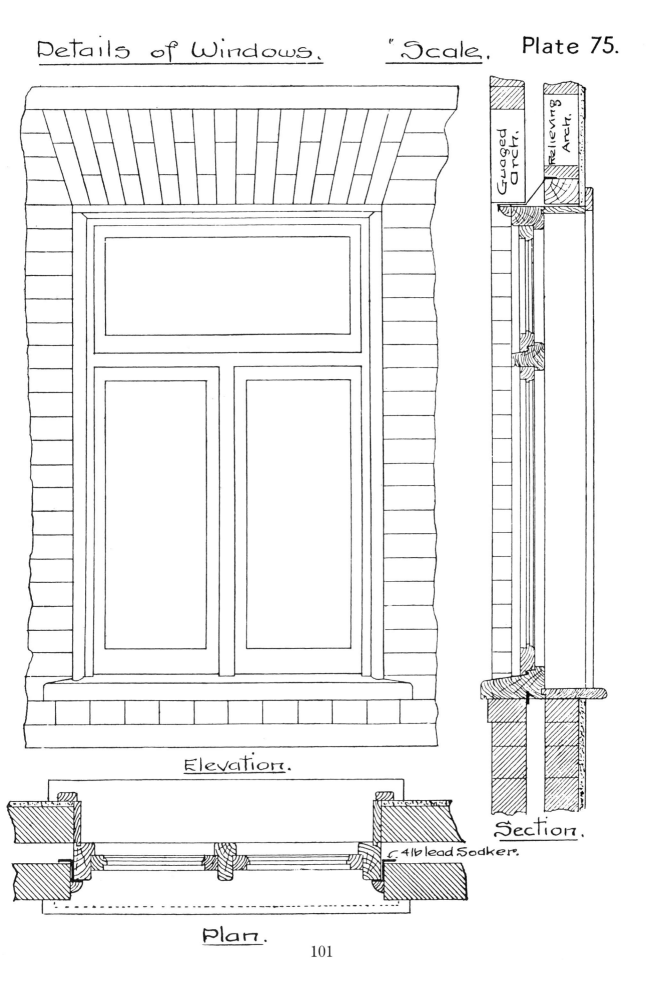

Guaged Arch.

Relieving Arch.

Elevation.

Section.

c 4lb lead Sodker.

Plan.

Plate 76.

Details of Bay Window, 1" Scale.

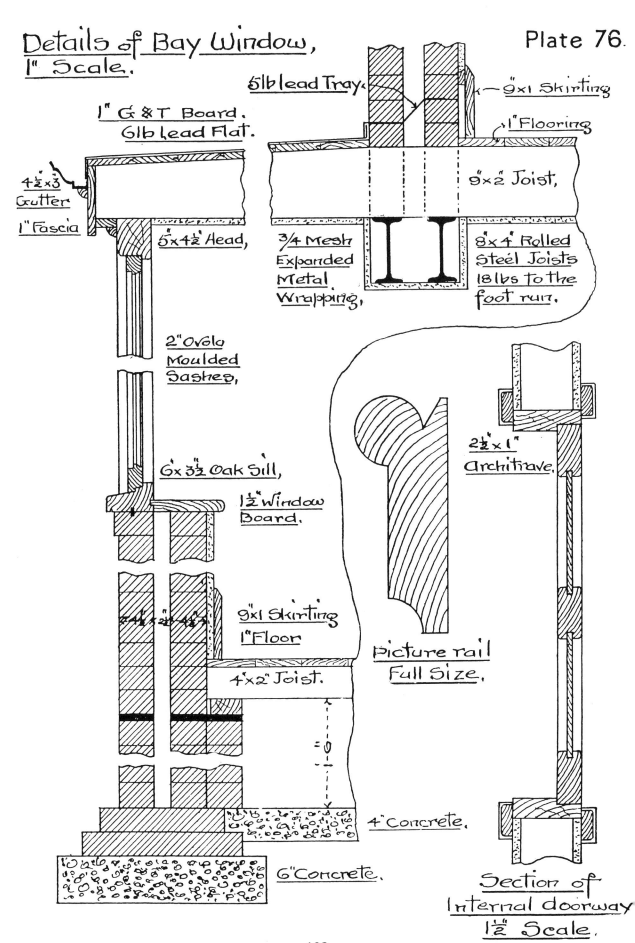

5lb lead Tray.

9"x1 Skirting

1" G & T Board. 6lb Lead Flat.

1" Flooring

4½"x3" Gutter

9"x2 Joist,

1" Fascia

5"x4½ Head,

3/4 Mesh Expanded Metal Wrapping,

8"x4" Rolled Steel Joists 18 lbs to the foot run.

2" Ovolo Moulded Sashes,

6"x3½ Oak Sill,

1½" Window Board.

2½"x1" Architrave.

9"x1 Skirting 1" Floor

4"x2" Joist.

Picture rail Full Size.

4" Concrete.

6" Concrete.

Section of Internal doorway 1½" Scale.

Newel Cap, & Handrail,
Half_full Size.

Section thro Landing,
Quarter Full Size.

SPECIFICATION OF WORKS required to be done in the erection of VILLA RESIDENCE in accordance with the Drawings numbered 70 to 77.

PRELIMINARY AND GENERAL.

GIVE all notices to the local authorities as the case may require, Notices. and pay all fees.

The contractor to take all responsibility for the setting out Setting out. of the work.

Erect temporary hoarding six feet high along the front of Hoarding. works, and provide proper door in same, with lock and key.

Provide all requisite scaffolding and plant for the proper Plant. execution of the works.

Provide for watching and lighting during the execution of Watching. the work.

Pay gas and water companies' charges for making connec- Fees. tions to their mains and fixing meters.

Provide all requisite temporary coverings to exposed work Coverings. during the progress of the work, also sawdust to protect floors.

Each trade to attend upon, cut away for, and make good Attend on Trades. after all others, and do all necessary jobbing work to complete the works.

Give all requisite facilities to sub-contractors (if any), pro- Sub-con- tractors. viding plant and scaffolding as required.

In all cases where P.C. or list prices or nett quotations are P.C. Amounts. stated, the contractor is to add for his profit, and for any requisite packing, carriage, or fixing.

Latrines. Provide latrines for the use of the workmen, take proper precautions to prevent same from becoming a nuisance. Disinfect from time to time, empty and remove, and fill in at completion.

Water. Provide water for the works, including what is wanted for testing the sanitary work.

Cart Away. Clear and cart away all rubbish as it may accumulate during the work and at completion thereof.

Scrub Floors. Scrub floors clean windows inside and out, and leave all clean at completion.

Provisional Sum. Provide the provisional sum of Ten pounds (£10) for expenditure in such extra work as the surveyor may direct; any portion not so expended shall be deducted from the amount due to the contractor.

EXCAVATOR.

Top Soil. Remove top soil over site of building to a depth of 9″.

Foundations. Excavate for foundations, part return, fill in and ram.

Filling Trenches. The trenches to be filled in as soon as walls are above ground level, after approval by the surveyor.

Under Floors. Excavate under boarded floors to allow for a clear space of 1′ 6″ from underside of joists to top of concrete bed.

Do all requisite excavation under tiled floors.

Trenches for Pipes. Excavate for gas and water pipes to the required depth, to conform with the companies' regulations, and fill in and ram after pipes are laid.

Water in Trenches. If water is found in the trenches, this must be baled or pumped out and the trenches kept dry until filled in.

Planking. Do all requisite planking, shoring or strutting, for maintaining the sides of trenches.

Surplus Earth. The whole of the surplus earth from the excavations is to be used for the levelling up of the site. The contractor is to allow in his estimate for wheeling and carting same.

SPECIFICATION FOR VILLA RESIDENCE

CONCRETOR.

The concrete to be composed of six parts of clean, washed, **Materials.** grey gravel, broken to pass a 2″ ring, two parts of clean, sharp, washed sand and one part of Portland cement.

The materials for concrete to be thoroughly mixed together **Mixing.** on clean platforms, being turned twice dry and twice whilst being wetted to a proper consistency.

No concrete or cement mortar to be used after it has commenced to set.

Brick rubble may be used for concrete if broken to pass a **Brick Rubble.** 2″ ring and properly cleaned and sifted.

Put concrete foundations as shown on the drawings. **Foundations.**

Lay a bed of concrete 4″ thick under boarded floors, and **Under Floors.** 6″ thick under tiled floors and hearths, also to yard floor.

Lay a bed of concrete 16″ wide and 4″ thick under all **Under Drains.** drains, and haunch up sides of drains with concrete as specified in drainage.

DRAINAGE.

Excavate for drains as shown on drawings, and provide and **Pipes.** lay to proper lines and levels 4″ and 6″ best salt-glazed stone-ware socketed pipes, providing all requisite bends, junctions, and other fittings.

The joints to be first caulked with tarred gasket and then **Joints.** properly filled and filleted with cement mortar.

The drains to rest on a bed of concrete 16″ wide and **Concrete to Drains.** 4″ thick; the sides of drains to be haunched up with concrete.

The whole of the drains to be laid to satisfy the local **Testing.** authority. Proper facilities and attention to be given to the inspector when testing.

The inspection chambers to be built in 9″ brickwork in **Inspection Chambers.** cement mortar on 6″ concrete foundations; the inside facings to be of best salt-glazed bricks. Provide all requisite half-channel pipes. Bends and fittings to be best salt-glazed. Put best salt-glazed bull-nosed brick benchings. Put strong galvanised step-irons every foot in depth where chambers are more than 2′ 0″ in depth.

Covers. The inspection covers to be of galvanized cast-iron, with cement-filled top.

Provide and build in proper syphon with raking arm and stopper to intercepting chamber.

F.A. Inlet. Take off 4″ pipe from intercepting chamber to point shown on drawing and carry up 2′ 0″ above ground, and finish with mica flap inlet valve.

Gullies. Provide and fix at the foot of rainwater pipes 6″ rainwater gullies, to be Messrs Sharp, Jones & Co.'s No. 75, with knuckle inlet and cast-iron gratings. The gullies to take bath, sink, and lavatory wastes to be Messrs Sharp, Jones & Co.'s " Branksome " pattern, with cast-iron gratings.

BRICKLAYER.

Bricks. The bricks to be hard, sound, well-burnt, true in shape, of good and approved quality.

Facings. The facings to be of best selected Bridgwater bricks, pointed down at finish with a neat weather-struck joint in cement.

The inside walls to be left rough for plaster, except walls of w.c. and coals, which are to have struck joints as the work proceeds and twice lime-whitened at finish.

Rise of Brickwork. Brickwork to be built to rise one foot in every four courses; vertical and horizontal joints to be kept true in line.

Lime. The lime to be freshly burnt Blue Lias lime from an approved maker.

Cement. The cement to be Portland cement from an approved maker, and to conform to the British Standard specification for Portland cement (1910), to be the quality known and described as medium setting.

SPECIFICATION FOR VILLA RESIDENCE

The sand to be clean, sharp, and free from earthy matter, Sand. and to be washed if directed.

The mortar to be composed of one part of lime to three Mortar. parts of sand.

Cement mortar to be composed of one part of cement to two parts of sand.

The external walls to be built hollow with $2\frac{1}{2}''$ cavity and Hollow Walls. bounded together with galvanized wrought-iron wall-ties, No. 446 to the cwt., placed $3'\ 0''$ apart horizontally and $12''$ vertically, with additional ties around openings.

The cavity and wall-ties to be kept clean by placing battens in cavity and lifting same as the work proceeds. Leave cleaning holes where directed over door and window heads, also at ground level; the bricks at these points to be bedded in sand temporarily, and properly bedded in mortar at completion.

The chimneys above roofs, sleeper and fender walls, and Brickwork in Cement Mortar. $4\frac{1}{2}''$ walls to be built in cement mortar.

Build $4\frac{1}{2}''$ sleeper and fender walls on one course of $9''$ Sleeper Walls. brickwork.

Put to all walls, including sleeper and fender walls, a damp- Damp Course. proof course of double course of slate, set and pointed in cement, joints to be lapped.

Build in where directed No. 15, $3'' \times 9''$ galvanized cast-iron Air Bricks. ventilating bricks.

Build in No. 3, $9'' \times 9''$ galvanized cast-iron ventilating bricks to w.c., coals, and larder.

Provide $200'\ 0''$ run $1\frac{1}{4}''$ No. 16 B.W.G. galvanized hoop- Hoop-iron Bond. iron, to be used as bond, part cut to short lengths and fixed to frames.

Do all requisite beam-filling between timbers. Beam-filling.

Bed plates and lintels. Bed Plates.

Provide and build in all requisite coke breeze fixing bricks. Fixing Bricks.

The external arches over door and window openings to be Gauged Arches. executed in gauged work with best selected red rubber bricks set in lime putty. The joints to be not more than $\frac{1}{8}''$ in thickness.

Relieving Arches. Turn relieving arches over all door and window openings, to be 9″ deep.

Trimmer Arches. Turn half-brick trimmer arches in cement to hearths on first floor.

Chimney Heads. Build chimney heads to detail, with oversailing courses and double course of tile creasing on top.

Chimney Pots. Provide and fix approved chimney pots, price 5s. each, and haunch in cement.

Parge and Core. Parge and core flues.

Piers under Kitchen Sink. The piers under kitchen sink to be built in $4\frac{1}{2}''$ best white glazed brickwork, with bull-nosed external angles, in cement mortar.

Boundary Piers. The two boundary piers at front to be built in 14″ × 14″ brickwork in cement mortar, with best selected Bridgwater facings and joints neatly struck as the work proceeds.

Fix Grates. Fix grates, mantels, and kitchener.

Bed and Point. Bed and point frames in hair mortar.

Point Flashings. Rake out and point flashings in cement.

Hoist and fix rolled steel joists.

Hearth Spaces. Fill in hearth spaces on ground floor with dry brick rubble and well ram to receive concrete.

Tiled Floors. Pave the floors of larder, w.c., kitchen entrance and hearth, also verandah, with Messrs Carter & Co.'s best selected $4\frac{1}{4}'' \times 4\frac{1}{4}''$ red paving tiles.

The paving to yard at back of house to be executed with 6″ × 6″ best red quarry tiles.

The floor of coals to be paved with best hard pottery bricks.

Hearths. The hearths to be finished with 3″ × 3″ best selected glazed tiles, with border tiles to match.

Tiled Dado. The walls of kitchen to be lined with 6″ × 3″ best selected white glazed tiles to a height of 3′ 6″. The jambs and frieze of kitchen fireplace to be lined with similar tiles to finish underneath shelf.

Provide all requisite internal and external angle tiles, also capping tile with rounded edge.

The floor tiles to be laid and grouted in cement and properly cleaned off at finish with sawdust. **Laying Tiles.**

The wall tiling to be bedded in cement and grouted in with Parian cement, and properly cleaned off at finish.

MASON.

Build in to entrance doorways, w.c. doorway, also doorway to flat 12″ × 6″ Purbeck stone steps, finely tooled one side and edge, with squared ends and back jointed, the steps to be 9″ longer than opening width. **Steps.**

The kerb to verandah to be 9″ × 6″ Purbeck stone, finely tooled one side and edge, and back jointed. Put 9″ × 3″ similar kerb to yard tiling. **Kerb.**

Provide and fix No. 2, 14″ × 12″ × 6″ tooled Purbeck stone templates under ends of rolled steel joists. **Templates.**

Put to boundary piers No. 2 finely tooled Purbeck stone pier caps 18″ × 18″ × 6″ worked to a detail. **Pier Caps.**

SLATER.

Cover the roofs with best Bangor "Countess" slating laid to a 3″ lap on 2″ × ¾″ sawn fir battens and nailed with two 1½″ compo nails to each slate.

Put double course of slate at eaves.

Do all requisite cutting to hips, valleys, verges, and ridges.

Note.—The hips and ridges will be covered with 6-lb. lead. See specification of Plumber.

PLASTERER.

The lime to be fresh, well-burnt, stone lime, and to be run into putty at least one month before being used. **Lime.**

Sand.   The sand to be clean and sharp and washed if directed.

Hair.   Hair to be the best long cow hair, and to be well beaten when dry, and mixed with the mortar.

Laths.   All laths to be lath and half, and to be riven out of sound Baltic fir, butted at joints, and with joints broken at 2′ 0″ intervals.

Ceilings.   Lath, plaster, float, and set ceilings, slopes of stairs, partitions, also ceiling of verandah.

Walls.   Render, float, and set to all the interior walls, with the exception of outside w.c. and coals.

Angles.   The salient angles throughout to be in Portland cement and finished with Keene's cement and slightly rounded.

Render Floors.   The floors of larder, w.c., kitchen entrance, verandah, and hearths to be rendered in cement $\frac{3}{4}$″ thick and floated to a level face to receive tiled floors.

Render Walls.   The jambs and frieze of kitchen fireplace, also walls of kitchen to a height of 3′ 6,″ to be rendered in cement and floated to a face to receive tiled dado.

Casing to Rolled Steel Joists.   The rolled steel joists to bay window to be wrapped around with $\frac{3}{4}$″ mesh expanded metal, and rendered in Portland cement and finished in Parian cement.

CARPENTER AND JOINER.

Timber.   The timber throughout to be of good and approved quality Baltic red fir, free from sap, shakes, large loose or dead knots, and all other defects, and to be cut die square.

The joinery to be made from best quality seasoned Christiania deals, or from deals of equal quality.

Spacing of Timbers.   The timbers to be spaced not more than 12″ apart in the clear and trimmed for fireplaces and chimneys.

Trimmers.   The trimming joists and rafters to be 1″ thicker than the ordinary timbers.

Centres, etc.   Provide, fix, and strike all requisite centres and turning pieces.

SPECIFICATION FOR VILLA RESIDENCE

Put firring-up pieces where necessary, and do all requisite **Firring-up.** cradling and bracketing.

Provide and fix all lintels, to be 1″ in depth for every foot of **Lintels.** opening width, and no lintel to be less than 3″ deep.

Do all requisite plugging to walls. **Plugging.**

Provide all requisite backings, grounds, and other fixings; **Grounds, etc.** also all requisite smith's work and ironmongery, with all nails, screws, holdfasts, bolts, etc. All screws for brass work to be brass.

The sizes of timbers to be as follows :—Ground-floor joists **Sizes of** 4″ × 2″. Sleepers 4″ × 2″. First-floor joists 9″ × 2″; trimmer joists **Timber.** 9″ × 3″. Plates 4½″ × 3″. Herring-bone struts 2½″ × 1½″—one row to each room. Ceiling joists and rafters 4″ × 2″. Ties 4″ × 2″. Purlins 6″ × 3″. Ridge 9″ × 1½″. Hips and valleys 9″ × 1½″. Battens 2″ × ¾″. Fascia board, 7″ × 1¼″. Soffit board 9″ × 1″. Fascia and soffite boards to be wrought. Ridge and hip rolls to be 2″ rounded.

Cover the roofs with ½″ rough boarding, on the boarding **Roof Board-** lay approved black sheathing felt horizontally, lapped 3″, and **ing, etc.** nailed with ½″ galvanized clout-nails. Put 1¼″ × ¼″ counter battens nailed on top of felt over each rafter, and to sides of hips and valleys.

Put to chimneys proper 1″ gutter boards and bearers. **Gutter Boards.**

The flat over bay window to have 9″ × 2″ joists cut to fall **Flat over** to gutter. Put 7″ × 3″ trimmer to ends of joists at angle of bay. **Bay Window.** Cover the flat with 1″ grooved and tongued boards, properly cleaned off flush for lead, and put 2″ wood rolls for lead. Fascia board 9″ × 1¼″, soffit board 3″ × 1″, with 1¼″ quarter round moulding nailed to frame, and similar moulding nailed to fascia under gutter.

The stud partitions to have 4″ × 3″ heads and sills, 4″ × 2″ **Stud** uprights and horizontal ties, all properly framed and spiked **Partitions.** together.

Trim for trap-door in ceiling, and put 1½″ solid rebated **Trap Door.**

linings with $1\frac{1}{4}''$ framed and panelled trap-door hung with $2\frac{1}{2}''$ wrought-steel butts, and put $3''$ brass bolt.

Provide and lay $36'\,0''$ super $1''$ rough board to form floor for tank in roof.

Sizes of Joiner's Work. The dimensions and thicknesses of joiner's work described in this specification are the sizes out of which the joinery is prepared and not the finished thicknesses. All joiner's work to be wrought and finished with a smooth, even surface.

The joiner's work as far as possible to be started immediately on the signing of the contract. The doors are to be framed together, but not cramped up, strip stacked and left for drying and glued up when directed by the surveyor. The door frames and window frames to be built in.

Verandah. The verandah to be framed with $5''\times5''$ posts, $5''\times3''$ plate, $3''\times3''$ transom and muntins, $3''\times3''$ curved bracket pieces. The flat to have $9''\times2''$ joists firred to falls. Cover the flat with $1''$ grooved and tongued flooring properly cleaned off flush at finish. Fascia board $10''\times1\frac{1}{4}''$; put $1\frac{1}{4}''$ quarter round moulding under eaves gutter. The handrail to be $3''\times3''$ moulded red fir, pinned into walls at ends and mitred at angle. The balusters to be tapered $2\frac{1}{2}''$ to $2''$ and $1''$ thick, tenoned into $3''\times2''$ bottom rail.

Floors. The floors throughout to be laid with $5''\times1''$ best red flooring, with square butt joints and cleaned off flush at finish. Provide sawdust for the protection of the floors when laid. Put mitred borders to hearths.

Matwell Sinking. Form sinking for mat $3'\times0''\times2'\,0''\times2''$ deep, with $3''$ mitred border around.

Door Linings. Put to all internal door openings $1\frac{3}{4}''$ solid rebated linings full width of walls and plaster.

Window Linings. The linings to windows to be $\frac{7}{8}''$ thick tongued to frames.

Window Boards. Put $1\frac{1}{4}''$ tongued and nosed window boards with returned ends to all windows.

Skirting. Put $9''\times1''$ rounded and chamfered skirting to dining-room, drawing-room, and hall; all other skirtings to be similar, only 7″ × 1″. Provide all requisite 2″ × ¾″ grounds, backings, and plugging for fixing same. The top ground to be bevelled to form key for plastering.

The architraves throughout to be 2½″ × 1″, with rounded **Architrave.** edges. Put 3″ × 1¼″ base blocks to architraves at doorways 10″ and 7½″ in height, housed for skirtings.

Put 2½″ × 1″ chamfered, grooved, and moulded picture rail **Picture Rail.** to all rooms, except bathroom.

The interior doors to be 6′ 8″ × 2′ 8″ × 2″, 4 panel, with edges **Interior Doors.** of framing slightly rounded, hung to linings with No. 2, 4″ wrought-steel butts, and fitted with 6″ two-bolt mortice lock and furniture, price 10s., to doors opening on to hall and landing, the remaining doors to have locks and furniture, price 8s. per set.

The French casement to dining-room to have 4½″ × 3″ rebated **French Casement.** and rounded frame, grooved for linings, with 6″ × 3″ rebated, sunk, weathered, and throated transom. The doors to be 2″ framed and panelled, with edges of framing slightly rounded, top panels prepared for glass, and with loose fixing beads, hung with 4″ wrought-steel butts, No. 2, to each door, and fitted with 6″ two-bolt, full rebated, mortice lock and furniture, price 12s. 6d. Put 2″ ovolo-moulded fanlight over, hung with 3″ wrought-steel butts at top, opening outwards, and fitted with 16″ Preston's patent brass fanlight opener and cords complete. Put 3″ × 2″ grooved and moulded weather-boards on outside of doors.

Put to front entrance doorway 5″ × 4″ rebated and rounded **Front Entrance Door.** frame, grooved for linings, with 6″ × 3″ rebated, sunk, weathered and throated transom. Door to be 2″ seven-panelled, with edges of framing slightly rounded, bottom rail to be weathered on top edge, top panel prepared for glass, with loose fixing beads, hung with No. 3, 4″ wrought-steel butts, and fitted with 6″ two-bolt mortice lock and furniture, price 10s. Put 2″ ovolo-moulded fanlight over, hung on top, opening outwards, with 3″ wrought-steel butts. Put Preston's 16″ patent brass fanlight opener and cords complete. Put on each entrance door N.P. "New departure" bell.

Kitchen Entrance Door. The kitchen entrance to have $4\frac{1}{2}″ \times 3″$ rebated and rounded frame, grooved for linings. Door to be 2″ square framed bead and butt, hung to jambs with No. 2, 4″ wrought-steel butts, and fitted with 6″ two-bolt mortice lock and furniture, price 8s. 6d.

Coal-house Door. Put to coal-house doorway $4″ \times 3″$ rebated and rounded jambs, and 1″ V-jointed, ledged, and braced door, with No. 3, $6″ \times 1″$ chamfered ledges and $6″ \times 1″$ chamfered braces, hung with 16″ wrought Tee-hinges, and fitted with 6″ two-bolt rim lock and strong brass furniture, price 5s. 6d.

Fix to back of jambs $3″ \times 2″$ rebated runners, and provide 1″ wrought movable runner boards to a height of 4′ 0″.

Windows. The windows throughout to have $4\frac{1}{2}″ \times 3″$ rebated and twice rounded frames, grooved for linings, $8\frac{1}{2}″ \times 4″$ oak, rebated, rounded, sunk, weathered and throated cills, grooved for water-bar and window board, $6″ \times 3″$ transoms, $4\frac{1}{2}″ \times 3″$ muntins, 2″ ovolo-moulded sashes, with $1\frac{1}{4}″$ bars where shown. All bottom sashes to be side hung. Fanlights to be hung at top, opening outwards; all to be hung with 3″ wrought-steel butts. The bottom sashes to be fitted with casement stays, price 2s. each, and fasteners, price 2s. each. The fanlights to have 16″ Preston's patent brass fanlight openers and cords complete.

Bay Window. The bay window to have $4\frac{1}{2}″ \times 3″$ wall posts, $4\frac{1}{2}″ \times 4″$ angle posts, bevelled, grooved, and tongued together, $5″ \times 4\frac{1}{2}″$ head—all rebated, twice rounded and throated. $6″ \times 3\frac{1}{2}″$ oak, rebated, sunk, weathered and throated cill, grooved for water-bar and window board. Put $1\frac{1}{4}″$ fascia around top, put $1\frac{1}{4}$ quarter round moulding under eaves gutter, and also under soffit board. Sashes to be 2″ ovolo-moulded, side hung on $3\frac{1}{2}″$ wrought-steel butts, fitted with casement stays and casement fasteners, price 2s. each.

Door to Flat over Verandah. Put to doorway over flat $4\frac{1}{2}″ \times 3″$ rebated and twice rounded jambs and head, grooved for linings, $7″ \times 4″$ oak cills to side-lights. Door to be seven-panelled, with edges of framing rounded, bottom panels to be raised and with weathered bottom rail, top panel prepared for glass in small squares. Put $2''$ ovolo-moulded side-lights in small squares to match door. Door to be hung with No. 2, $4''$ wrought-steel butts; side-lights hung with $3''$ wrought-steel butts. Put $6''$ two-bolt mortice lock and furniture, price 10s., to door. The side-lights to be fitted with casement stays, price 2s. each, and fasteners, price 2s. each.

Note.—All door jambs to be dowelled to steps with $6'' \times \frac{3}{4}''$ wrought-iron dowels.

Put around the outside of all door and window frames $1\frac{1}{4}'' \times 1\frac{1}{4}''$ quarter round moulding to stop joint of frame with brickwork. **Moulding around Frames.**

The staircase to be constructed with $2''$ wall string, with $1\frac{1}{2}'' \times 1''$ rounded moulding nailed on top edge to stop joint with plaster. $2''$ cut outer string, $1\frac{1}{2}''$ treads with rounded nosings, with returned and mitred ends on outer string, $1''$ risers, rebated and mitred to outer string and with $\frac{1}{4}''$ moulded bracket pieces. $1\frac{1}{2}'' \times \frac{1}{2}''$ Scotia moulding, returned and mitred to outer string. $5'' \times 5''$ newels tapered to $4''$ on top, morticed and housed for strings and handrail. $6'' \times 6'' \times 3''$ moulded mahogany caps, dowelled to newels, $1\frac{1}{4}''$ tapered balusters, $1''$ apron board, $1\frac{1}{2}''$ rounded nosing morticed for balusters. Put $2'' \times 1'$ moulded cover piece on bottom edge of apron to cover joint with plaster. The stairs to be properly housed, glued, and blocked together. The winders and ramps to stairs to be grooved and cross-tongued and properly glued together. Put $4'' \times 3''$ fir carriage pieces, splayed and fitted to floor and trimmers and well spiked. Put half newel spiked to wall on ground floor, with $9'' \times 3''$ curved arch piece tenoned to same and to main newel of stairs. **Staircase.**

The spandrail under stairs to have $1\frac{1}{2}''$ panelled framing with rounded edges properly framed to suit angle of stairs. **Spandrail.**

Put doorway in end for access to lavatory with $4'' \times 2''$ wall post, head, and transom, the newel to form the other post. Hang to same 2″ four-panel door similar to other interior doors, with lock and furniture complete. Put 1″ lining board across top of frame on outside to suit level of soffite of stairs. The fanlight over to be 2″ ovolo-moulded.

Lavatory under Stairs. Put across cupboard, where shown on plan, partition of 3″ × 2″ studding, and cover each side with ¾″ V-jointed match-board to form back for lavatory basin. Put 1″ top on 3″ × 2″ framed bearers, to be level with top of basin, and finish around top with 4″ × 1″ plain skirting.

Linen Cupboard on Landing. The linen cupboard on landing to have 1½″ panelled end and front, with edges of framing slightly rounded, of full height from floor to ceiling. The cupboard to be in two heights: the bottom portion 6′ 6″ high, the top portion 2′ 6″ high; to have two framed and panelled doors hung to frame with 3″ wrought-steel butts, fitted with 3½″ two-lever brass cupboard locks and 1½″ oval brass turn buckles. Fit up in cupboard six tiers of 1″ shelves 11″ wide, the shelves to be returned across ends of cupboard.

Panelling to Wardrobe. Put similar panelling to form back of wardrobe off front bedroom, of full height from floor to ceiling. The doors to wardrobe to be 2″, all as described for linen cupboard. Fit up in top portion of cupboard No. 2, 1″ shelves 11″ wide, and returned across ends. The lower portion of wardrobe to have 5″ × 1″ chamfered rail, and provide and fix No. 6″ brass wardrobe hooks. Put two-bolt 6″ mortice lock and furniture, price 8s. 6d. to lower door; the top door to have 1½″ oval brass turn buckles.

Cover to Cistern. Provide 1″ ledged matchboard cover to cistern in roof.

Shelving. Provide and fix in larder and elsewhere as directed 80 feet run of 11″ × 1″ wrought shelving on proper cleats and brackets.

Draining Board. Provide and fix to kitchen sink 1¼″ wrought-teak drain-ing board, hollow grooved, and with 4″ × 1″ teak skirting fixed to walls.

Front Fence. The front fence to be constructed with English oak throughout. The four gate-posts to be 7′ 0″ long, 5″ × 5″, wrought, with natural butts left on. Put 8″ × 8″ × 3″ moulded caps dowelled to tops of posts. The intermediate posts to be 7′ 0″ long, 4″ × 4″, with natural butts left on, placed at intervals of not more than 7′ 0″. The tops to stand 3″ above capping of fence and rounded. Rails to be $3\frac{1}{2}$″ × $3\frac{1}{2}$″ cut arris, tenoned and cogged to posts, and fastened with oak tre-nails. Cover the fence with 4″ × $\frac{3}{4}$″ × $\frac{1}{2}$″ sawn pales, fastened to rails with $2\frac{1}{2}$″ galvanized rose-head nails. Put 3″ × 2″ chamfered and grooved capping on top, the ends of capping to be cogged to posts. Gravel board to be 6″ × $1\frac{1}{4}$″, let into posts $\frac{3}{4}$″, and fastened with galvanized nails. Put 3″ × 2″ stumps 2′ 6″ long between posts, and fasten gravel board to same. The two entrance gates to be $2\frac{1}{4}$″ thick to detail. Hang gates to posts with 24″ galvanized hooks and twists. Provide and fix galvanized gate latches, price 3s. each.

Erect close-boarded fence 4′ 6″ high to the two sides and back, to have 4″ × 4″ sawn oak posts 7′ 0″ long, with natural butts left on, placed 8′ 0″ apart, 4″ × 3″ cut arris oak rails, the fence to be morticed and tenoned together, and the rails housed to posts and covered with 4″ × $\frac{3}{4}$″ country cut fir boarding, nailed to rails with 2″ galvanized nails. The gravel board to be 6″ × 1″ fir, let into posts and fastened with galvanized nails. Put 3″ × 2″ oak stumps 2′ 6″ long between posts, and fasten gravel board to same.

Side and Back Fences.

Note.—The side and back fences to be erected before the building is commenced.

SMITH AND FOUNDER.

Provide all smith and founder's work, also ironmongery as described elsewhere, or as may be requisite for the proper execution of the work.

Provide, hoist and fix over bay window No. 2 rolled steel joists 12 feet long, 9″ × 4″, 21 lbs. to the foot run, to be obtained from Messrs Dorman, Long & Co.

Rolled Steel Joists.

Chimney Bars. Provide for all chimney openings $2'' \times \frac{1}{2}''$ wrought-iron cambered arch bars with tanged ends.

Water Bars. Provide $1'' \times \frac{1}{8}''$ galvanized wrought-iron window bars cut to requisite lengths for all window cills.

Eaves Gutter. Provide and fix to eaves $4\frac{1}{2}'' \times 3''$ cast-iron moulded eaves gutter, with all requisite angles, outlets, and stopped and returned ends. Joints to be made with red lead and properly bolted, and fixed to fascia with strong galvanized mushroom-topped screws.

Rain-water Pipes. The rain-water pipes to be $2\frac{1}{2}''$ cast-iron, and fixed with $3''$ galvanized round-headed nails. Provide all requisite swan necks and shoes.

Grates, Mantels, and Kitchener. Provide the sum of £25 (twenty-five pounds) for grates, mantels, kitchener, and copper, to be selected by the proprietor and fixed by the contractor.

PLUMBER.

Provide all requisite solder, tacks, wall hooks, etc., and carefully execute all plumbing work in gutters, aprons, flashings, soakers, etc. Milled lead to be used.

All joints to be wiped.

Aprons to be $12''$ wide, flashings $7''$ wide, and stepped where necessary. Where roofs abut against raking walls put $14'' \times 7''$ soakers of 4-lb. lead, one to each slate, and secured with a galvanized iron nail. Put 6-lb. lead gutters behind chimneys.

Put $18'' \times 18''$ lead aprons where ridges abut on roof slopes.

Flats and aprons to be of 6-lb. lead, flashings 5-lb. lead, soakers 4-lb. lead. All lead to be laid to proper falls.

Valleys. Lay valley gutters of 6-lb. lead $18''$ wide, joints to lap $4''$.

Hips and Ridges. Cover the hips and ridges with 6-lb. lead, $18''$ wide, properly dressed over rolls, the ridges to lap $6''$, hips $4''$. Provide all requisite 7-lb. lead tacks, $3''$ wide, placed not more than $2'\ 6''$ apart.

SPECIFICATION FOR VILLA RESIDENCE

Lay the flats over verandah and bay window with 6-lb. lead, **Flats to Verandah and Bay Window.** laid to a fall of $1\frac{1}{2}''$ in 10 feet. The rolls to be placed not more than 2' 6" apart, centre to centre. Put 5-lb. lead cover flashings.

Build in over door and window openings on ground floor, **Trays.** also over angle bay window, and the roof of w.c., and coals, 5-lb. lead trays, to be the width shown on detail.

Put 4-lb. lead soakers to the sides of all door and window **Flashings to Frames.** frames, to be turned around front edge of frame and copper nailed 3" apart, the inside edge to be turned back to inside of face of outer $4\frac{1}{2}''$ wall—see detail.

Put 4" L.C.C. galvanized cast-iron vent-pipe at head of **Vent Pipe.** drain, carried up over roof of w.c., and above roof of main building 3' 0", and put copper wire dome on top. Provide and fix No. 2 galvanized bends of similar weight.

Put similar soil-pipe for first-floor w.c., and provide Y-junction for connection of lead soil-pipe from w.c.

The joints to be first caulked with tow and run with lead, **Jointing of Soil and Vent Pipes.** and caulked tight with a caulking iron.

Provide and fix in kitchen 2' 6" × 1' 6" × 10" high-back fire- **Kitchen Sink.** clay kitchen sink, white glazed inside and out, with 2" brass plug and vulcanite washer complete, with No. 3, $\frac{1}{2}''$ brass taps, marked "hot," "cold," and "main." Put 2" lead trap with brass cap and cleaning eye and 2" lead waste discharging on to gully.

The weight of lead pipe to be as follows, viz. :—

$\frac{3}{4}''$ lead pipe $7\frac{1}{2}$ lbs. per yard run.
$1\frac{1}{4}''$,, 13 ,, ,,
$1\frac{1}{2}''$,, $16\frac{1}{2}$,, ,,
2" ,, 25 ,, ,,
4" ,, 76 ,, per 10 feet length.

The outside w.c. to have w.c. apparatus with pan and trap, **Outside W.C.** $1\frac{1}{4}'$ lead flush-pipe and flushing cistern, with chain and pull complete, polished mahogany hinged seat, and pair of cast-iron painted brackets, price £4.

First-floor W.C. The first-floor w.c. to have low-down closet set complete, price £5, 10s. Connect w.c. to soil-pipe with 4″ drawn lead-pipe, and provide brass socket and thimble for this connection.

Overflows. Put $\frac{3}{4}$″ lead pipe overflows from w.c. cisterns, carried 6″ through wall and turned down at ends.

Lavatory. Provide and fix under staircase 24″ flat-back fireclay lavatory basin, with circular front, white glazed inside and out, with two nickel-plated taps, marked " hot " and " cold," and nickel-plated washer, plug, and chain complete. Put $1\frac{1}{2}$″ lead trap with brass cap and cleaning eye, and $1\frac{1}{2}$″ lead waste-pipe, carried through wall and discharging over gully outside.

Bath. Provide and fix iu bathroom 6′ 0″ rolled edge first-quality parallel porcelain enamelled cast-iron bath, with trap and nickel-plated fittings and overflow complete, price £8. Put 2″ lead waste-pipe carried through wall and discharging into cistern-head. Provide and fix $2\frac{1}{2}$″ L.C.C. galvanized cast-iron down-pipe. The cistern-head to be 12″ flat-back galvanized cast-iron, of approved pattern.

Testing. The whole of the sanitary fittings and plumber's work to be tested at completion to the satisfaction of the local authority's inspector.

WATER FITTER.

Charges. Pay water company's charges for connection to main, laying on supply, and fixing meter.

Pipes and Fittings. The water-pipes and fittings to be the best galvanized wrought-iron steam tube, with screwed and socketed ends.

Cistern. Provide and fix in roof 80-gallon galvanized wrought-iron riveted cistern, No. 14 gauge. Put 2″ galvanized iron pipe overflow discharging on to roof. Provide proper screw union connection to cistern.

Cylinder. Provide and fix on cast-iron brackets by the side of kitchen fireplace, 50-gallon galvanized wrought-iron riveted hot-water cylinder, $\frac{1}{8}$″ plate.

SPECIFICATION FOR VILLA RESIDENCE

Provide and fix at the back of kitchen range, the full width **High-pressure Boiler.** of fire, a $\frac{3}{8}''$ plate, wrought-iron high-pressure welded boot boiler, with manhole and arch flue, drilled for pipe connections, and provided with $\frac{3}{4}''$ dead weight safety valve and $\frac{3}{4}''$ emptying pipe with brass bib tap.

From meter lay on $\frac{3}{4}''$ supply to cistern in roof, and put **Main Supply.** $\frac{3}{4}''$ high-pressure ball valve and silencer. Take off $\frac{1}{2}''$ branch from this pipe and finish over kitchen sink.

Connect cistern in roof to high-pressure boiler with $\frac{3}{4}''$ pipe. **Hot Water Supply.** The flow and return pipes from boiler to cylinder to be $1\frac{1}{4}''$ pipe.

Take off from cylinder $1''$ flow and return pipes, and continue $1''$ exhaust pipe and turn over top of cistern.

Take off from flow-pipe $\frac{3}{4}''$ branches to supply bath, kitchen sink, and lavatory.

Lay on cold supply from cistern in roof to the two w.cs., **Cold Water Supply.** flushing cisterns, bath, kitchen sink, and lavatory with $\frac{1}{2}''$ pipe.

Provide all requisite brass unions, elbows, tees, bends, **Fittings.** springs, etc.

Provide and fix where directed No. 3, $\frac{3}{4}''$ and No. 2, $\frac{1}{2}''$ brass **Stop-cocks.** stop-cocks.

GAS FITTER.

Pay gas company's charges for laying on gas and fixing **Charges.** meter, also for testing service at completion.

The gas-pipes to be of the best quality galvanized wrought- **Pipes.** iron.

From meter carry on $\frac{1}{2}''$ supply, with $\frac{3}{8}''$ branches off same **Supply.** to the following points, viz.:—Three bedrooms, bathroom, w.c. on first floor, kitchen, dining-room, drawing-room, lavatory, and two points in hall.

Provide and fix where directed No. 2, $\frac{1}{4}''$ brass stop-cocks. **Stop-cocks.**

Put to the drawing-room and dining-room two-light **Gas Fittings.** pendants, price 23s. each complete.

The hall to have single light pendant, price 12s. complete; kitchen to have similar pendant, price 10s. The bracket to hall to be inverted pattern, price 9s.

The brackets to bedrooms, bathroom, and lavatory to be inverted pattern, price 7s. each.

The whole of the fittings to be approved by the proprietor, and to be fitted with inverted burners with by-passes, mantles, and globes complete.

Testing. The whole of the gasfittings to be tested at completion to the satisfaction of the surveyor.

GLAZIER.

The glass to be of the best quality of its respective kinds, free from bubbles, scratches, and other defects, carefully cut to fit the rebates, bedded in putty, back puttied and sprigged where requisite. The British polished plate glass to be the best quality $\frac{1}{4}''$ thick, full bedded in putty and wash leather, and front puttied.

Glaze the angle bay window, front entrance door and fanlight, window in hall, front bedroom window, french casement, and fanlight to dining-room with best polished British plate glass, as above described.

The windows of larder, w.c., lavatory, and bathroom to be glazed with best quality " Muranese" glass. The remainder of the glazing to be executed with best selected 21-oz. British sheet glass in putty and properly sprigged.

Clean the glass inside and out at completion.

PAINTER.

Paint. The paint to be prepared with genuine old whitelead and genuine linseed oil.

No following coat to be put on until the previous coat has been inspected and approved.

SPECIFICATION FOR VILLA RESIDENCE

The ironwork throughout to have one coat of red-lead paint, **Painting to Ironwork.** and three coats of "Torbay" paint finished stone colour.

All ironwork to be thoroughly cleaned before painting is done.

Knot, stop, prime, and paint four coats to all exterior wood- **Painting to Woodwork.** work; the interior woodwork to have three coats in addition to the priming coat.

The sashes to be finished "ivory" white; all other exterior **Colours.** work in two tints of stone colour.

The interior woodwork to be painted in tints selected by the **Varnishing Woodwork.** surveyor, and to have one coat of best hard-drying white varnish.

Rub down and french polish handrail to staircase. **Polish Handrail.**

The walls of hall, dining-room, staircase, and around landing **Painted Dado.** to have a painted dado, 3′ 3″ high from floor to top of border line.

Put one-inch border line of darker colour. **Border Line.**

The dado to be painted three coats of "Indestructible" paint to approved tint.

The walls above dado, and to other rooms to have one **Distemper.** coat of Hall's "primi" size, and two coats of Hall's distemper to approved tints, with frieze of different colour.

The walls throughout to be thoroughy cleaned down before colouring or painting is done.

The ceilings throughout to have two coats of approved white distemper.

Clean down and twice lime-whiten the walls of outside w.c. **Lime-whiten.** and coals.

The whole of the ground-floor joists, sleepers, and underside **Stop Rot.** of floor boards to have one coat of creosote before being fixed.

The side and back fences to have two coats of creosote.

Touch up all painted work where requisite, clean grates, black stoves, and leave all clean and tidy at completion.

BUILDING CONSTRUCTION DRAWING

A CLASS-BOOK FOR THE ELEMENTARY STUDENT AND ARTISAN

BY

RICHARD B. EATON

LECTURER ON BUILDING CONSTRUCTION, POOLE SCHOOL OF
ART AND TECHNOLOGY

Part IV

JOINERY DRAWINGS, SPECIFICATIONS AND MEASUREMENTS

24 PLATES

London
E. & F. N. SPON, Ltd., 57 HAYMARKET, S.W. 1
New York
SPON & CHAMBERLAIN, 120 LIBERTY STREET
1919

PREFACE

THE accompanying work dealing with *Joinery Drawing* is of similar character to the work on *Building Construction Drawing* already published, dealing however more particularly with the trade of the joiner.

The drawings and details generally are fully dimensioned, and show the joiner's work in its accustomed setting. Specifications are appended for all the joinery, and in some instances for other portions of work, such as coverings to flats, finishings connected therewith, and glazing.

Detailed measurements of the drawings are also given, additional allowances being made for horns, and the finished cut. These measurements are added in the hope that the student and apprentice will find them an advantage in the study of his trade.

RICHARD B. EATON.

"LAKESIDE," SELDOWN, POOLE,
September 1919.

PLATE **78**.

Various Sections for Door Jambs.

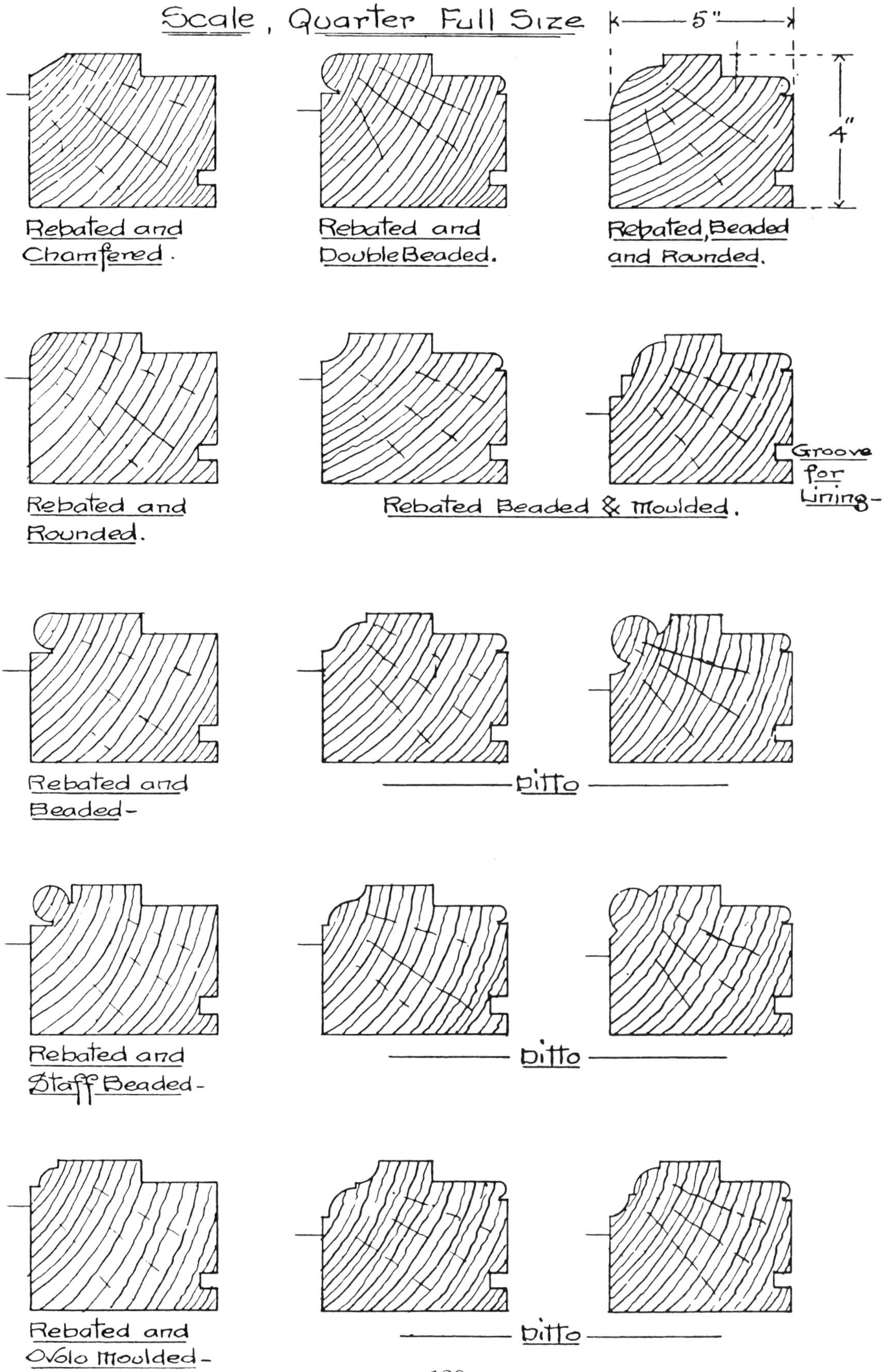

Scale, Quarter Full Size

5"

4"

Rebated and
Chamfered.

Rebated and
Double Beaded.

Rebated, Beaded
and Rounded.

Rebated and
Rounded.

Rebated Beaded & Moulded.

Groove
for
Lining-

Rebated and
Beaded-

———— Ditto ————

Rebated and
Staff Beaded-

———— Ditto ————

Rebated and
Ovolo Moulded-

———— Ditto ————

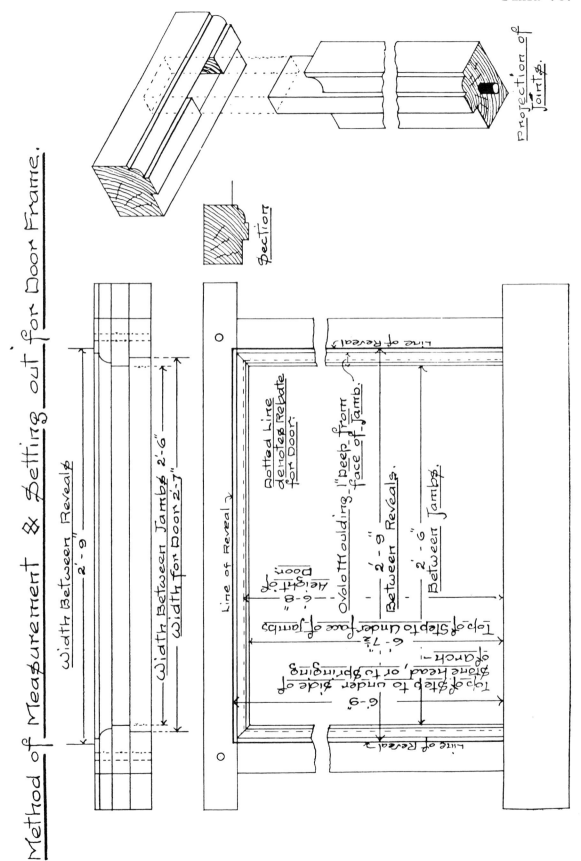

PLATE 79.

Method of Measurement & Setting out for Door Frame.

Projection of Joints.

Section

Width Between Reveals
2'-9"

Width Between Jambs 2'-6"
Width for Door 2'-7"

Line of Reveal

Line of Reveal

Dotted Line denotes Rebate for Door

Ovolo Moulding 1" Deep from face of Jamb.

2'-9"
Between Reveals

2'-6"
Between Jambs

Height of Door
6'-8"

Top of Step to underface of Jambs
6'-7½"

Top of Step to under side of Stone Head, or to Springing of arch
6'-9"

Line of Reveal

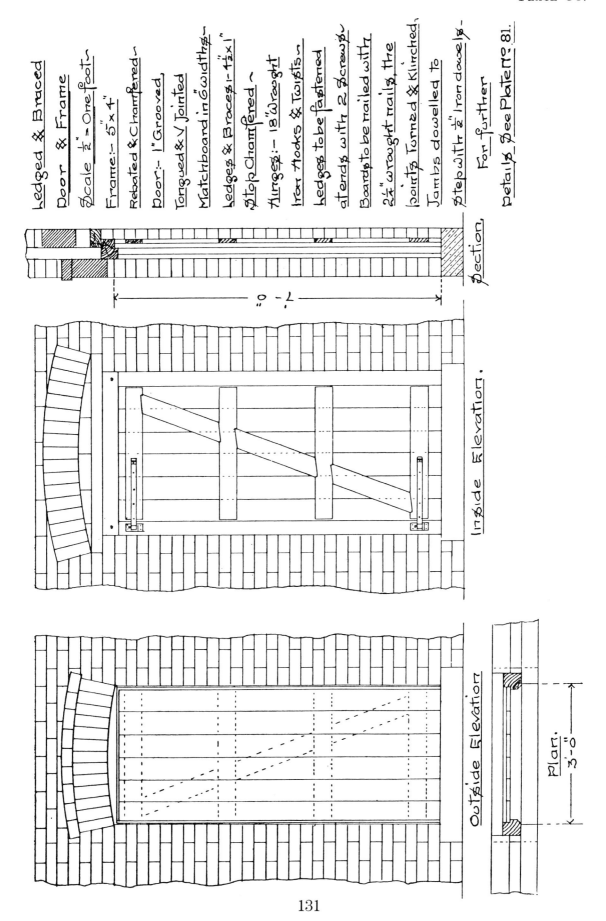

PLATE 80.

Ledged & Braced
Door & Frame
Scale $\frac{1}{2}$ = One Foot~
Frame:- 5"× 4"
Rebated & Chamfered~
Door:- 1" Grooved
Tongued & V Jointed
Matchboard in 6 widths~
Ledges & Braces 1- 1½"×1"
Stop Chamfered ~
Hinges:- 18" Wrought
Iron Hooks & Twists~
Ledges to be fastened
at ends with 2 Screws,
Boards to be nailed with
2¼" wrought nails, the
points Turned & Klinched,
Jambs dowelled to
Step with ½" Iron dowels ~
For Further
Details See Plate Nº 81.

Section.

Inside Elevation.

Outside Elevation.

Plan.

3'-0"

7'-0"

131

PLATE **81.**

Details of Ledged Door & Frame.

Scale $1\frac{1}{2}'' =$ One foot.

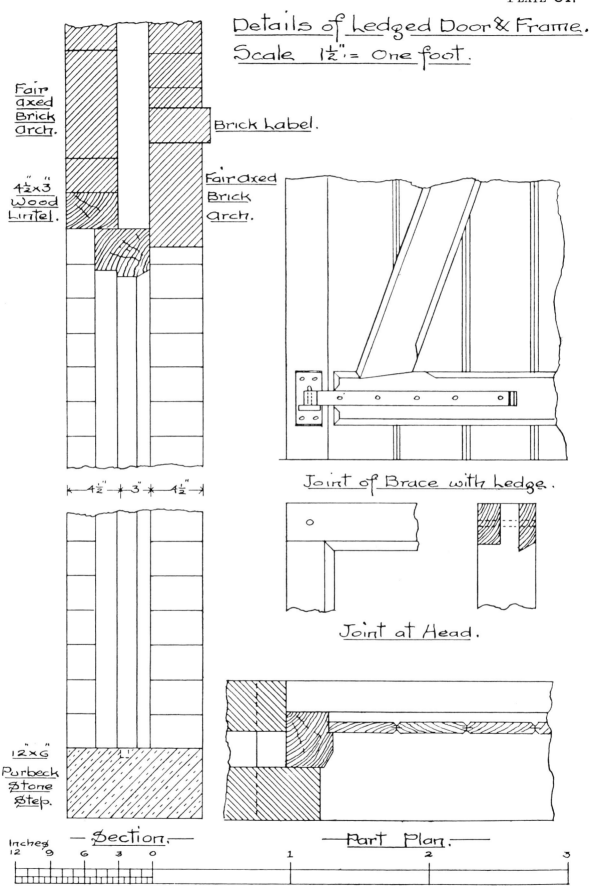

Fair axed Brick Arch.

Brick Label.

$4\frac{1}{2}''\times 3''$ Wood Lintel.

Fair axed Brick Arch.

$\mapsto 4\frac{1}{2}'' \ast 3'' \ast 4\frac{1}{2}'' \to$

Joint of Brace with Ledge.

Joint at Head.

$12''\times 6''$ Purbeck Stone Step.

— Section. —

— Part Plan. —

Inches
12 9 6 3 0   1   2   3

132

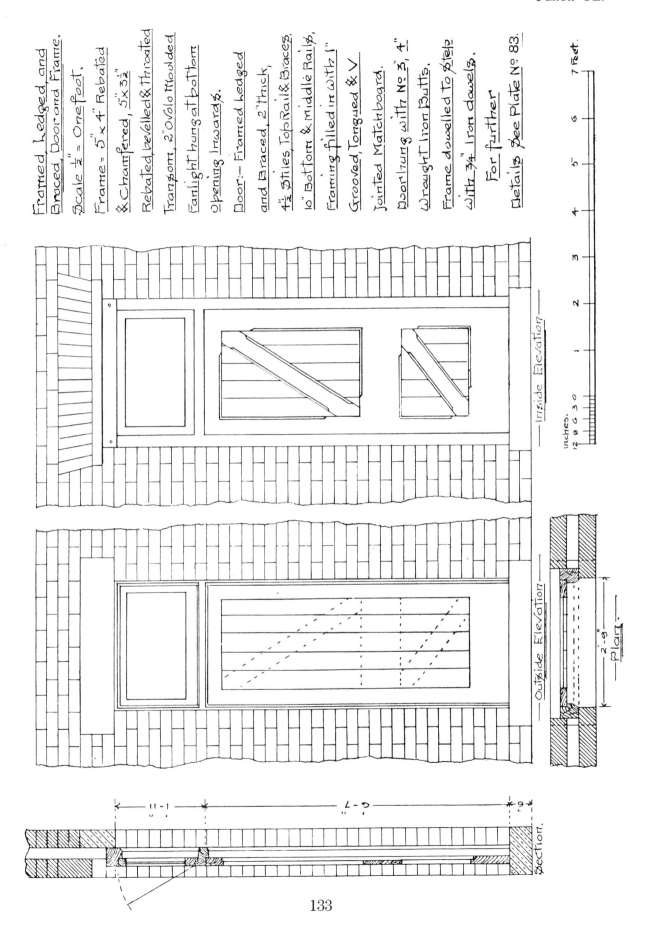

PLATE 82.

Framed Ledged and Braced Door and Frame.

Scale ½" = One Foot.

Frame = 5" x 4" Rebated & Chamfered, 5" x 3½" Rebated bevelled & Throated Transom, 2" Ovolo Moulded Fanlight hung at bottom opening inwards.

Door:- Framed Ledged and Braced, 2" thick, 4½" Stiles Top Rail & Braces, 10" Bottom & middle Rails, Framing filled in with 1" Grooved, Tongued & V Jointed Matchboard. Door hung with No 3, 4" Wrought Iron Butts. Frame dowelled to Step with ¾" Iron dowels. For further Details See Plate No 83.

Inside Elevation

Outside Elevation

Plan

Section.

inches.
12 9 6 3 0   1   2   3   4   5   6   7 Feet.

11-1"

5-7"

6"

2-9"

PLATE 83.

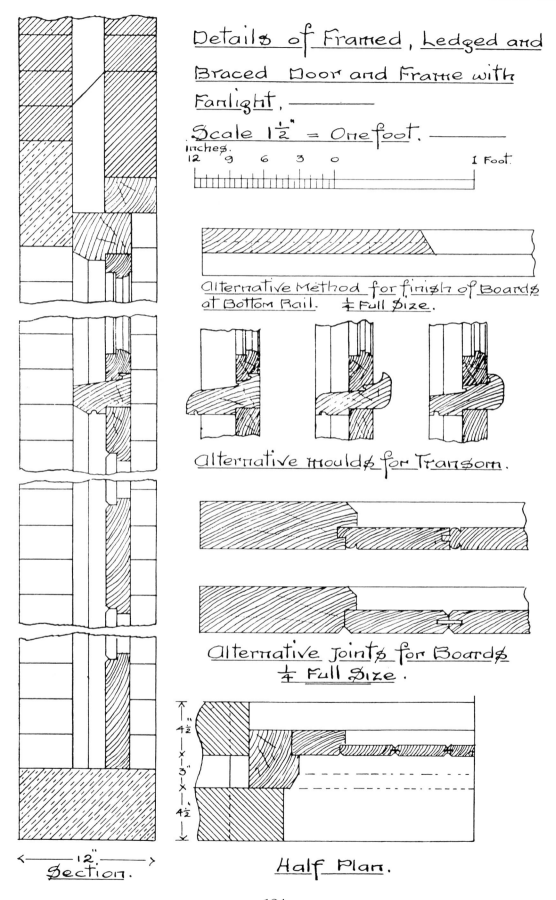

Details of Framed, Ledged and Braced Door and Frame with Fanlight.————

Scale $1\frac{1}{2}''$ = One foot.————

inches.
12 9 6 3 0   1 Foot.

Alternative Method for finish of Boards at Bottom Rail. $\frac{1}{4}$ Full Size.

Alternative moulds for Transom.

Alternative Joints for Boards $\frac{1}{4}$ Full Size.

$4\frac{1}{2}''$ × $3''$ × $4\frac{1}{2}''$

Half Plan.

<————— 12'' —————>
Section.

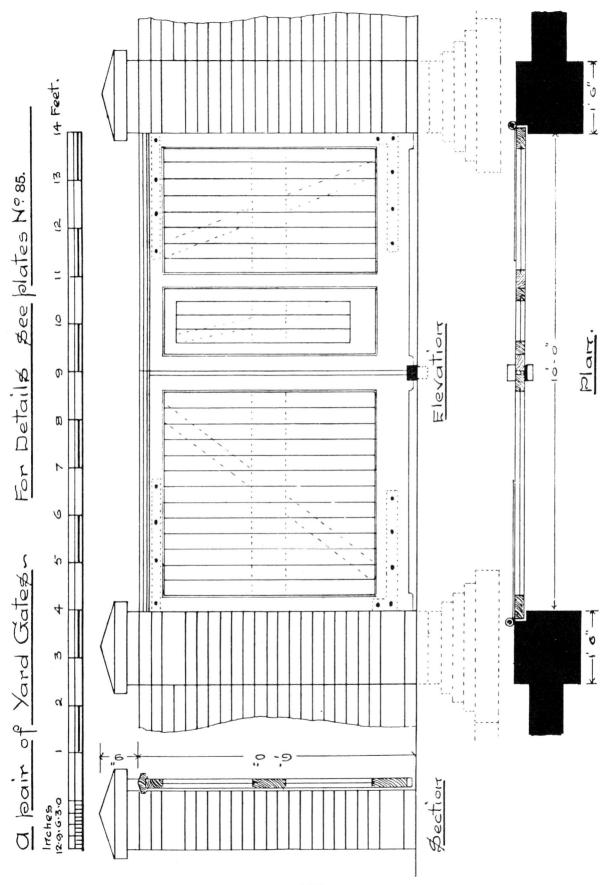

A Pair of Yard Gates.   For Details See Plates No. 85.

PLATE 84.

Elevation

Section

Plan

Inches
12·9·6·3·0

1 2 3 4 5 6 7 8 9 10 11 12 13 14 Feet.

135

PLATE 85.

A pair of Yard Gates,   Details.

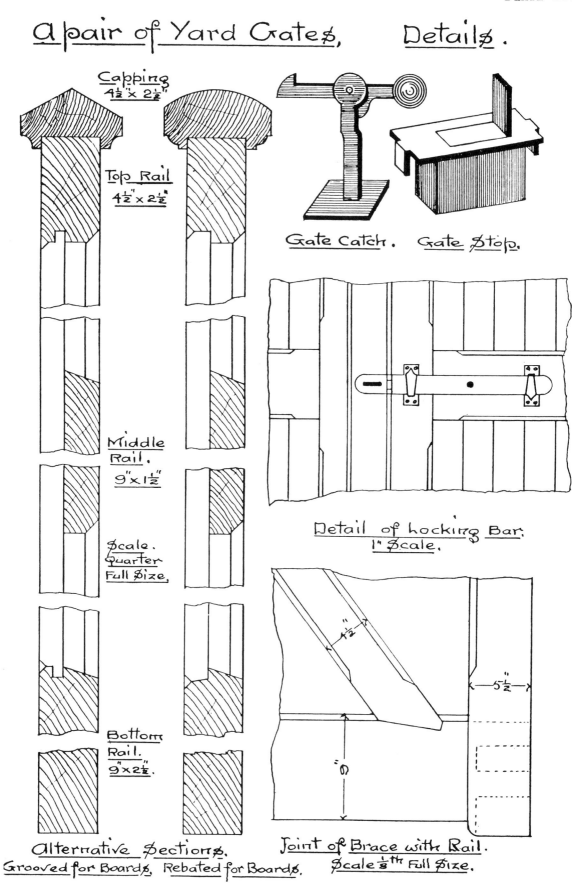

Capping
4½" x 2½"

Top Rail
4½" x 2½"

Gate Catch.   Gate Stop.

Middle
Rail.
9" x 1½"

Scale.
Quarter
Full Size.

Detail of Locking Bar.
1" Scale.

Bottom
Rail.
9" x 2½"

Alternative Sections.
Grooved for Boards. Rebated for Boards.

4½"

5½"

9"

Joint of Brace with Rail.
Scale ⅛th Full Size.

PLATE 86.

Front Entrance Door & Frame with Segmental Head & Fanlight.

For Details _ See Plate Nos 87 & 88.

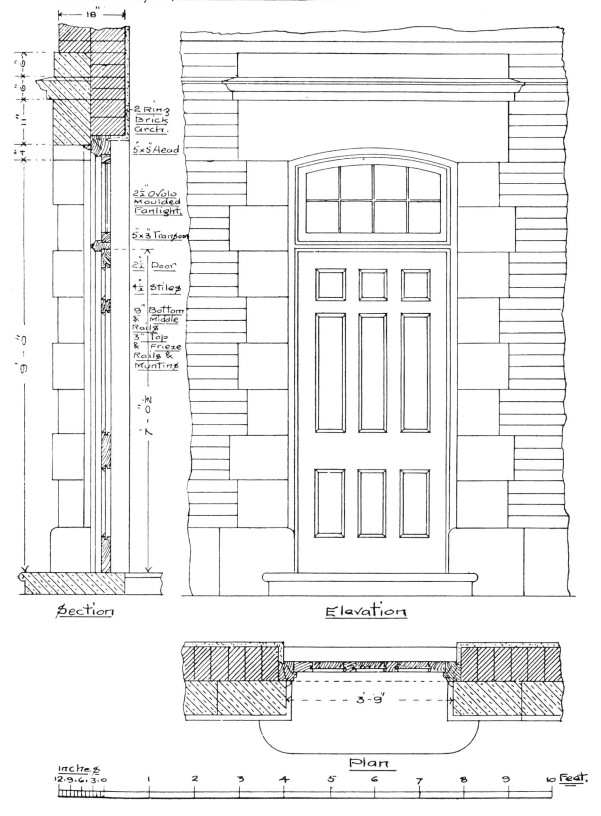

18"

2 Ring Brick Arch.

5×5 Head

2½ Ovolo Moulded Fanlight.

5×3 Transom

2½ Door

4½ Stiles

9" Bottom & Middle Rails
3" Top & Frieze Rails & Munting

Section

Elevation

3'-9"

Plan

Inches
12.9.6.3.0 1 2 3 4 5 6 7 8 9 10 Feet.

137

PLATE 87.

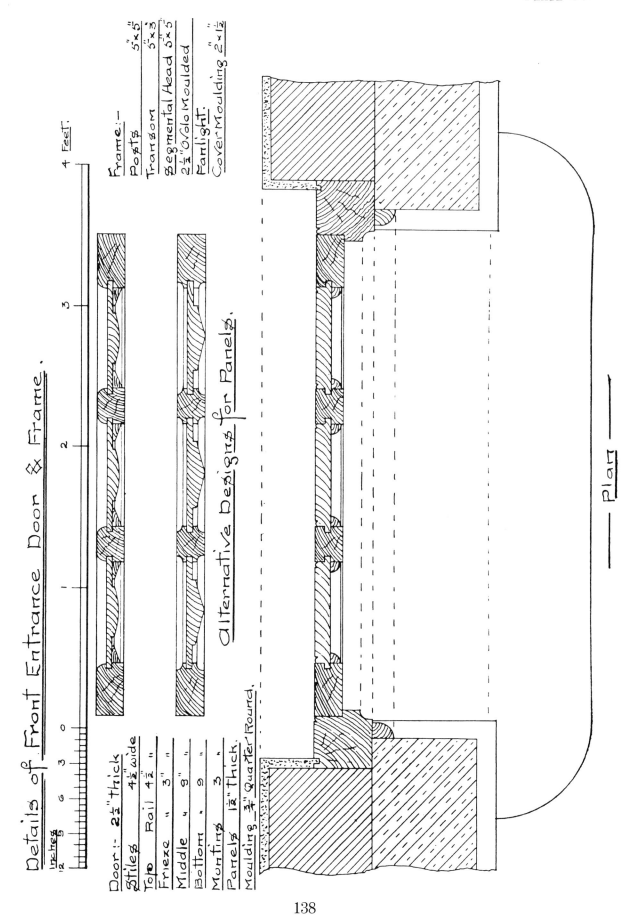

Details of Front Entrance Door & Frame.

Inches
12 9 6 3 0 1 2 3 4 Feet.

Frame:—
Posts 5"×5"
Transom 5"×3"
Segmental Head 5"×5"
2½" Ovalo Moulded
Fanlight.
Cover Moulding 2×1½"

Door:— 2½" thick
Stiles 4½" wide
Top Rail 4½"
Frieze " 3" "
Middle " 9" "
Bottom " 9" "
Muntins 3" "
Panels 1½" thick
Moulding ¾" Quarter Round.

Alternative Designs for Panels.

Plan

138

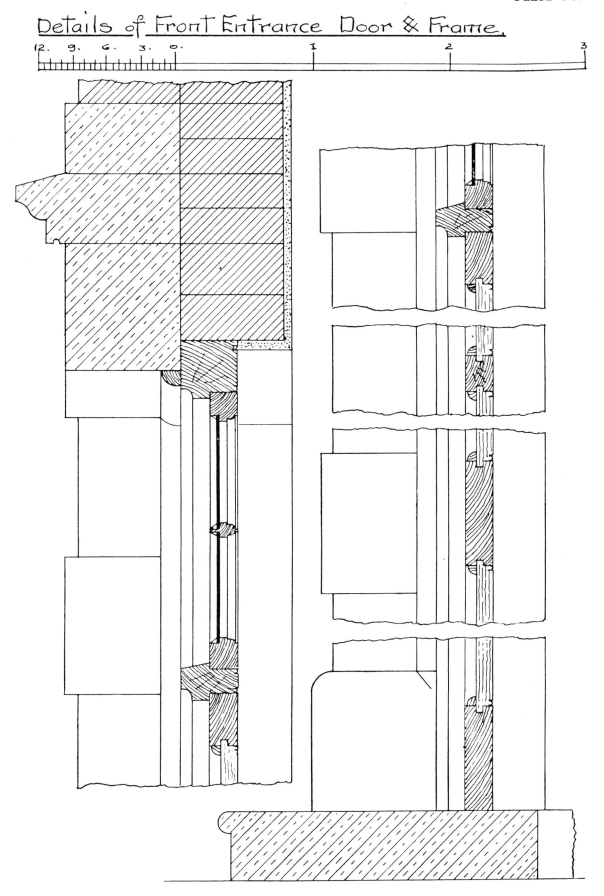

PLATE 88.

Details of Front Entrance Door & Frame.

12. 9. 6. 3. 0   1   2   3

PLATE 89.

Entrance Door & Frame with Fanlight & Sidelights.
For Details   See Plate No 90.

Section

Elevation

Plan.
6'-9"

Centre x for arch

140

PLATE 90.

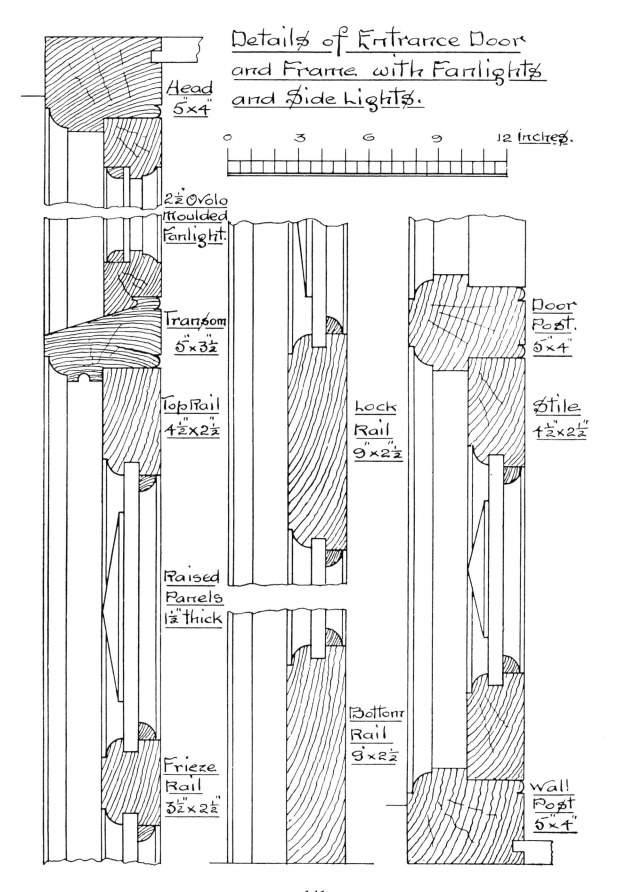

Details of Entrance Door and Frame with Fanlights and Side Lights.

Head
5"×4"

2½" Ovolo
Moulded
Fanlight.

Transom
5"×3½"

Top Rail
4½"×2½"

Raised
Panels
1½" thick

Frieze
Rail
3½"×2½"

Lock
Rail
9"×2½"

Bottom
Rail
9"×2½"

Door
Post.
5"×4"

Stile
4½"×2½"

Wall
Post
5"×4"

0   3   6   9   12 inches.

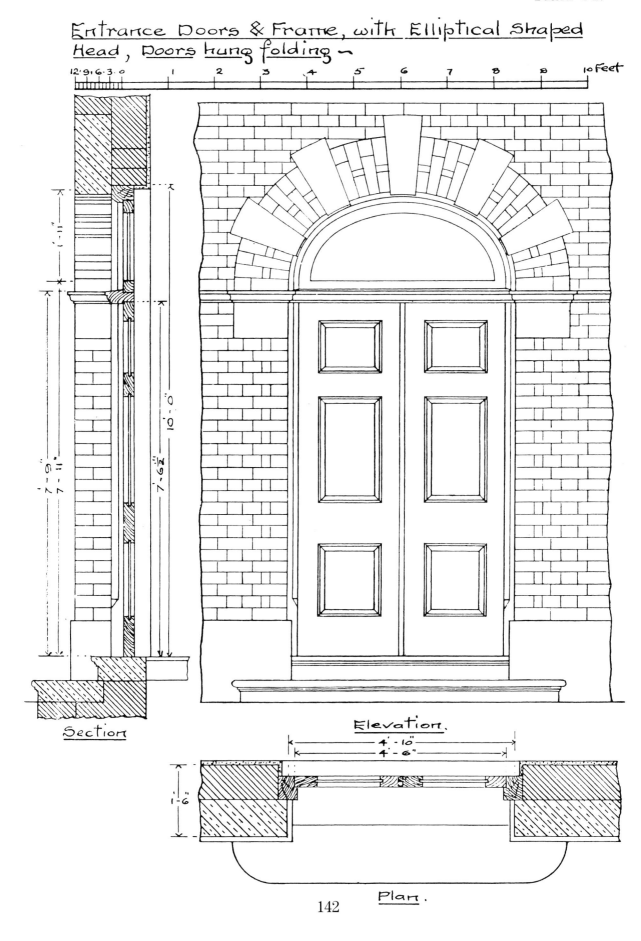

PLATE 91.

Entrance Doors & Frame, with Elliptical Shaped Head, Doors hung folding ~

Section

Elevation.

Plan.

142

PLATE 92.

Details of Entrance Doors & Frame with Elliptical Shaped Head.

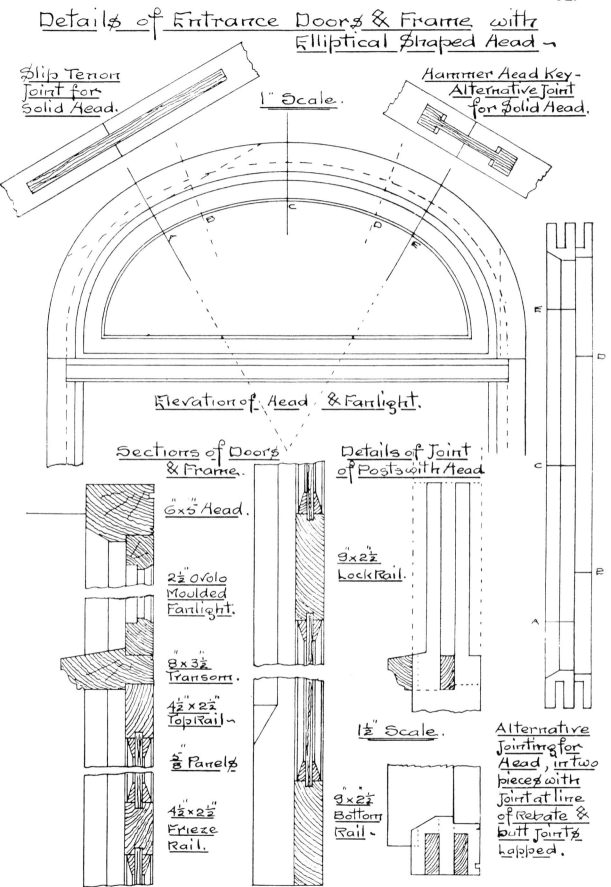

Slip Tenon Joint for Solid Head.

1" Scale.

Hammer Head Key. Alternative Joint for Solid Head.

Elevation of Head & Fanlight.

Sections of Doors & Frame.

6"x5" Head.

2½" Ovolo Moulded Fanlight.

8"x3½" Transom.

4½"x2½" Top Rail.

⅝" Panels

4½"x2½" Frieze Rail.

Details of Joint of Posts with Head

9"x2½" Lock Rail.

1½" Scale.

9"x2½" Bottom Rail.

Alternative Jointing for Head, in two pieces with Joint at line of Rebate & butt Joints lapped.

PLATE 93.

Entrance Doorway and Sidelights.
Door Frame 5"x4", Door 2", 6 panels, Sidelights Frame 5"x3", Sashes 2" Ovolo Moulded.

Elevation.

Plan.

144

PLATE 94.

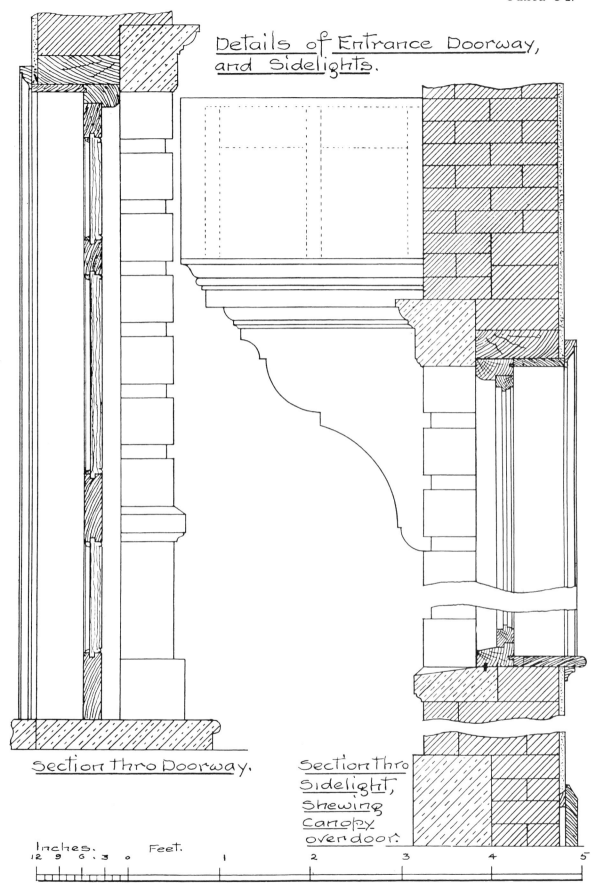

Details of Entrance Doorway, and Sidelights.

Section thro Doorway.

Section thro Sidelight, shewing Canopy over door.

Inches.   Feet.
12 9 6 3 0   1   2   3   4   5

PLATE **95.**

Framed and Panelled Doors.

Stiles, Top Rails, Frieze Rails & Muntins 4½" wide, Lock rails & Bottom rails 9" wide.

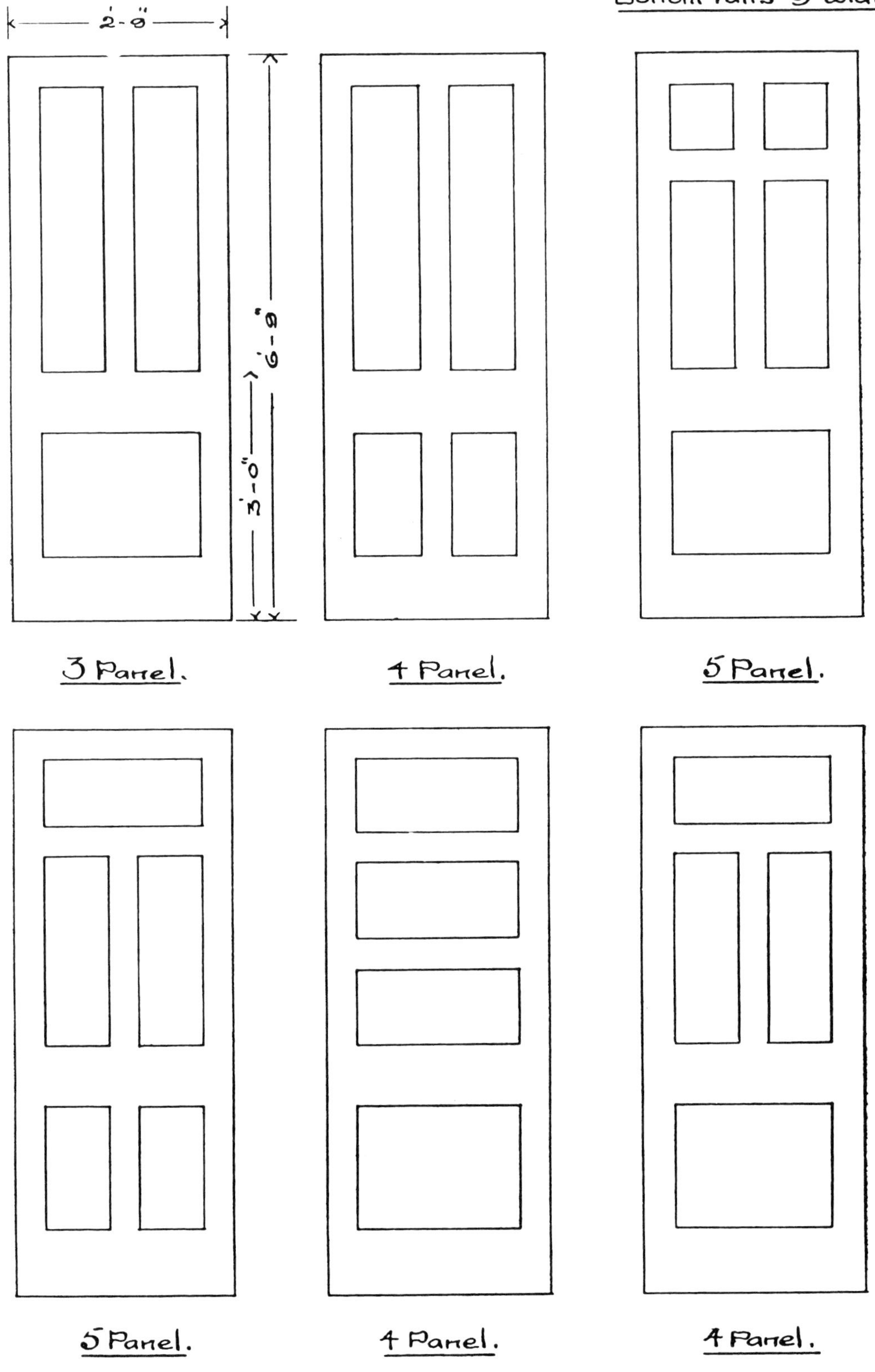

3 Panel.

4 Panel.

5 Panel.

5 Panel.

4 Panel.

4 Panel.

PLATE 96.

The Joints of a Framed & Panelled Door:-

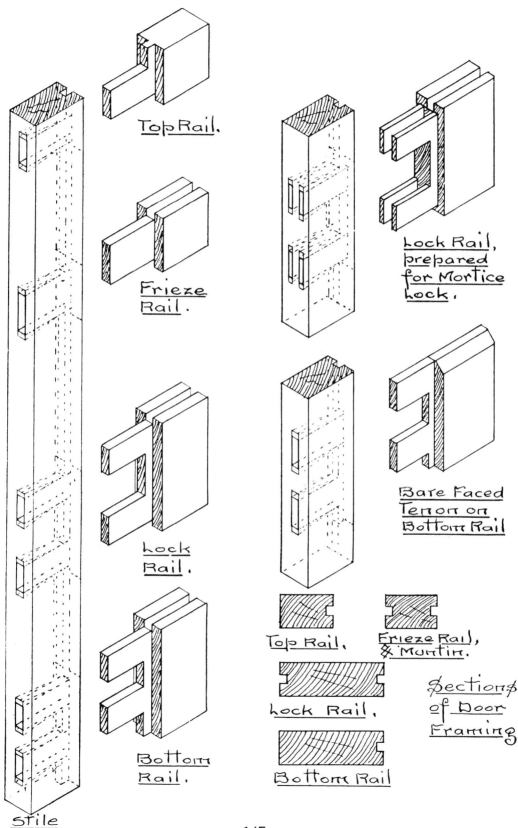

Top Rail.

Frieze Rail.

Lock Rail, prepared for Mortice Lock.

Lock Rail.

Bare Faced Tenon on Bottom Rail

Bottom Rail.

Top Rail.

Frieze Rail, & Muntin.

Lock Rail.

Bottom Rail

Sections of Door Framing

stile

147

PLATE **97**.

Internal Door Linings, Plain Stopped, Single Rebated, Double Rebated, Skeleton Framed, & Framed Panelled & Rebated.

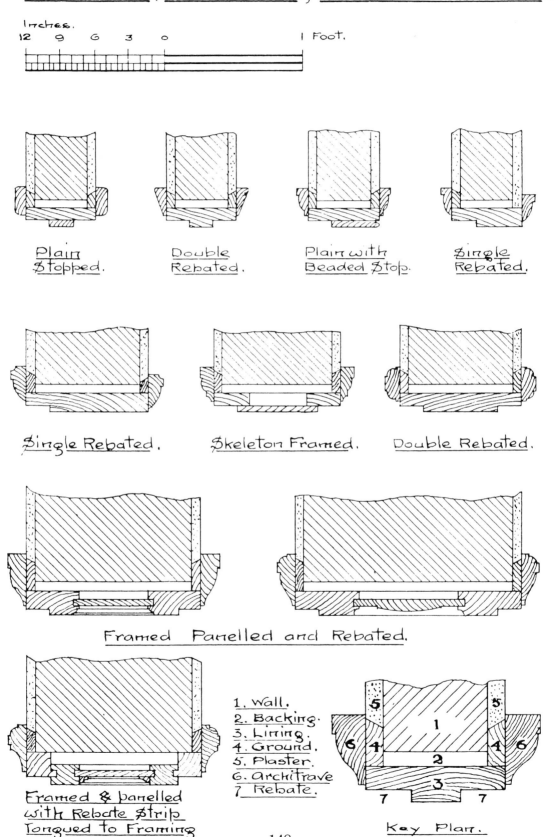

Inches.
12 9 6 3 0   1 Foot.

Plain Stopped.

Double Rebated.

Plain with Beaded Stop.

Single Rebated.

Single Rebated.

Skeleton Framed.

Double Rebated.

Framed Panelled and Rebated.

Framed & panelled with Rebate Strip Tongued to Framing

1. Wall.
2. Backing.
3. Lining.
4. Ground.
5. Plaster.
6. Architrave
7. Rebate.

Key Plan.

PLATE 98.

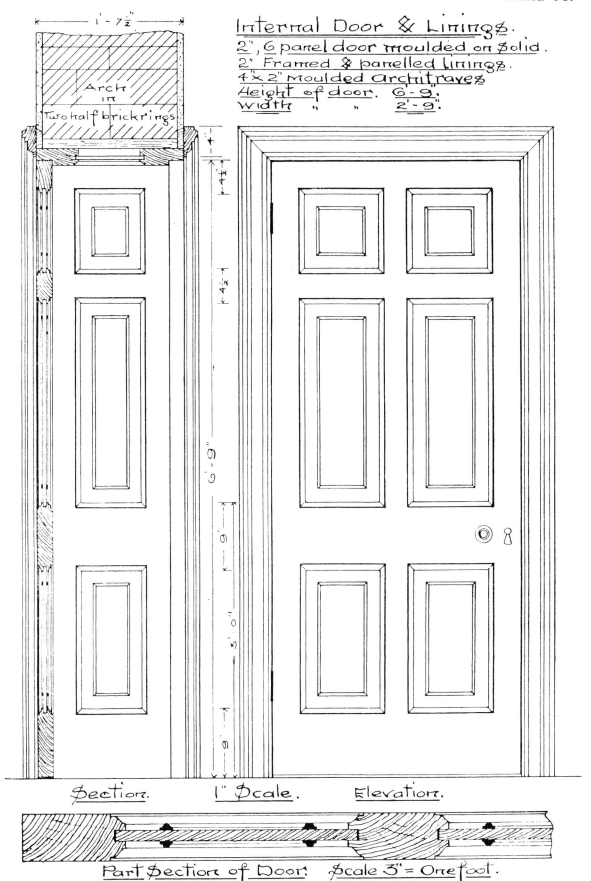

Internal Door & Linings.
2", 6 panel door moulded on Solid.
2" Framed & panelled Linings.
4"×2" moulded Architraves
Height of door. 6-9".
Width " " 2'-9".

1'-7½"

Arch in Two half brick rings

4"
4½"
4½"
6'-9"
9"
3'-0"
9"

Section.   1" Scale.   Elevation.

Part Section of Door.   Scale 3"= One foot.

149

PLATE 99.

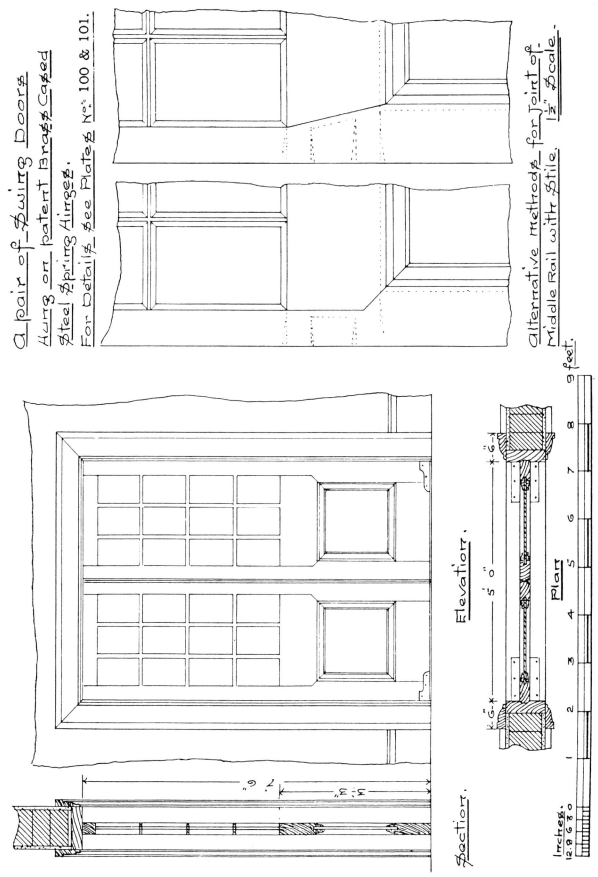

A pair of Swing Doors Hung on patent Brass Cased Steel Spring Hinges. For Details see Plates Nos. 100 & 101.

Alternative methods for joint of Middle Rail with Stile.

½" Scale.

Elevation.

Plan.

Section.

150

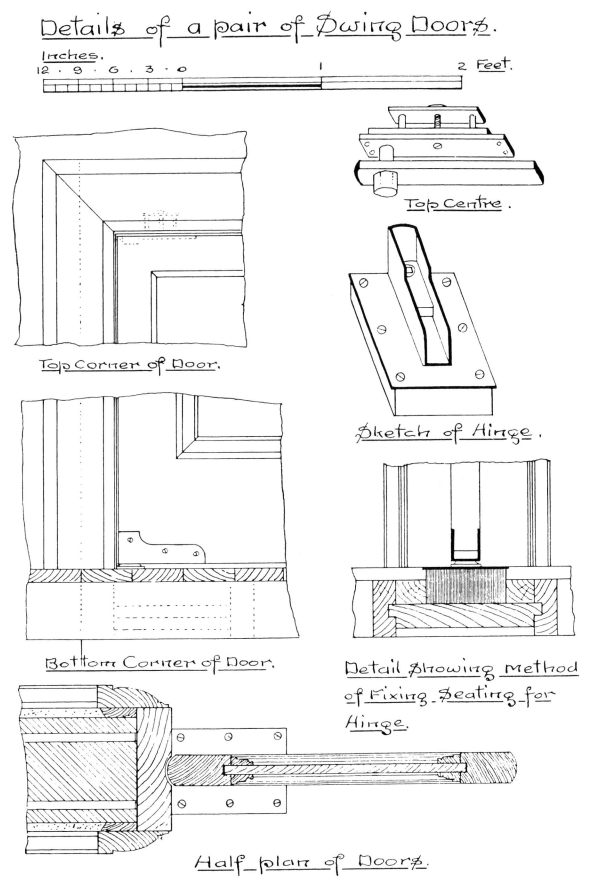

PLATE 100.

Details of a pair of Swing Doors.

Inches.
12 . 9 . 6 . 3 . 0   1   2 Feet.

Top Centre.

Top Corner of Door.

Sketch of Hinge.

Bottom Corner of Door.

Detail Showing Method of Fixing Seating for Hinge.

Half-plan of Doors.

151

PLATE 101.

Details of a pair of Swing Doors.
Scale, Half Full Size.

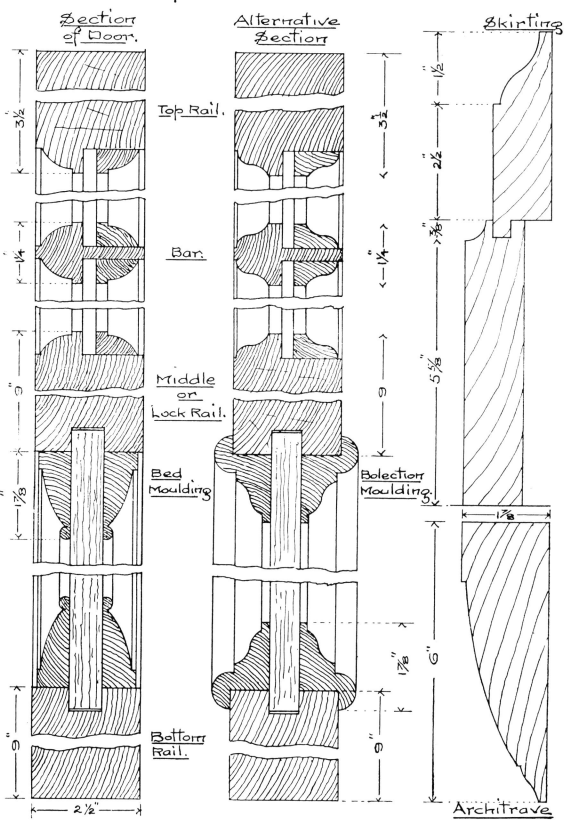

Section of Door.

Alternative Section

Skirting

3½ 1¼ 9" 1⅞" 9"

Top Rail.

Bar.

Middle or Lock Rail.

Bed Moulding

Bottom Rail.

3½ 1¼ 9"

Bolection Moulding.

1⅞" 9"

1½ 2½ ⅜ 5⅝ 1⅞ 6"

Architrave

SPECIFICATION OF BACK ENTRANCE DOOR AND FRAME. (Plates 80, 81.)

The back entrance door frame to have 5″ × 4″ wrot, rebated and chamfered jambs and head, the jambs to be dowelled to step with $\frac{3}{4}$″ diameter wrought-iron dowels.

The door to be of 1″ V-jointed matchboard in 6″ widths, with 1″ × $4\frac{1}{2}$″ stop chamfered ledges and braces.

Fasten the ends of ledges to boards with $1\frac{3}{4}$″ iron screws, two to each end, the boards to be fastened to ledges with $2\frac{1}{4}$″ wrought-iron nails, with ends turned and clinched.

The door to be hung with 18″ wrought-iron hooks and twists, and fitted with 6″ two-bolt rim lock and Mace's $2\frac{1}{4}$″ strong brass furniture, and two 8″ iron barrel bolts.

MATERIALS REQUIRED FOR LEDGED AND BRACED DOOR AND FRAME. (Plates 80, 81.)

	Length.		Total Length.			Description.
	′	″	′	″		
2	7	4	14	8	run	Jambs.
1			4	0	,,	Head.
			18	8	.,	5″ × 4″ rebated and chamfered frame.
6	7	1	42	6	,,	6″ × 1″ tongued and grooved V-jointed boards.
4	2	10	11	4	,,	Ledges.
3	2	2	6	6	,,	Braces.
			17	10	,,	$4\frac{1}{2}$″ × 1″ stop chamfered ledges and braces.
2						3″ × $\frac{3}{4}$″ diameter wrought-iron dowels.
1					pair	18″ wrought-iron hooks and twists.
4						$2\frac{1}{2}$″ × $\frac{5}{16}$″ round-head bolts, nuts and washers.
14						$1\frac{1}{2}$″ No. 12 iron screws.
1						6″ two-bolt rim lock.
1					set	2″ Mace's brass-rim lock furniture.
2						8″ tower bolts and screws.
16						$1\frac{3}{4}$″ No. 12 iron screws.
150						$2\frac{1}{4}$″ wrought-iron nails.

SPECIFICATION OF FRAMED, LEDGED DOOR AND FRAME. (Plates 82, 83.)

The door frame to have $5'' \times 4''$ wrot, rebated and chamfered jambs, and head with $5'' \times 3\frac{1}{2}''$ transom, and fanlight over. The frame to be dowelled to step with $3''$ diameter wrought-iron dowels.

Put $2''$ ovolo-moulded and rebated fanlight hung at bottom, opening inwards; put Leggot's patent fanlight opener with cords complete. Glaze the fanlight with best selected British sheet glass, properly bedded, sprigged, and front puttied.

The door to be $2''$ thick, framed, ledged and braced, with $4\frac{1}{2}''$ stiles, braces, and top rail, the bottom and middle (or lock) rail to be $10''$, all properly framed together, rebated and stop chamfered. The filling to framing to be of $1''$ V-jointed grooved matchboard, with loose wood tongues. All joints of boards and tongues, also backs of ledges, braces, and framing, to be painted with good red-lead paint when putting together. Hang the door with $1\frac{1}{2}$ pairs of $4''$ wrought-steel butts and $1\frac{1}{2}''$ screws. Provide and fix $6''$ two-bolt rim lock and $2\frac{1}{4}''$ Mace's strong brass-rim lock furniture.

FRAMED, LEDGED DOOR AND FRAME

MATERIALS REQUIRED FOR FRAMED, LEDGED AND BRACED DOOR AND FRAME. (PLATES 82, 83.)

	Length.	Total Length.		Description.
2	8′ 9″	17′ 6″		Jambs.
1		3 9		Head.
		21 3	run	5″ × 4″ rebated and chamfered frame.
1		3 3	,,	5″ × 3½ rebated, weathered, chamfered and throated transom.
2				3″ × ¾″ diameter wrought-iron dowels.
2	6 9	13 6		Door stiles.
1	2 9	2 9		Door top rail.
		16 3	run	4½″ × 2″ rebated and stop chamfered stiles and top rail.
1		3 8		
1		2 5		
		6 1	run	4½″ × 1″ stop chamfered braces.
1		2 9	,,	10″ × 2″ rebated and stop chamfered rail.
1		2 9	,,	10″ × 1¼″ stop chamfered rail.
5	5 6	27 6	,,	5″ × 1″ V-jointed matchboard grooved for wood tongues.
4	5 6	22 0		1″ × ⅛″ oak tongues.
1½			pair	4″ wrought-steel butts and 1½″ screws.
1			set	2¼″ Mace's strong brass-rim furniture.
80				1¾″ wrought-iron nails.
2	1 10	3 8		Stiles for fanlight.
1		2 9		Top rail for fanlight.
		6 5	run	2¼″ × 2″ rebated and moulded sash stiles and top rail.
1		2 9	,,	3″ × 2″ rebated and moulded sash stiles and bottom rail.
1				Leggot's patent fanlight opener and cord.
1			pair	3″ wrought-steel butts and 1½″ screws.
1	2′ 4″ × 1′ 4″		=	3′ 1″ 4‴ sup. 21 oz. best selected British sheet glass.

SPECIFICATION FOR A PAIR OF YARD GATES.
(PLATES 84, 85.)

THE yard gates to be $2\frac{1}{2}''$ thick, framed, ledged and braced, V-jointed on outside, stop chamfered on the inside, the top edges of bottom and middle rails to be weathered.

Stiles to be $5\frac{1}{2}''$ wide, top rails $4\frac{1}{2}''$ wide, bottom rails $9''$ wide, middle rails $9'' \times 1\frac{1}{2}''$, braces $4\frac{1}{2}'' \times 1\frac{1}{2}''$; put $4\frac{1}{2}'' \times 2\frac{1}{2}''$ moulded and weathered capping to top of gates. Fill in between framing with $1''$ V-jointed double-faced matchboard in narrow widths, securely nailed to rails and braces; the edges of boards to be tongued to framing, and V-jointing returned on ends of boards. The joints of rails throughout, also backs of rails and edges of boards and framing, to have one coat of good red-lead paint when putting together.

The gates to be hung with $2\frac{1}{2}'' \times \frac{1}{2}''$ wrought-iron strap hinges; the top hinges to be $3'$ long, and bottom hinges $2'\ 6''$ long; provide the requisite $\frac{1}{2}''$ round-headed bolts with nuts and washers. The hooks to have long jaws with tanged ends, and to be let into pierstones, and securely leaded in.

Provide and fix in concrete surround, No. 2 wrought-iron gate catches. Put as stop for gate when closed proper box gate stop with lifting stop. Provide No. 1 18″ wrought-iron monkey-tail bolt.

Provide in one gate for small door to be similarly framed, braced, and boarded as gates, hung to framing with No. 3, 4″ wrought-steel butts and $1\frac{1}{2}''$ screws, and fitted with strong galvanized night latch with three keys.

Provide and fix proper wrought-iron hinged locking-bar to gates, and put strong galvanized padlock with No. 3 keys.

A PAIR OF YARD GATES

MATERIALS REQUIRED FOR A PAIR OF YARD GATES.
(PLATES 84, 85.)

	Length.		Total Length.			Description.
	′	″	′	″		
4	6	0	24	0		$5\frac{1}{2}'' \times 2\frac{1}{2}''$ grooved chamfered and stop chamfered stiles.
2	5	2	10	4		$4\frac{1}{2}'' \times 2\frac{1}{2}''$ grooved chamfered and stop chamfered top rails.
2	5	2	10	4		$9' \times 2\frac{1}{2}''$ grooved chamfered and bevelled bottom rails.
1			5	2		
1			3	5		
			8	7	run	$9' \times 1\frac{1}{2}''$ stop chamfered and bevelled middle rails.
2	2	9	5	6		
2	2	4	4	8		
			10	2	run	$4\frac{1}{2}'' \times 2\frac{1}{2}''$ stop chamfered braces.
2	4	9	9	6		Stiles for small door.
1			1	6		Top rail for small door.
			11	0	run	$4\frac{1}{2}'' \times 2\frac{1}{2}''$ grooved and chamfered stiles and top rail for small door.
1			1	6	,,	$7'' \times 2\frac{1}{2}''$ grooved chamfered and bevelled bottom rail for small door.
1			1	6	,,	$9'' \times 1\frac{1}{2}''$ stop chamfered and bevelled middle rail for small door.
1			1	6		
1			1	10		
			3	4	run	$4'' \times 1\frac{1}{2}''$ stop chamfered braces for small door.
21	4	8	98	0		For gates.
3	3	10	11	6		For small door.
			109	6	run	$4'' \times 1''$ V-jointed matchboard.
2	5	2	10	4		$4\frac{1}{2}'' \times 2\frac{1}{2}''$ grooved, moulded and weathered capping.
1					pair	$2\frac{1}{2}'' \times \frac{1}{2}''$ wrought-iron hinges 3′ long.
1					,,	$2\frac{1}{2}'' \times \frac{1}{2}''$ wrought-iron hinges 2′ 6″ long.
18						$3'' \times \frac{1}{2}''$ round-head bolts, nuts and washers.

MATERIALS REQUIRED FOR A PAIR OF YARD GATES (PLATES 84, 85)— *Continued.*

	Length.	Total Length.		Description.
4			pair	Wrought-iron gate hooks with long jaws and tanged ends.
2				Wrought-iron gate catches.
1				Cast-iron box gate stop.
1				18″ monkey-tail bolt.
1				26″ wrought-iron hinged locking-bar.
1				Strong galvanized padlock.
1				4″ wrought-steel butts and 1½″ screws.
1				Galvanized iron-cased night latch and three keys.
300				2″ wrought-iron nails.

SPECIFICATION OF ENTRANCE DOOR AND FRAME WITH SEGMENTAL HEAD. (PLATES 86, 87, 88.)

THE frame to have 5″ × 4″ wrot, rebated, moulded and beaded jambs and segmental head, 5″ × 3″ rebated, moulded, weathered and beaded transom. Put around outside of jambs 2″ × 1½″ rounded fillet to cover joint with stonework. The frame to be dowelled to step with 3″ × ¾″ diameter wrought-iron dowels.

The door to be 2½″ thick, nine panelled, with bead and flush panels to inside, the panels on outside face of door to be moulded with ¾″ round, bed moulding. The stiles and top rail to be 4½″ wide, bottom and middle rails 9″ wide, muntins 3″ wide. Hang door to frame with No. 3, 4″ wrought-steel butts and 1½″ screws. Put 6″ two-bolt mortice lock and furniture, also No. 2, 9″ brass barrel bolts.

The fanlight to be 2½″ thick, ovolo-moulded and rebated, with 1¼″ bars.

Glaze the fanlight with 21 oz. best selected British sheet glass, properly bedded, sprigged, and front puttied.

MATERIALS REQUIRED FOR ENTRANCE DOOR AND FRAME WITH SEGMENTAL HEAD. (PLATES 86, 87, 88.)

	Length.		Total Length.			Description.
	'	"	'	"		
2	9	4	18	8	run	5" × 4" rebated, moulded and beaded jambs.
1			4	9	,,	Head cut circular out of 9" × 5", or from two pieces similar length of 9" × 2½", and jointed at line of rebate, worked to same section as jambs.
1			4	2	,,	4½" × 2½" rebated, weathered and moulded transom.
2	8	2	16	4	,,	2" × 1½" rounded fillet to cover joint of frame with stonework.
1			4	0	,,	2" × 1½" rounded fillet worked circular for head.
2						3" × ¾" diameter wrought-iron dowels.
2	7	3	14	6		Stiles for door.
1			3	6		Top rail for door.
			18	0	run	4½" × 2½" grooved stiles and top rail.
1			3	6		Frieze rail.
2	1	9	3	6		Muntins.
2	3	0	6	0		,,
2	1	0	2	0		,,
			15	0	run	3" × 2½" twice-grooved frieze rail and muntins.
2	3	6	7	0	,,	9" × 2½" grooved bottom, and twice-grooved lock rail.
3	1	7	4	9		
3	2	9	8	3		
3		10	2	6		
			15	6	run	9½" × 1¼" rebated and beaded panels, with ends cut and bead mitred in.
			45	0	,,	¾" quarter-round bed moulding mitred around panels.
1½					pairs	4" wrought-steel butts and 1½" screws.

MATERIALS REQUIRED FOR ENTRANCE DOOR AND FRAME WITH
SEGMENTAL HEAD (PLATES 86, 87, 88)—*Continued.*

	Length.		Total Length.			Description.
	′	*″*	*′*	*″*		
1						6″ two-bolt mortice lock and furniture.
2	1	9	3	6		Stiles for fanlight.
1			3	6		Bottom rail for fanlight.
			7	0	run	$2\frac{1}{2}″ \times 2\frac{1}{2}″$ rebated and moulded sash stiles and bottom rail.
1			3	6	,,	Head cut circular out of $5″ \times 2\frac{1}{2}″$.
2	1	10	3	8		
1	1	11	1	11		
1			3	5		
			9	0	run	$2\frac{1}{2}″ \times 1\frac{1}{4}″$ moulded and rebated sash bar.
4		$9″ \times 9″$				Panes 21 oz. best selected British sheet
2		$10″ \times 9″$				glass. Four panes to have top edge
2		$9″ \times 9″$				cut circular.

SPECIFICATION OF ENTRANCE DOOR AND FRAME WITH SIDE-LIGHTS. (PLATES 89, 90.)

PUT to entrance doorway 5″ × 4″ rebated, moulded and beaded frame with segmental head, 5″ × 4″ double rebated, moulded and beaded door-posts. Transom to be 5″ × 3½″ double rebated, moulded, weathered and beaded. The frame to be dowelled to step with 3″ × ¾″ diameter wrought-iron dowels.

Fill in over transom with 2½″ ovolo-moulded and rebated fanlights and fitted with movable fixing beads, the centre light to be hung at bottom, opening inwards, and to be fitted with brass roller stays at side, and brass spring fastener and cords complete.

The sidelights to be 2½″ thick, framed and panelled, with diminishing stiles and raised panels. The stiles to be 4½″ wide at bottom and diminishing to 3″ at top, top rail 3″ wide, bottom and middle rails 9″ wide, the top panels to be prepared for leaded lights, and fitted with movable fixing beads. The framing to be moulded on solid.

The door to be 2½″ thick, four panelled, framed and moulded on solid, with raised panels. Stiles, top rails, and muntins to be 4½″ wide, bottom and middle rails to be 9″ wide; put quarter-round moulding around panels on inside of door. The door to be hung with No. 3, 4″ wrought-steel butts and 1½″ screws. Put to door 6″ two-bolt mortice lock and gun-metal furniture with long plates. Provide and fix Yale night latch with three keys complete.

The top panels in side-lights, also fanlights, to be filled in with plain leaded lights glazed with best selected British muffled sheet glass.

MATERIALS REQUIRED FOR ENTRANCE DOOR AND FRAME WITH SIDE-LIGHTS AND FANLIGHT. (Plates 89, 90.)

	Length.		Total Length.			Description.
	′	″	′	″		
2	9	9	19	6	run	5″ × 4″ wall-posts, rebated, moulded and beaded.
2	10	2	20	4	,,	5″ × 4″ door-posts, twice rebated, moulded and beaded.
1			7	3	,,	5″ × 3½″ transom, rebated, weathered, moulded and throated.
1			7	9	,,	Head cut circular out of 9″ × 5″ or from two pieces 9″ × 2½″, and jointed at line of rebate; worked to same detail as wall-posts.
4						3″ × ¾″ diameter wrought-iron dowels.
2	7	3	14	6		
1			3	2		
			17	8	run	4½″ × 2½″ stiles and top rail to door grooved and moulded.
1			3	2	,,	
1			2	6		
			5	8	run	3½″ × 2½″ frieze rail, and muntin twice grooved and moulded.
1			3	2	,,	9″ × 2½″ bottom rail, grooved and moulded.
1			3	2	,,	9″ × 2½″ lock rail, twice grooved and moulded.
1			2	6	,,	11″ × 1½″ panel, raised and bevelled.
2	2	6	5	0	,,	13½″ × 1½″ panel, raised and bevelled.
1			2	6	,,	22″ × 1½″ panel, raised and bevelled.
			30	0	,,	¾″ quarter-round moulding mitred around panels.
2	2	5	4	10		
2	2	7	5	2		
2	2	8	5	4		
2	1	6	3	0		
1			3	2		
			21	6	run	2½″ × 2½″ sash stile and bottom rails to fanlight rebated and moulded.

ENTRANCE DOOR AND FRAME WITH SIDE-LIGHTS

Materials required for Entrance Door and Frame with Side-lights and Fanlight (Plates 89, 90)—*Continued.*

	Length.		Total Length.			Description.
	′	″				
2	1	6	3	0		
1			3	2		
			6	2	run	$2\frac{1}{2}'' \times 2\frac{1}{2}''$ top rails to fanlight worked circular.
4	7	3	29	0	,,	$4\frac{1}{2}'' \times 2\frac{1}{2}''$ stiles for side-lights diminished to $3''$ at top, rebated and moulded, bottom grooved for panels.
2	1	6	3	0	,,	$3'' \times 2\frac{1}{2}''$ top rails to side-lights rebated and moulded.
2	1	6	3	0	,,	$9'' \times 2\frac{1}{2}''$ middle rails to side-lights rebated and moulded and grooved for panels.
2	1	6	3	0	,,	$9'' \times 2\frac{1}{2}''$ bottom rails to side-lights grooved and moulded.
2	1	10	3	8	,,	$10'' \times 1\frac{1}{2}''$ panels raised and bevelled.
			11	0	,,	$\frac{3}{4}''$ quarter-round moulding mitred around panels.
4	3	7	14	4		
8	1	1	8	8		
2	2	9	5	6		
2	2	0	4	0		
4	2	2	8	8		
			41	2	run	$\frac{3}{4}'' \times \frac{3}{8}''$ movable fixing beads mitred around rebates of fanlights and side-lights.
2						$8''$ brass roller stays to fanlight.
1						Brass fanlight catch and cords.
2						Small brass Lazy pulleys.
1						Small brass cleat hook.
$1\frac{1}{2}$					pairs	$4''$ wrought-steel butts and screws.
1					,,	$3''$ wrought-steel butts and screws.
1						$6''$ two-bolt mortice lock and furniture with long plates.

Length.	Total Length.		Description.
2			10″ strong brass barrel bolts.
2	3′ 6″ × 1′ 0″	= 7′ 0″.	
2	2′ 0″ × 1′ 0″	= 4′ 0″.	
1	2′ 8″ × 2′ 3″	= 6′ 0″.	
			17′ 0″ sup. plain-leaded lights glazed with best selected 21 oz. British sheet glass.
	4′ 8″	run	Extra only to top edges made to circular shapes.

SPECIFICATION OF ENTRANCE DOORS AND FRAME WITH ELLIPTICAL-SHAPED HEAD. (PLATES 91, 92.)

THE door frame to have 6″ × 5″ wrot, rebated, stop chamfered and beaded jambs, grooved for inside linings. The head to be 6″ × 5″, elliptical shaped as detail, cut out of the solid, jointed where shown, and fastened with hammer-headed keys. As an alternative the head may be made up in two thicknesses, with joint at line of rebate and screwed together, the joints to overlap. Transom to be 8″ × 3½″, rebated, weathered, beaded, throated and moulded. The jambs to be dowelled to step with 3″ × ¾″ wrought-iron dowels.

The doors to be 2½″ thick, three panelled, square framed both sides, and bed moulded. Stiles, top rail and frieze rail to be 4½″ wide, bottom rail and lock rail 9″ wide, panels ⅝″ thick, bed moulding 1¾″ × ¾″. The centre joint of doors to be rebated and beaded. Hang doors to jambs with 5″ heavy brass butts, 1½ pairs to each door. Provide and fix No. 2, 10″ strong brass barrel bolts for one door and 6″ full rebated two-bolt mortice lock with gun-metal furniture complete to the other door.

The fanlight to be 2½″ thick, ovolo-moulded and rebated, loose with fixing beads for glass; hang fanlight to transom with one pair 3½″ strong brass butts. Put approved fanlight opener and cords complete.

Glaze the fanlight with ¼″ best selected polished British plate glass bedded in putty and wash-leather, and sprigged and front puttied.

MATERIALS REQUIRED FOR ENTRANCE DOORS AND FRAME WITH ELLIPTICAL-SHAPED HEAD. (PLATES 91, 92.)

	Length.		Total Length.			Description.
	′	″	′	″		
2	9	0	18	0	run	6″ × 5″ rebated, stop chamfered and beaded jambs.
2	2	3	4	6	,,	Head out of 8″ × 6″ worked circular same section of jambs (haunches).
1			3	5	,,	Head out of 8″ × 6″ worked circular same section of jambs (centre).
2						Hammer-headed keys 14″ long out of 3″ × 2½″ oak, and No. 4 small oak wedges.
2						3″ × ¾″ diameter iron dowels.
4	7	8	30	8	run	4½″ × 2½″ grooved stiles for doors.
2	2	4	4	8	,,	4½″ × 2½″ grooved top rails for doors.
2	2	4	4	8	,,	4½″ × 2½″ twice grooved frieze rails.
2	2	4	4	8	,,	9″ × 2½″ twice grooved lock rails.
2	2	4	4	8	,,	9″ × 2½″ once grooved bottom rails.

MATERIALS REQUIRED FOR ENTRANCE DOORS AND FRAME WITH
ELLIPTICAL-SHAPED HEAD (PLATES 91, 92)—*Continued.*

	Length.	Total Length.		Description
2		$1'\ 3'' \times 1'\ 5'' \times \frac{5}{8}''$		Panels.
2		$2'\ 4'' \times 1'\ 5'' \times \frac{5}{8}''$		,,
2		$1'\ 8'' \times 1'\ 5'' \times \frac{5}{8}''$		,,
24	1 4	32 0	run	$1\frac{3}{4}'' \times \frac{3}{4}''$ bed moulding.
8	1 7	12 8	,,	,, ,, ,,
8	2 4	18 8	,,	,, ,, ,,
8	1 2	9 4	,,	,, ,, ,,
3			pairs	5'' heavy brass butts and $1\frac{1}{2}''$ screws.
2				10'' heavy brass barrel bolts.
1				6'' two-bolt full rebated mortice lock and gun-metal furniture.
1		4 7	run	$3'' \times 2\frac{1}{2}''$ rebated and moulded bottom rail to fanlight.
2	1 8	3 4	,,	Head to fanlight worked circular out of $7'' \times 2\frac{1}{2}''$.
1		3 0	,,	Head to fanlight worked circular out of $8'' \times 2\frac{1}{2}''$.
1			pair	$3\frac{1}{2}''$ brass butts and screws.
1				Fanlight opener and cords.
2				Brass Lazy pulleys.
1				Brass fanlight catch and cords.
1	$4'\ 1'' \times 1'\ 7''$		=	6' 5'' 7''' sup. best selected polished British plate glass cut to circular shape at top.

SPECIFICATION OF ENTRANCE DOORWAY AND SIDE-LIGHTS. (Plates 93, 94.)

THE entrance doorway to have 5″ × 3″ wrot, rebated and rounded jambs, grooved for linings, and dowelled to step with 3″ × ¾″ diameter wrought-iron dowels.

Door to be 2½″ thick, six panelled, square framed, with bead and flush panels to outside; inside to be bed moulded with ¾″ round moulding. Hang door with No. 3, 5″ wrought-steel butts and 1½″ screws. Provide and fix to door strong Yale night latch and furniture, No. 2, 10″ brass barrel bolts, No. 1 brass door chain, No. 1, gun-metal centre knob, and No. 1, letter-plate in polished gun-metal with 8″ × 1½″ opening.

The side-lights to be 2½″ thick, ovolo-moulded and rebated, and provided with loose fixing beads for leaded lights. Frames to be of similar section as door frame, and with weathered and grooved sills. The side-lights to have plain leaded lights, glazed with best selected muffled British sheet glass. Put to door-frame and side-lights 7½″ × 1″, linings tongued to frames. The window boards to be 10½″ × 1½″, tongued to sills, and with rounded nosing with mitred and returned ends. Put under nosing of window boards 2″ × 1½″ moulding, with mitred and returned ends. The architrave moulding to be 3″ × 1½″, securely fixed to linings, and mitred at angles.

The hood over entrance door to have 5″ wrot and shaped brackets tenoned to plates; the moulding around top of brackets to be similar in section to that on the stone window heads, and must intersect with same at wall line. The plates for roof to be 15″ × 4″ morticed for brackets, with beaded moulding planted on, mitred at angles, and returned to face of wall and continued under eaves moulding. The plates to run 4½″ into wall, and securely pinned. Provide No. 2, ½″ bolts, 2′ 6″ long, for securing brackets to wall. The roof to have $6'' \times 1''$ ridge, $5'' \times 2''$ wrot and chamfered rafters; the outside rafters to have $3'' \times 3''$ moulding planted on, and mitred at angle, and continued to wall lines at eaves. Cover the roof with $\frac{7}{8}''$ V-jointed matchboard in narrow widths; on this lay 6 lb. milled lead turned up $4''$ to face of wall on slope of roof, and put 5 lb. stepped cover flashing securely pinned to wall with lead wedges and neatly stopped in with cement at finish. The edges of lead at eaves and barge to be copper-nailed $3''$ apart. Provide three screwed and soldered dots to each slope of roof.

MATERIALS REQUIRED FOR ENTRANCE DOORWAY AND SIDE-LIGHTS. (Plates 93, 94.)

	Length.	Total Length.		Description.
2	7′ 2″	14′ 4″	run	Jambs.
		4 0		Head.
		18 4	run	$5'' \times 3''$ rebated, beaded, grooved and rounded frame.
2				$3'' \times \frac{3}{4}''$ diameter wrought-iron dowels.
2	7 0	14 0		Stiles for door.
1		3 5		Top rail for door.
		17 5	run	$4\frac{1}{2}'' \times 2\frac{1}{2}''$ grooved stiles and top rail for door.
1		3 5		Frieze rail.
1		1 7	} Muntins.	
1		1 6		
1		2 7		,,
		9 1	run	$4\frac{1}{2}'' \times 2\frac{1}{2}''$ twice grooved frieze rail and muntins.
1		3 5		$9'' \times 2\frac{1}{2}''$ twice grooved lock rail.
1		3 5		$9'' \times 2\frac{1}{2}''$ once grooved bottom rail.

MATERIALS REQUIRED FOR ENTRANCE DOORWAY AND SIDE-LIGHTS
(PLATES 93, 94)—*Continued.*

Length.		Total Length.			Description.
	'	"	'	"	
2			1	3	×	1' 2½" × 1½" panels) rebated and beaded,
2			2	4	×	,, ,, ,, } with ends cut and
2			1	5	×	,, ,, ,,) bead mitred in.
12	1	3	15	0		
4	1	2	4	8		
4	2	3	9	0		
4	1	5	5	8		
			34	4		¾" quarter-round moulding mitred around panels outside.
1½					pairs	5" wrought-steel butts and 1½" screws.
1						Yale night latch and three keys.
2						10" brass barrel bolts.
1						Centre door-knob in polished gun-metal.
1						Letter-plate 8" × 1½", opening in polished gun-metal.
4	4	9	19	0		
2	2	4	4	8		
			23	8	run	5" × 3" rebated, beaded, grooved and rounded frame to side-lights.
2	2	4	4	8	,,	5" × 3" rebated, weathered, grooved and rounded sills.
4	4	4	17	4		Stiles.
2	1	10	3	8		Top rails.
			21	0	run	2½" × 2½" rebated and moulded sash stiles and top rails to side-lights.
2	1	10	3	8		3" × 2½" rebated and moulded bottom rails.
			21	0	,,	¾" × ⅜" movable fixing beads to fasten leaded lights.
2	3	9	× 1	4	=	10' sup. plain leaded lights glazed with best selected 21 oz. British muffled sheet glass.

Materials required for Entrance Doorway and Side-lights (Plates 93, 94)—*Continued.*

	Length.		Total Length.			Description.
	′	″	′	″		
2	7	1	14	2		Inside linings to door frame.
1	4	0	4	0		,, ,, ,, ,, ,,
4	4	9	19	0		,, ,, ,, side-lights.
2	2	4	4	8		,, ,, ,, ,,
			41	10	run	$7\frac{1}{2}'' \times 1''$ inside linings tongued to door frame and side-lights, and fixed to proper grounds.
2	3	0	6	0	,,	$10\frac{1}{2}'' \times 1\frac{1}{2}''$ tongued and nosed window boards, with mitred and returned ends.
2	3	0	6	0	,,	$2'' \times 1\frac{1}{2}''$ moulding under nosing of window boards, with returned ends.
4	5	0	20	0		Architrave to side-lights.
2	2	10	5	8		,, ,, ,,
2	7	4	14	8		,, ,, doorway.
1			4	6		,, ,, ,,
			44	10	run	$3'' \times 1\frac{1}{2}''$ moulded architrave fixed to linings and mitred at angles.

HOOD OVER DOOR.

	Length.		Total Length.			Description.
2	2	9	5	6	run	$15'' \times 4''$ plates morticed for brackets.
2						Shaped brackets 3′ 7″ long, 2′ wide, 5″ thick, out of oak, grooved, tongued and jointed up. The grain of wood to run parallel with salient points of moulded edge of bracket.
4	2	4	9	4		
2		9	1	6		
			10	10	run	$3' \times 2\frac{1}{2}''$ moulding planted on brackets and mitred at angles.

MATERIALS REQUIRED FOR ENTRANCE DOORWAY AND SIDE-LIGHTS (HOOD OVER DOOR) (PLATES 93, 94)—*Continued.*

	Length.	Total Length.		Description.
	′ ″	′ ″		
4	2 6	10 0		
2	1 6	3 0		
		13 0	run	$1\frac{3}{4}'' \times 1\frac{1}{2}''$ beading planted on plate and mitred at angles.
2	3 8	7 4		To barge rafters.
2	2 9	5 6		To eaves.
		12 10	run	$3'' \times 3''$ moulding planted on barge rafters and at eaves and mitred at angles.
6	3 6	21 0	,,	$5'' \times 2''$ chamfered rafters.
1		2 9	,,	$6'' \times 1''$ ridge.
22	2 8	58 8	,,	$4'' \times \frac{7}{8}''$ V-jointed matchboard.
	7′ 6″ × 3′ 1″		=	23′ 1″ 6‴ sup. 6 lb. lead covering to roof.
6				Screwed and soldered dots.
2	4′ 6″ × 7″		=	5′ 3″ sup. 5 lb. lead stepped flashing.

SPECIFICATION OF INTERNAL DOOR AND LININGS. (PLATES 95, 96, 97, 98.)

THE internal door openings to have 2″ framed, panelled, rebated linings, moulded on solid, and with small moulding planted on panels. To be the full width of wall and plaster, and securely fixed to proper grounds. The joints at head to be grooved and tongued.

The door to be 2″ thick, six panelled, framed and moulded on solid both sides, with small marginal moulding planted on panels.

Stiles, top rail and frieze rail, and muntins to be $4\frac{1}{2}″$ wide, bottom and lock rails 9″ wide, panels $\frac{1}{2}″$ thick. Door to be hung with one pair 4″ wrought-steel butts and $1\frac{1}{2}″$ screws, and fitted with 6″ two-bolt mortice lock and gun-metal furniture.

MATERIALS REQUIRED FOR INTERNAL DOOR AND LININGS. (PLATES 95, 96, 97, 98.)

	Length.		Total Length.			Description.
4	7	0	28	0		Stiles to jamb lining.
2	3	2	6	4		Stiles to head lining.
			34	4	run	$5\frac{1}{2}″ \times 2″$ rebated, grooved and moulded on solid stiles to linings.
2	1	1	2	2	,,	$6\frac{1}{2}″ \times 2″$ end rails to head, rebated, grooved, and solid moulded and grooved for jamb lining.
1			1	1	,,	$4\frac{1}{2}″ \times 2″$ muntin twice grooved and moulded on solid.
2	1	1	2	2	,,	5″ × 2″ top rails to jamb linings grooved and moulded on solid and tongued to head lining.

MATERIALS REQUIRED FOR INTERNAL DOOR AND LININGS (PLATES 95, 96, 97, 98)—*Continued.*

	Length.		Total Length.			Description.
	′	″	′	″		
2	1	1	2	2	run	4½″ × 2″ frieze rails twice grooved and moulded on solid.
2	1	1	2	2	,,	9″ × 2″ middle rails twice grooved and moulded on solid.
2	1	1	2	2	,,	9″ × 2″ bottom rails once grooved and moulded on solid.
2		11	1	10	,,	9″ × ½″ panels.
2	1	7	3	2	,,	,, ,,
2	2	3	4	6	,,	,, ,,
2		11	1	10	,,	,, ,,
			11	4	,,	,, ,,
16		5	6	8		
4	1	3	5	0		
4	1	11	7	8		
8		7	4	8		
			24	0	run	1″ bead moulding planted on panels and mitred at angles.

DOOR.

	Length.		Total Length.			Description.
2	7	0	14	10	run	Stiles to door.
1			2	10	,,	
			16	10	,,	4½″ × 2″ stiles, and top rail grooved and moulded on solid.
1			2	10		Frieze rail.
1			1	10		Muntin.
1			2	6		,,
1			1	3		,,
			8	5	run	4½″ × 2″ frieze rail and muntins twice grooved and moulded on solid.

MATERIALS REQUIRED FOR INTERNAL DOOR AND LININGS (DOOR)
(PLATES 95, 96, 97, 98)—*Continued.*

	Length.		Total Length.			Description.
	′	″	′	″		
2	1	7	3	2		Bottom panels.
2	2	3	4	6		Centre panels.
2		11	1	10		Top panels.
			9	6	run	11″ × ½″ panels.
24		7	14	0		
8	1	3	10	0		
8	1	11	15	4		
8		7	4	8		
			44	0	run	1″ bead moulding planted on panels and mitred at angles.
1					pair	4″ wrought-steel butts and screws.
1						6″ two-bolt mortice lock and gun-metal furniture.
4	7	3	29	0		
2	3	6	7	0		
			36	0	run	4″ × 2″ moulded architraves fixed to linings and grounds and mitred at angles.

SPECIFICATION FOR A PAIR OF SWING DOORS.
(PLATES 99, 100, 101.)

PROVIDE and fix to opening $10\frac{1}{2}″ × 3″$ wrot jamb linings, hollow, rebated for doors.

The doors to be $2\frac{1}{2}″$ thick, wrot, square framed, panelled, and bolection moulded bottom panels, with diminishing stiles and top prepared for glass, ovolo-moulded and rebated, and provided with movable fixing beads for glass. Doors to be hung folding into two halves to swing both ways on patent brass-cased steel spring hinges with adjusting centres, the top centres to be adjustable also. The seating for hinge to be formed, as shown on the drawing, with 2″ solid, block tongued into joists, and with block on each side of hinge.

Stiles to be 5″ wide diminished to $3\frac{1}{2}$″ at top, top rail $3\frac{1}{2}$″ wide, bottom and middle rails 9″ wide, panels $\frac{3}{4}$″ thick, bolection moulding $1\frac{7}{8}$″ × $1\frac{1}{4}$″.

The doors to be glazed with $\frac{1}{4}$″ best selected polished British plate glass bedded in putty and wash-leather.

Put to each door No. 2, 14″ gun-metal swing-door handles, No. 4, 10″ strong brass barrel bolts. Provide No. 4 brass spring door stops, No. 2 to each door.

The architraves to be 6″ × 2″ moulded, securely fixed to grounds and mitred at angles.

MATERIALS REQUIRED FOR A PAIR OF SWING DOORS AND FRAME. (PLATES 99, 100, 101.)

	Length.		Total Length.			Description.
	′	″	′	″		
2	8	6	17	0	run	$10\frac{1}{2}$″ × 3″ hollow grooved jambs.
1			6	0	,,	$10\frac{1}{2}$″ × 3″ head.
4	7	9	31	0	,.	5″ × $2\frac{1}{2}$″ door stiles diminished to $3\frac{1}{2}$″ at top, rebated and moulded and prepared for glass, bottom grooved for panels, edges rounded.
2	2	7	5	2	,,	9″ × $2\frac{1}{2}$″ bottom rails to doors, grooved for panels.
2	2	7	5	2	,,	9″ × $2\frac{1}{2}$″ middle rails grooved for panels, top edge rebated and moulded.
2	2	7	5	2	,,	$3\frac{1}{2}$″ × $2\frac{1}{2}$″ top rails, rebated and moulded.
6	2	7	15	6	,,	
4	4	2	16	8		
			32	2	run	$2\frac{1}{2}$″ × $1\frac{1}{4}$″ rebated and moulded bars.

MATERIALS REQUIRED FOR A PAIR OF SWING DOORS AND FRAME
(PLATES 99, 100, 101)—*Continued.*

	Length.		Total Length.			Description.
	′	″	′	″		
48		8	32	0		
48	1	0	48	0		
			80	0	run	$1'' \times \frac{1}{2}''$ movable moulding fitted to rebates and mitred at angles.
16	1	9	28	0	,,	$1\frac{7}{8}'' \times 1\frac{1}{4}''$ bolection moulding to panels with mitred angles.
4	8	3	33	0		
2	6	2	12	4		
			45	4	run	$6'' \times 2''$ moulded architrave planted on jambs and mitred at angles.
2	1	2	2	4	,,	$5'' \times 2''$ fir blocks fitted between joists, and grooved for seating of hinge.
2	1	2	2	4	,,	$12'' \times 2''$ fir seating blocks tongued to joists.
4		11	3	8	,,	$2\frac{1}{2}'' \times 2''$ fir blocks at sides of hinges.
2						Brass-cased double-action floor springs with adjustable centres and top centres.
4						$14''$ gun-metal swing-door handles.
4						$10''$ strong brass barrel bolts.
4						Brass spring door-stops.
24						Panes best polished $\frac{1}{4}''$ British plate glass, each $12'' \times 7\frac{1}{2}''$, bedded in oil putty and wash-leather.

BUILDING CONSTRUCTION DRAWING

A CLASS-BOOK FOR THE ELEMENTARY STUDENT AND ARTISAN

BY

RICHARD B. EATON

LECTURER ON BUILDING CONSTRUCTION, POOLE SCHOOL OF
ART AND TECHNOLOGY

Part V

JOINERY DRAWINGS, SPECIFICATIONS AND MEASUREMENTS

26 PLATES

London
E. & F. N. SPON, Ltd., 57 HAYMARKET, S.W. 1
New York
SPON & CHAMBERLAIN, 120 LIBERTY STREET
1919

PREFACE

THE accompanying work dealing with *Joinery Drawing* is of similar character to the work on *Building Construction Drawing* already published, dealing however more particularly with the trade of the joiner.

The drawings and details generally are fully dimensioned, and show the joiner's work in its accustomed setting. Specifications are appended for all the joinery, and in some instances for other portions of work, such as coverings to flats, finishings connected therewith, and glazing.

Detailed measurements of the drawings are also given, additional allowances being made for horns, and the finished cut. These measurements are added in the hope that the student and apprentice will find them an advantage in the study of his trade.

RICHARD B. EATON.

"LAKESIDE," SELDOWN, POOLE,
October 1919.

PLATE 102.

Cased Frame & 2" Sashes, double hung.
Descriptive drawing of the various parts.

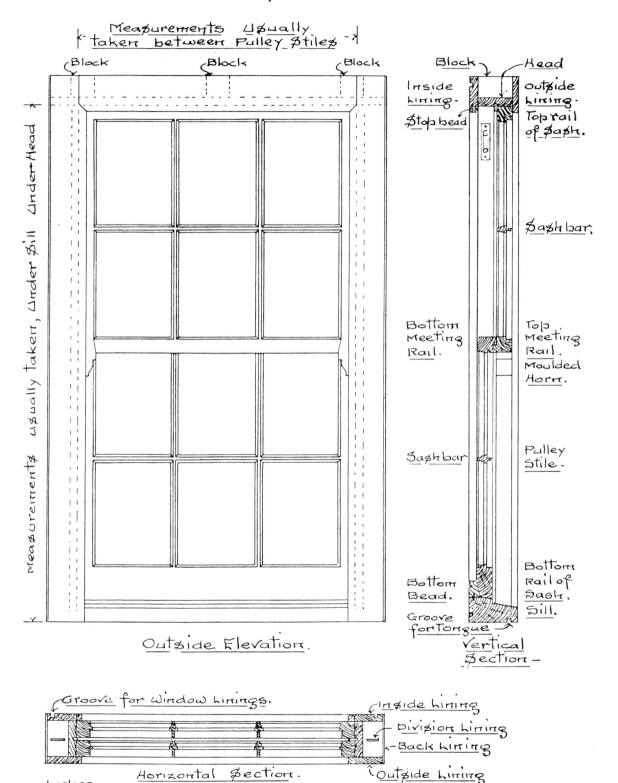

Measurements usually taken between Pulley Stiles

Block   Block   Block

Under Head

Measurements usually taken, Under Sill

Outside Elevation.

Block   Head
Inside lining.   Outside lining.
Stop bead   Top rail of Sash.

Sash bar.

Bottom Meeting Rail.

Top Meeting Rail. Moulded Horn.

Sash bar

Pulley Stile.

Bottom Bead.

Bottom Rail of Sash. Sill.

Groove for Tongue

Vertical Section.

Groove for Window Linings.

Inside lining
Division lining
Back lining

Horizontal Section.

Outside lining

Inches.
12 . 9 . 6 . 3 . 0   1   2   3   4 Feet.

PLATE 103.

Deal Cased Sash Frame, with 2" Sashes.

For Details, See Plates Nos. 104 & 105.

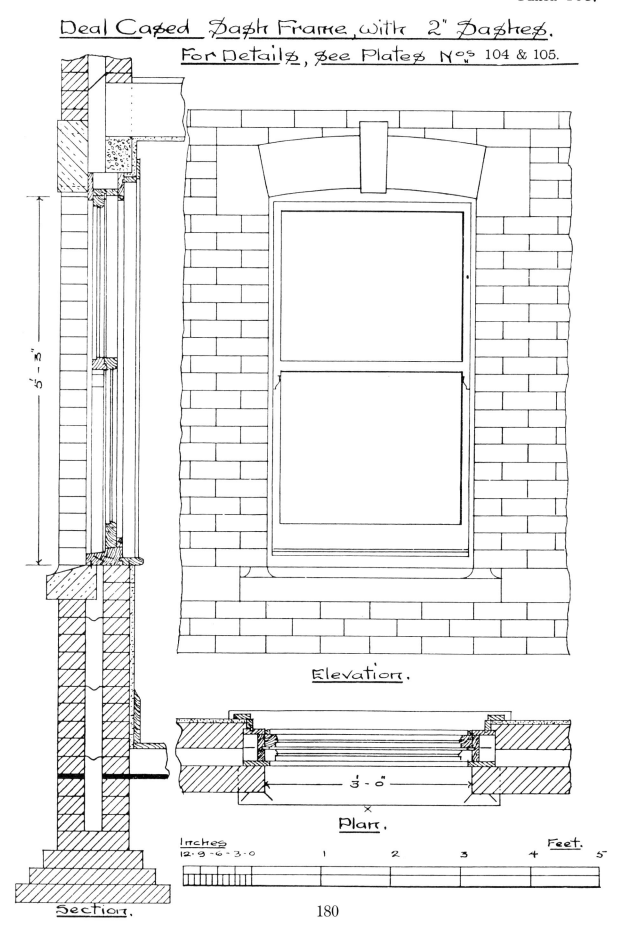

Elevation.

Plan.

Section.

Inches
12 · 9 · 6 · 3 · 0   1   2   3   4   Feet.   5

PLATE 104.

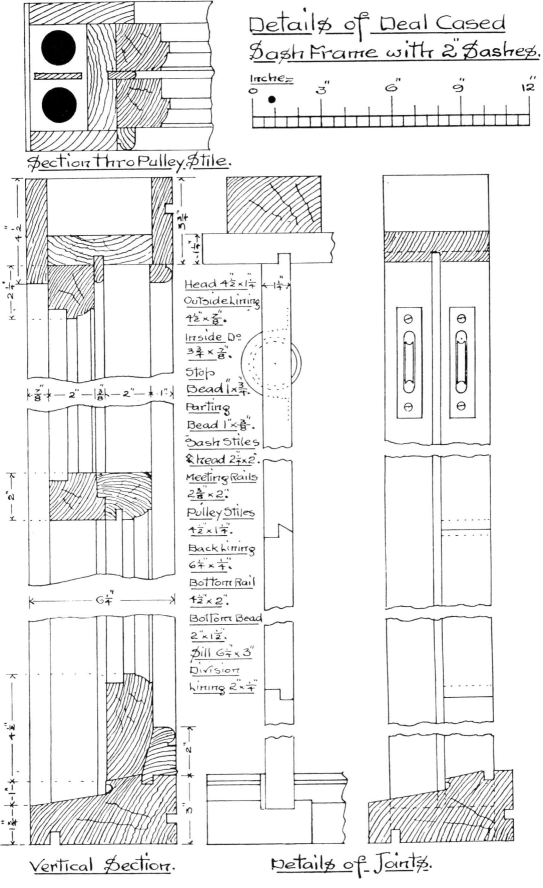

Section thro Pulley Stile.

Details of Deal Cased Sash Frame with 2" Sashes.

Inches 0 3" 6" 9" 12"

Head 4½"×1¼"
Outside Lining 4½"×⅞".
Inside D° 3¾"×⅞".
Stop Bead 1"×¾".
Parting Bead 1"×⅜".
Sash Stiles & Head 2¼"×2".
Meeting Rails 2⅜"×2".
Pulley Stiles 4½"×1¼".
Back Lining 6¼"×¼".
Bottom Rail 4½"×2".
Bottom Bead 2"×1½".
Sill 6¼"×3"
Division Lining 2"×¼".

Vertical Section.

Details of Joints.

181

PLATE 105.

Details of Sashes & Frame, with 2" Sashes,
1¾" Pulley Stiles & Head tongued to ⅞" Inside & Outside
Linings 6¼"x 3" Sill Double Sunk, weathered throated and
grooved for water bar, 1"x ¾" rounded Stop moulding ⅞₆ Parting
bead, 3" bottom moulding ¼" back & division linings.

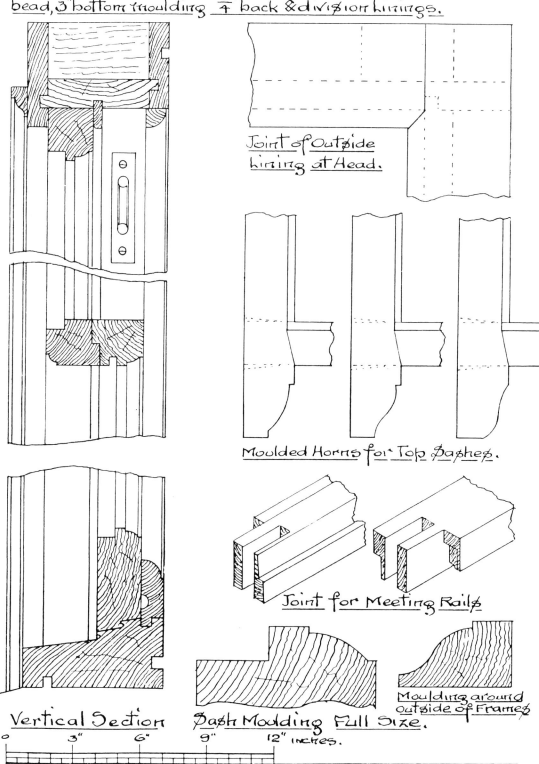

Joint of Outside Lining at Head.

Moulded Horns for Top Sashes.

Joint for Meeting Rails

Vertical Section   Sash Moulding Full Size.

Moulding around outside of Frames

0   3"   6"   9"   12" inches.

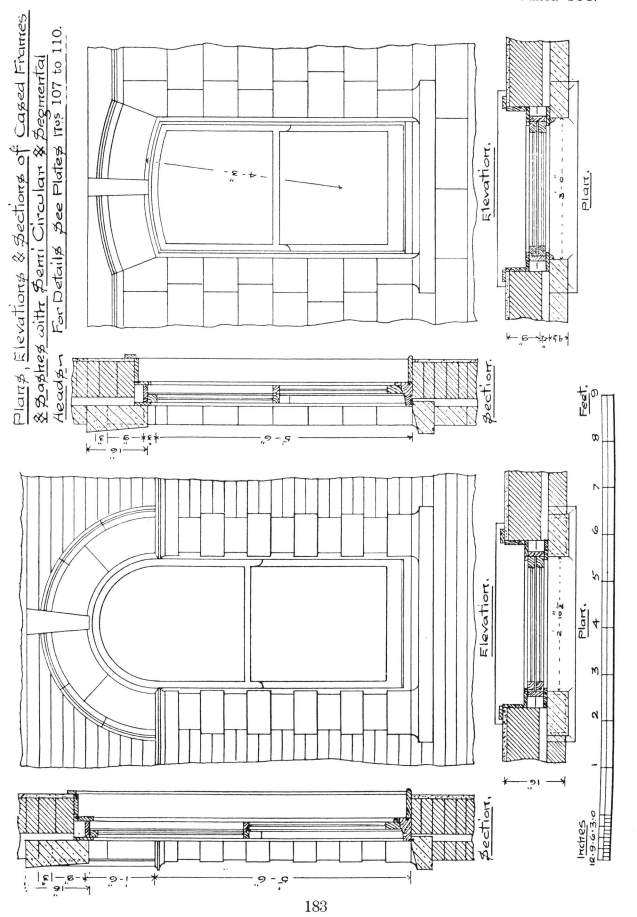

Plans, Elevations & Sections of Cased Frames & Sashes with Semi Circular & Segmental Heads. For Details See Plates Nos. 107 to 110.

PLATE 106.

Elevation.

Plan.

Section.

Elevation.

Plan.

Section.

Feet

Inches

183

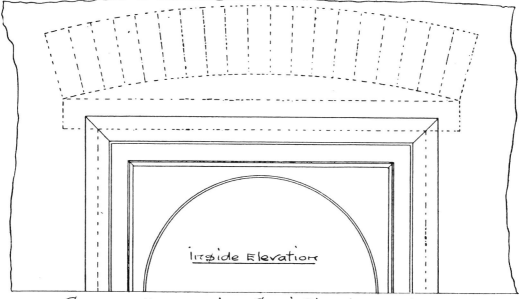

PLATE **107.**

Details of Sashes, with Semi Circular Head.

__Square Head Inside Semi Circular Outside.__

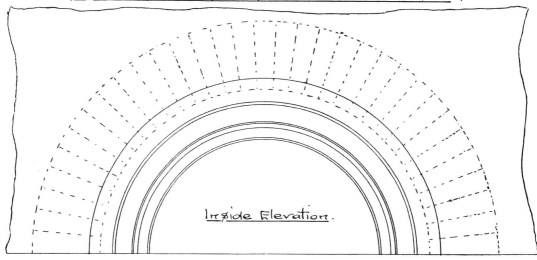

Inside Elevation.

__Semi Circular Inside and Outside__

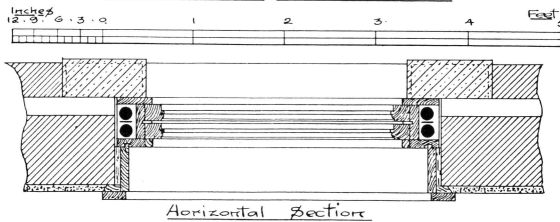

Inches
12. 9. 6. 3. 0.   1   2   3.   4   Feet 5

__Horizontal Section__

184

PLATE 108.

Details Shewing Joints of Sashes with Semi-Circular Head.

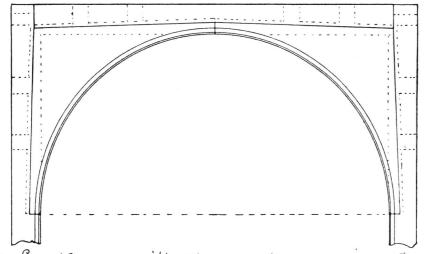

Sash for Frame with Square Head Inside, Semi Circular Outside.

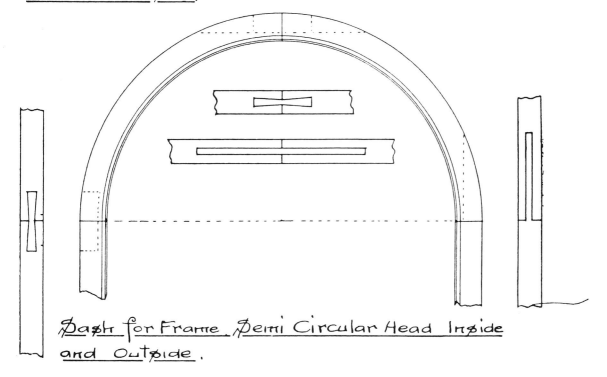

Sash for Frame, Semi Circular Head Inside and Outside.

Inches | Feet.

12. 9. 6. 3 0 1 2 3

PLATE 109.

Sash Frame with Semi Circular Head.

Details of Joints.   1½" Scale.
Alternative Methods.

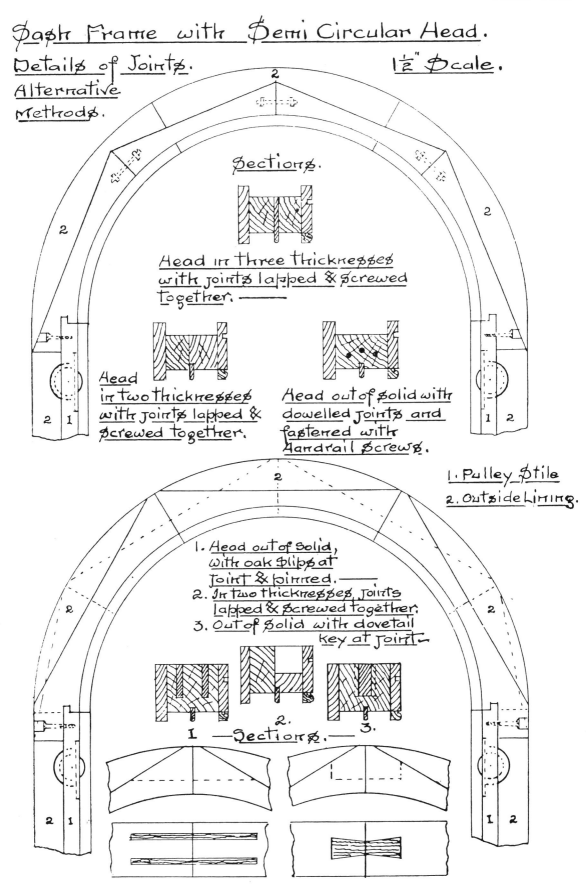

Sections.

Head in three thicknesses with joints lapped & screwed together.

Head in two thicknesses with joints lapped & screwed together.

Head out of solid with dowelled joints and fastened with handrail screws.

1. Pulley Stile
2. Outside Lining.

1. Head out of solid, with oak slips at joint & pinned.
2. In two thicknesses, joints lapped & screwed together.
3. Out of solid with dovetail key at joint.

1 — Sections. — 3.
2.

186

PLATE 110.

Details of Sash Frame with Segmental Head.

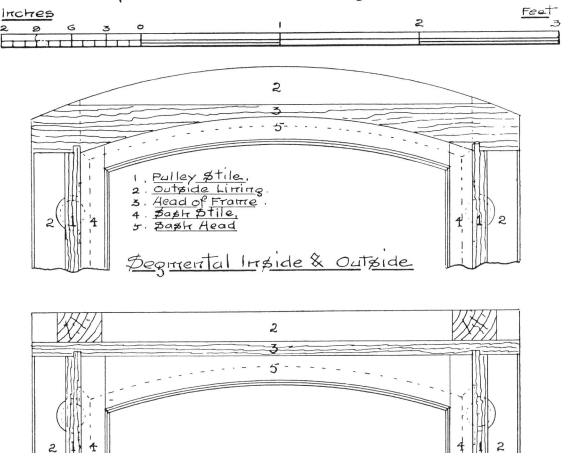

1. Pulley Stile.
2. Outside Lining.
3. Head of Frame.
4. Sash Stile.
5. Sash Head

Segmental Inside & Outside

Square Inside, Segmental Outside

Sections thro Pulley Stiles & Head, shewing Joints.

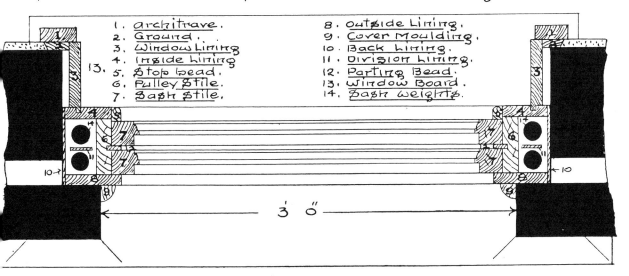

1. Architrave.
2. Ground.
3. Window Lining
4. Inside Lining
5. Stop bead.
6. Pulley Stile.
7. Sash Stile.
8. Outside Lining.
9. Cover Moulding.
10. Back Lining.
11. Division Lining.
12. Parting Bead.
13. Window Board.
14. Sash Weights.

3' 0"

—— Horizontal Section. ——

PLATE **111.**

Cased Frame & 2" Sashes, with 2" Fanlight over.

Outside Elevation.

Horizontal Section.

Inches

12. 9. 6. 3. 0   1   2   3   4   5   6   Feet.
                                                          7

188

PLATE 112.

Details of Cased Frame with Fanlight.

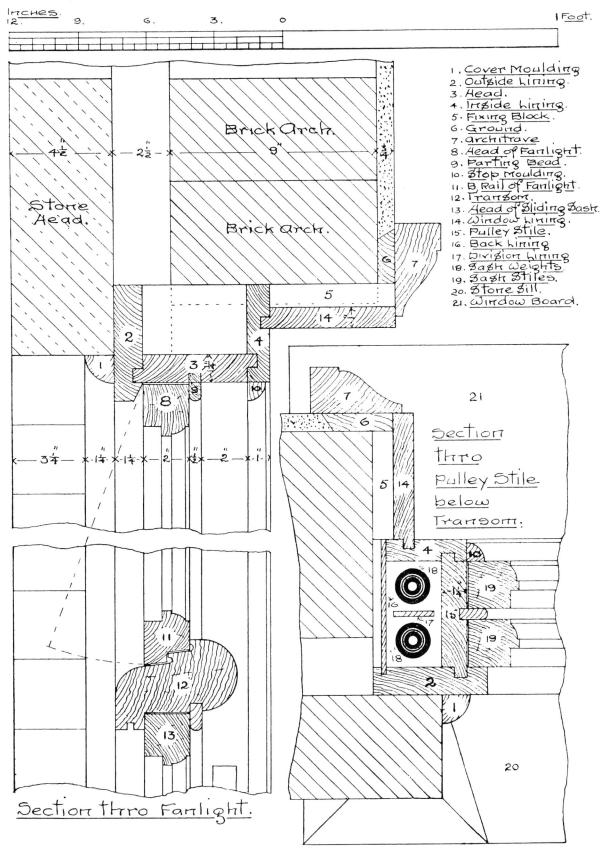

Inches.

12. 9. 6. 3. 0 1 Foot.

Brick Arch. 9"

4½" — 2½"

Stone Head.

Brick Arch.

1. Cover Moulding
2. Outside Lining.
3. Head.
4. Inside Lining.
5. Fixing Block.
6. Ground.
7. Architrave
8. Head of Fanlight.
9. Parting Bead.
10. Stop Moulding.
11. B. Rail of Fanlight.
12. Transom.
13. Head of Sliding Sash.
14. Window Lining.
15. Pulley Stile.
16. Back Lining
17. Division Lining
18. Sash Weights
19. Sash Stiles.
20. Stone Sill.
21. Window Board.

3¾" — 1¼" — 1½" — 2" — ½" — 2" — 1"

Section thro Pulley Stile below Transom.

Section thro Fanlight.

189

PLATE 113.

Details of Cased Frame with Fanlight.

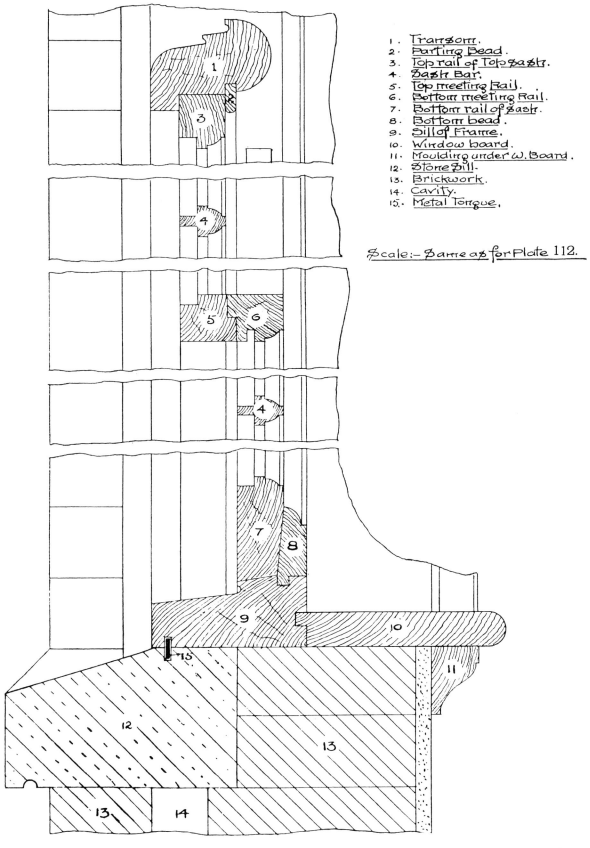

1. Transom.
2. Parting Bead.
3. Top rail of Top Sash.
4. Sash Bar.
5. Top meeting Rail.
6. Bottom meeting Rail.
7. Bottom rail of Sash.
8. Bottom bead.
9. Sill of Frame.
10. Window board.
11. Moulding under W. Board.
12. Stone Sill.
13. Brickwork.
14. Cavity.
15. Metal Tongue.

Scale:— Same as for Plate 112.

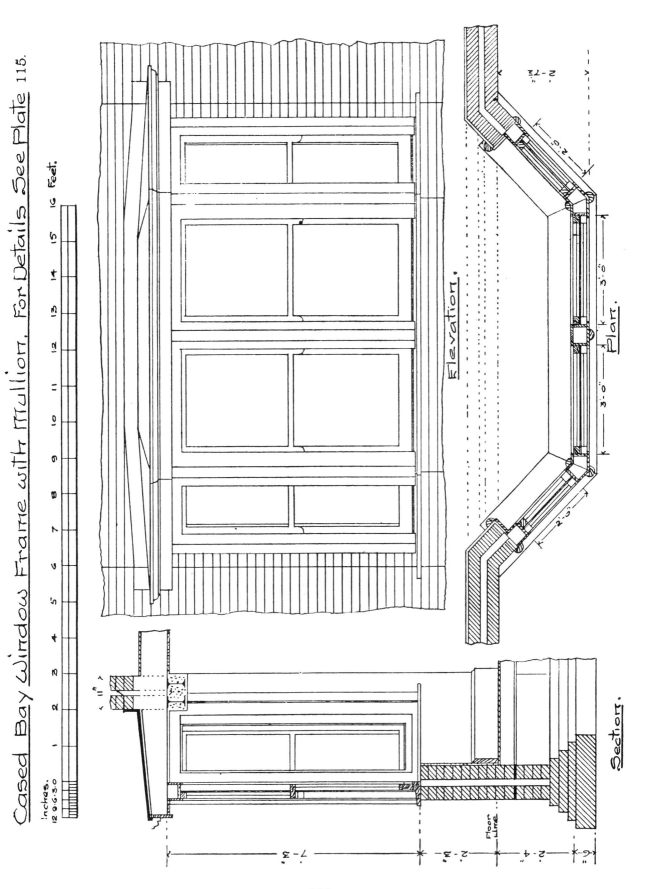

Cased Bay Window Frame with Mullion. For Details See Plate 115.

Inches.
12 9 6 3 0   1   2   3   4   5   6   7   8   9   10   11   12   13   14   15   16 Feet.

Elevation.

Plan.

Section.

Floor Line.

191

PLATE 115.

Details of Bay Window with Mullion.

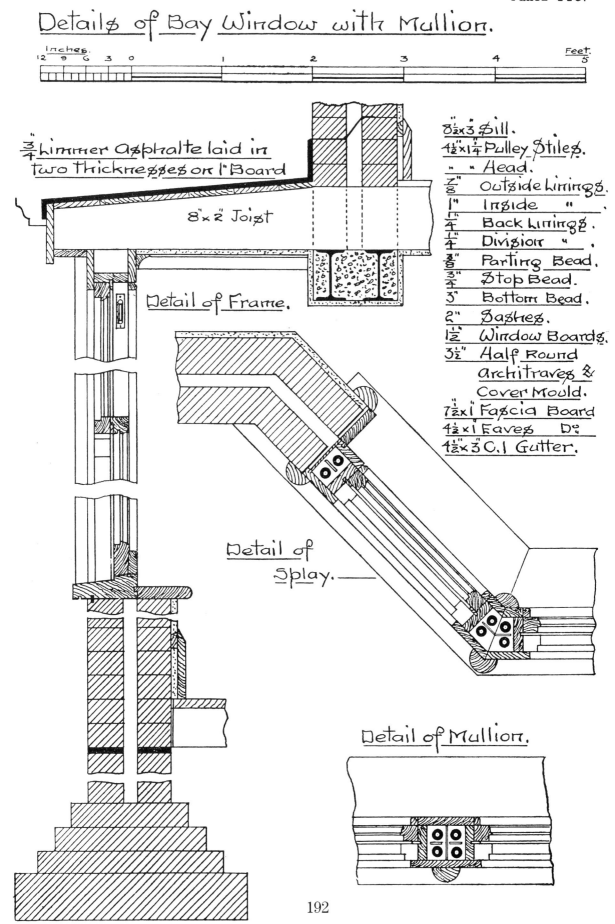

Inches.
12 9 6 3 0   1   2   3   4   Feet. 5

$\frac{3}{4}$" Limmer Asphalte laid in two Thicknesses on 1" Board

8"× 2" Joist

Detail of Frame.

Detail of Splay. —

Detail of Mullion.

8½"× 3" Sill.
4½"× 1¼" Pulley Stiles.
  "   " Head.
$\frac{7}{8}$" Outside Linings.
1" Inside   ".
$\frac{1}{4}$" Back Linings.
$\frac{1}{4}$" Division   ".
$\frac{3}{8}$" Parting Bead.
$\frac{3}{4}$" Stop Bead.
3" Bottom Bead.
2" Sashes.
1½" Window Boards.
3½" Half Round Architraves & Cover Mould.
7½"× 1" Fascia Board
4½"× 1" Eaves D°.
4½"× 3" C.I Gutter.

192

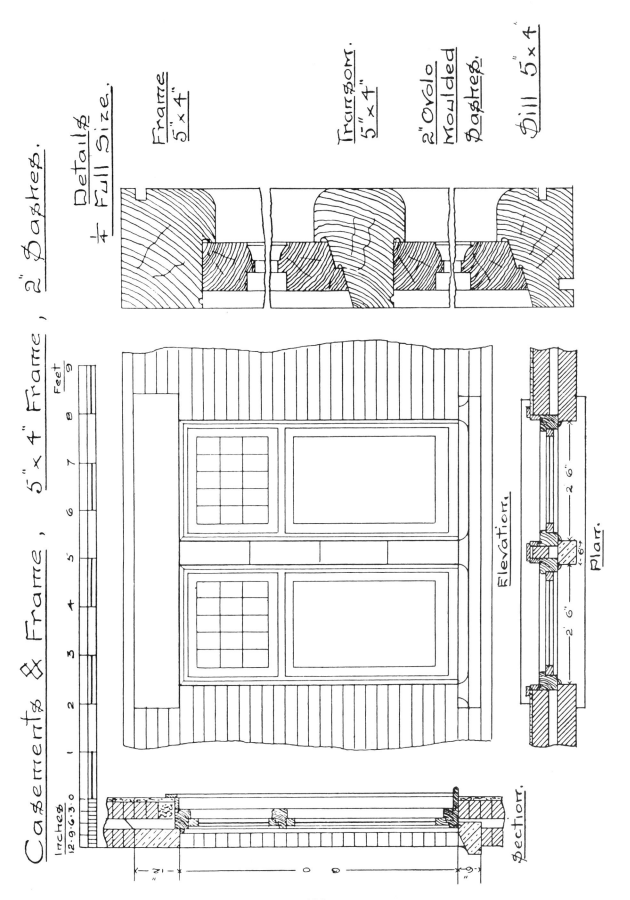

PLATE 116.

Casements & Frame, 5" × 4" Frame, 2" Sashes.

Details ¼ Full Size.

Frame 5" × 4"

Transom 5" × 4"

2" Ovolo Moulded Sashes.

Sill 5" × 4"

Inches
12·9·6·3·0

Feet
9 8 7 6 5 4 3 2 1

Elevation.

Plan.

2' 6"

1' 6"

2' 6"

Section.

193

PLATE 117.

Angle Casement Window.

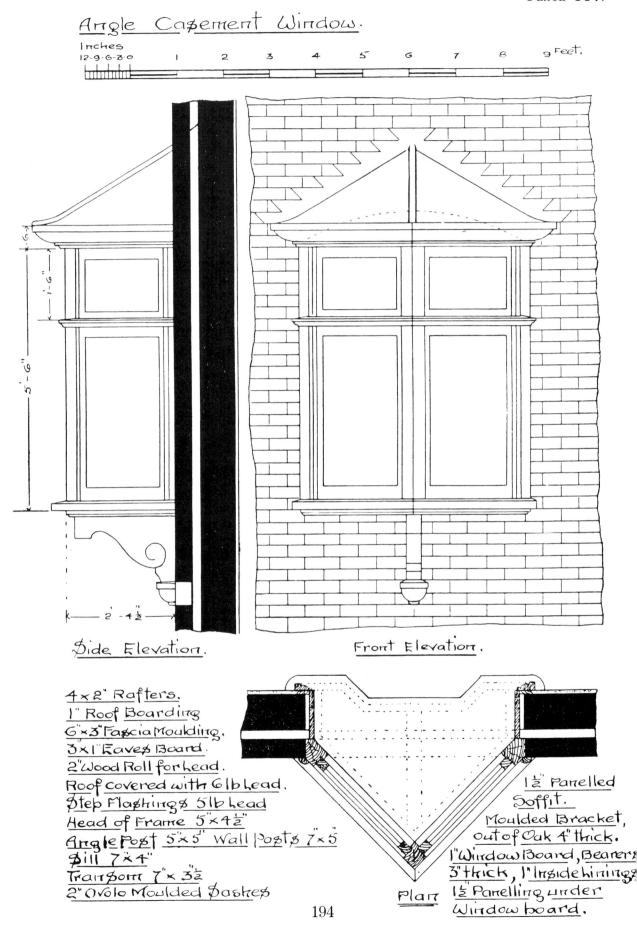

Inches
12·9·6·3·0   1   2   3   4   5   6   7   8   9 Feet.

6"
1'·6"
5'·6"

2'·4½"

Side Elevation.

Front Elevation.

4 × 2" Rafters.
1" Roof Boarding
6" × 3" Fascia Moulding.
3 × 1" Eaves Board.
2" Wood Roll for head.
Roof Covered with 6 lb Lead.
Step Flashings 5 lb Lead
Head of Frame 5" × 4½"
Angle Post 5" × 5" Wall Posts 7" × 5
Sill 7" × 4"
Transom 7" × 3½"
2" Ovolo Moulded Sashes

Plan

1½" Panelled
Soffit.
Moulded Bracket,
out of Oak 4" thick.
1" Window Board, Bearers
3" thick, 1" Inside lining
1½ Panelling under
Window board.

194

Plate 118.

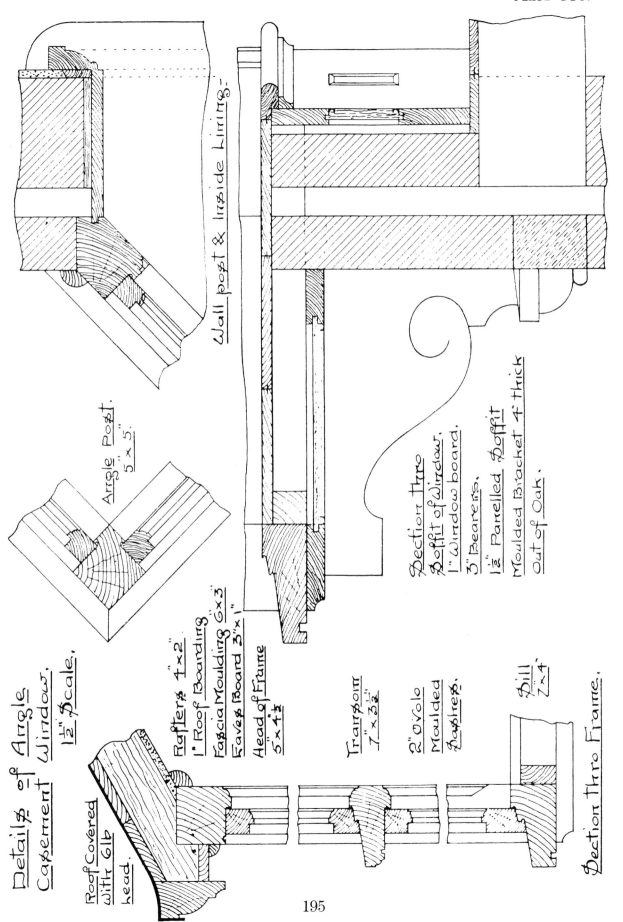

Wall post & Inside lining.

Angle Post.
5" × 5"

Details of Angle
Casement Window.
1½" Scale.

Roof Covered
with 6lb.
lead.

Rafters 4"×2"
1" Roof Boarding
Fascia Moulding 6×3
Eaves Board 3"×1"
Head of Frame
5"×4½

Transom
7"×3½

2" Ovolo
Moulded
Rafters.

Section thro
Soffit of Window.
1" Window board.
3" Bearers.
1½" Panelled Soffit
Moulded Bracket 4" thick
out of Oak.

Sill
7×4

Section thro Frame.

PLATE 119.

Bay Window. ——

Inches
12. 9. 6. 3. 0.   1   2   3   4   5   6   7   8   9   10 Feet.

Elevation

7'. 0"

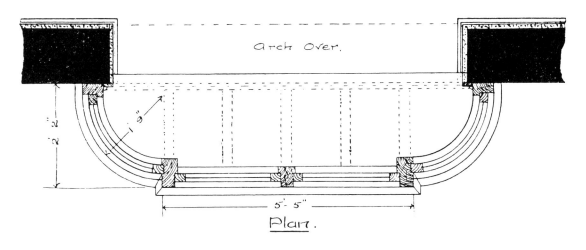

Arch over.

2'. 2"

1'. 9"

5'. 5"

Plan.

PLATE 120.

Details of Bay Window.

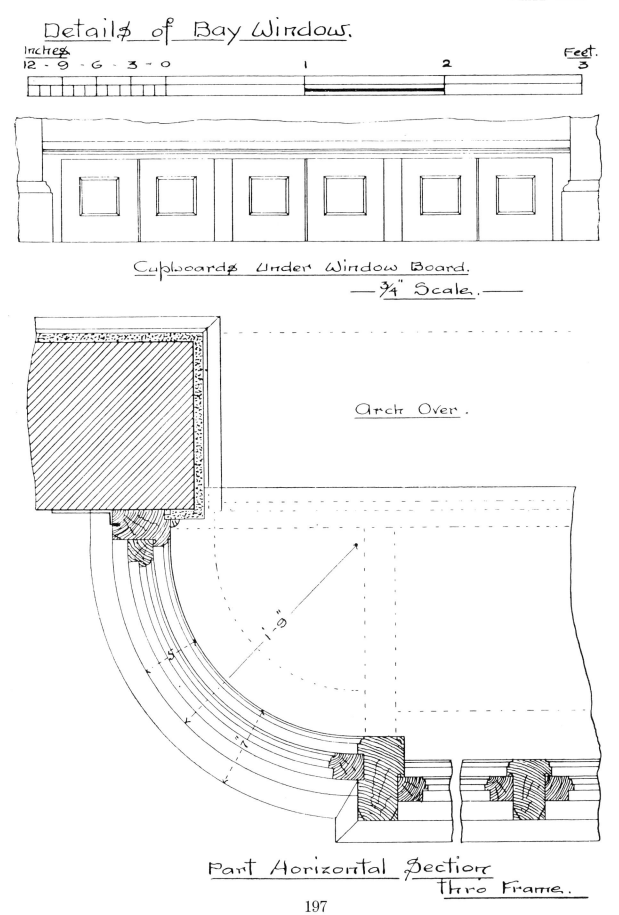

Cupboards Under Window Board.
—¾" Scale.—

Arch Over.

1'-9"

5

7

Part Horizontal Section
Thro' Frame.

PLATE 121.

Details of Bay Window.—

Inches
12 · 9 · 6 · 3 · 0   1 Foot

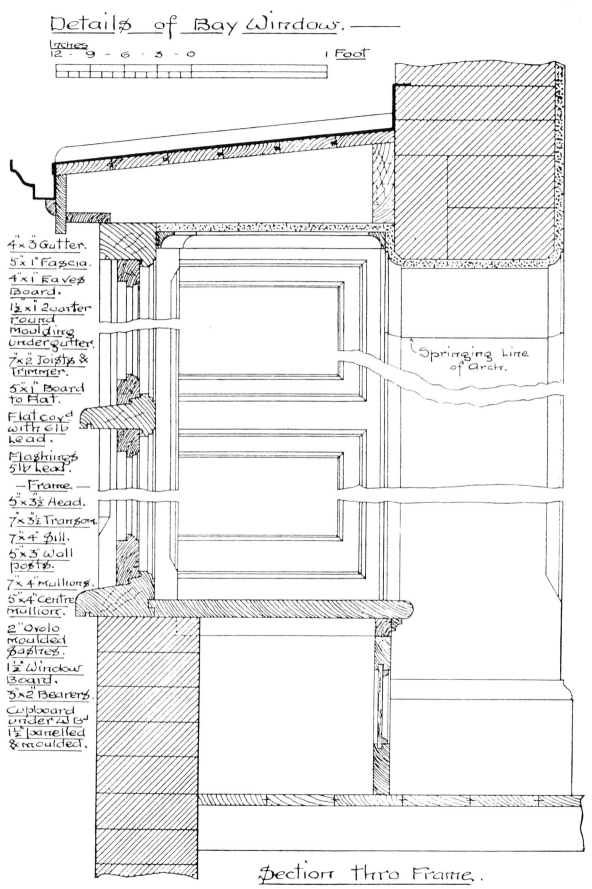

4" x 3" Gutter.

5" x 1" Fascia.

4" x 1" Eaves Board.

1½" x 1" Quarter round moulding under gutter.

7" x 2" Joists & Trimmer.

5" x 1" Board to Flat.

Flat cov'd with 6lb Lead.

Flashings 5lb Lead.

— Frame. —

5" x 3½" Head.

7" x 3½" Transom.

7" x 4" Sill.

5" x 3" Wall posts.

7" x 4" Mullions.

5" x 4" Centre mullion.

2" Ovolo moulded gashes.

1½" Window Board.

3" x 2" Bearers.

Cupboard under W. B. 1½" panelled & moulded.

Springing Line of Arch.

Section thro Frame.

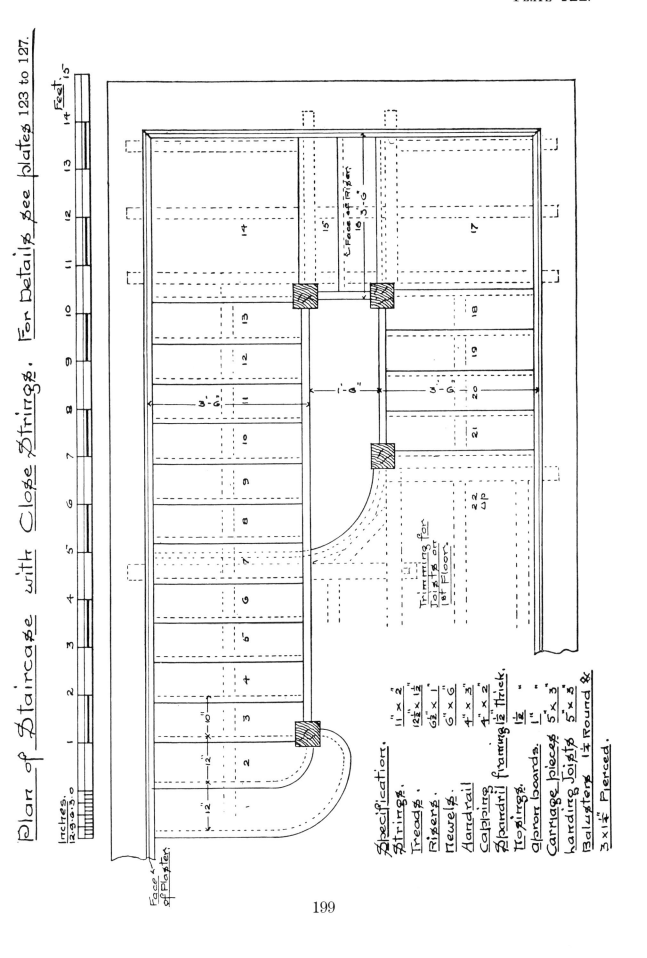

Plan of Staircase with Close Strings. For Details see plates 123 to 127.

PLATE 122.

Specification.

Strings.	$11'' \times 2''$
Treads.	$12\frac{1}{2}'' \times 1\frac{1}{2}''$
Risers.	$6\frac{1}{2}'' \times 1''$
Newels.	$6'' \times 6''$
Handrail	$4'' \times 3''$
Capping	$4'' \times 2''$
Spandril framing	$1\frac{1}{2}''$ thick.
Trostings.	$1\frac{1}{2}''$ "
apron boards.	$1''$ "
Carriage pieces	$5'' \times 3''$
Landing Joists	$5'' \times 3''$
Balusters	$1\frac{1}{4}''$ Round &
$3 \times 1\frac{1}{4}''$ Pierced.

Face of Plaster.

Trimming for Joists on 1st Floor.

Face of Riser 3'- 6"

199

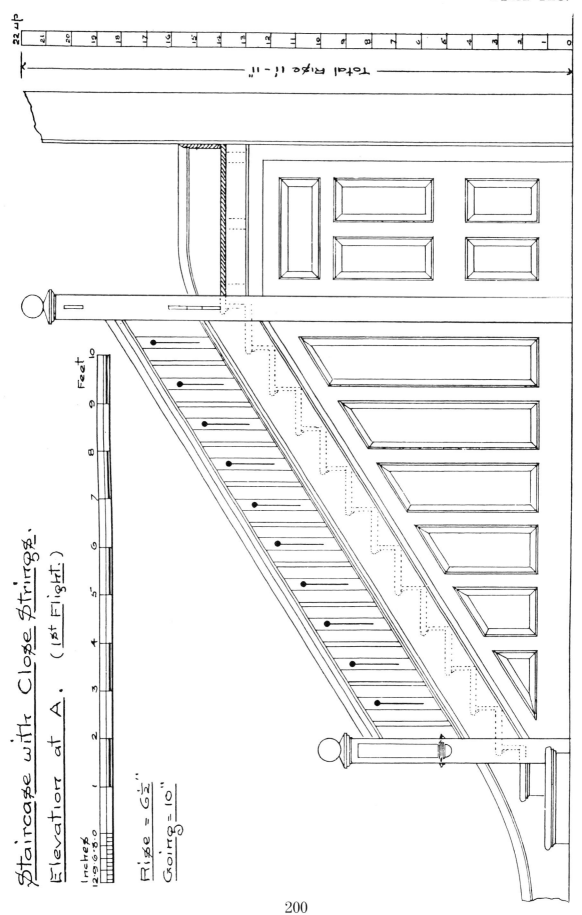

Staircase with Close Strings.

Elevation at A. (1st Flight.)

Rise = 6½"
Going = 10"

Total Rise 11'-11"

Feet

Inches

PLATE 123.

200

PLATE **124.**

Staircase with Close Strings.

Elevation at B. (2ⁿᵈ Flight.)

Inches.   Feet.

12·9·6·3 0   1   2   3   4   5   6   7   8   9   10

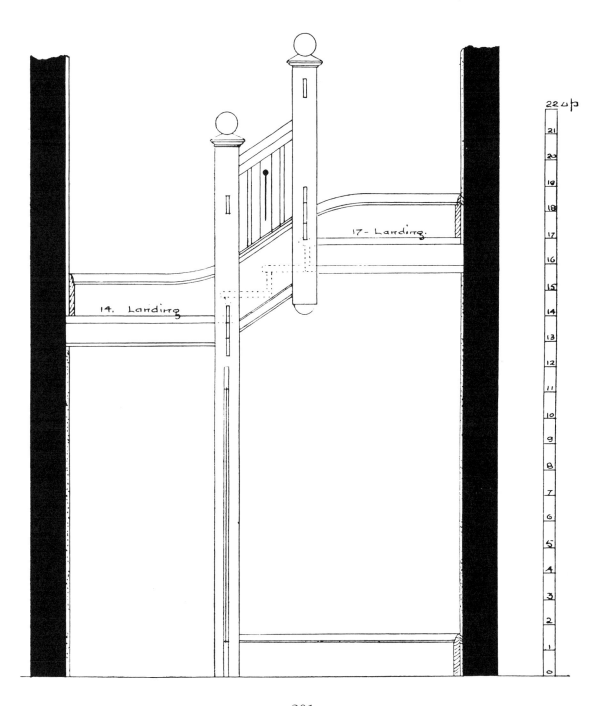

17 - Landing.

14. Landing

22 up
21
20
19
18
17
16
15
14
13
12
11
10
9
8
7
6
5
4
3
2
1
0

PLATE 125.

Staircase with Close Strings.
Elevation at C   3rd Flight.

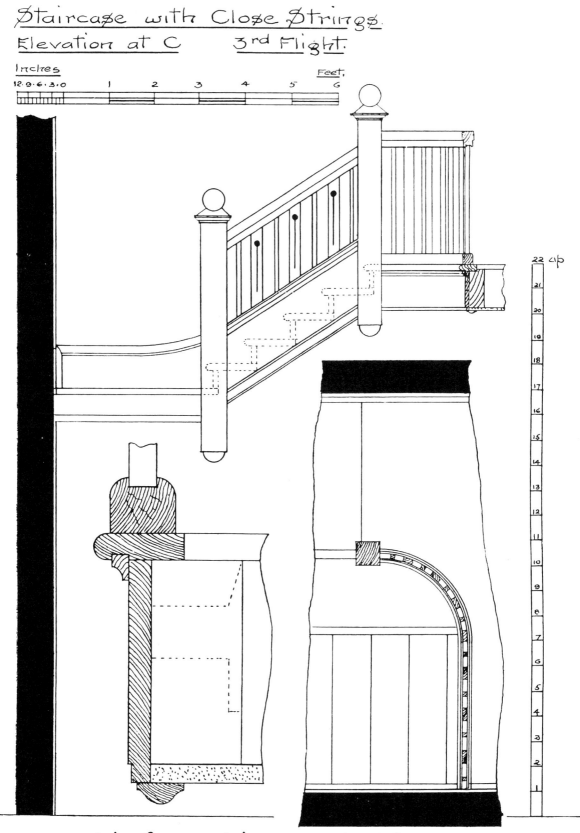

Detail of Apron Lining   Detail at Landing
Scale - ¼ Full Size.

PLATE 126.

Details of Staircase with Close Strings.

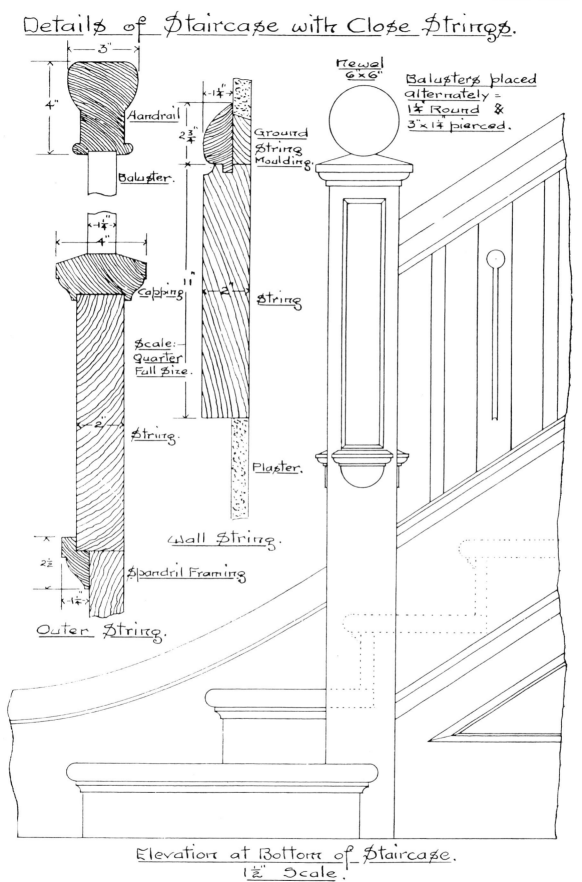

3"

4"

Handrail

Baluster.

1¼"

4"

Capping

11"

2"

String.

Scale:
Quarter
Full Size.

String.

Wall String.

Spandril Framing

2½

1¼"

Outer String.

1¼"

2¾"

Ground
String
Moulding.

2"

String

Plaster.

Newel
6"×6"

Balusters placed
alternately =
1¼ Round &
3"×1¼ pierced.

Elevation at Bottom of Staircase.
1½" Scale.

PLATE 127.

Details of Staircase with Close Strings.
1" Scale & ¼ Full Size.

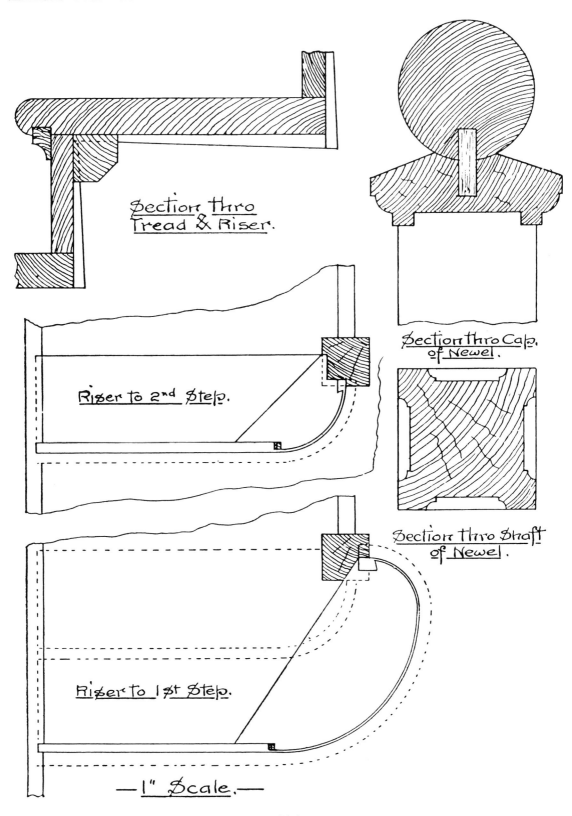

Section Thro
Tread & Riser.

Riser to 2nd Step.

Section Thro Cap.
of Newel.

Section Thro Shaft
of Newel.

Riser to 1st Step.

—1" Scale.—

SPECIFICATION FOR CASED FRAMES AND SASHES. (Plates 102, 103, 104, 105.)

THE windows to have $6\frac{1}{2}'' \times 3''$ sunk, weathered and throated sills, grooved for water bar, bottom bead, and window board, $1\frac{1}{4}''$ pulley stiles and heads grooved for parting bead and tongued for linings, $3\frac{3}{4}'' \times \frac{7}{8}''$ inside linings grooved for pulley stiles and window linings, $4\frac{1}{2}'' \times \frac{7}{8}''$ outside linings grooved for pulley stiles, $3'' \times 1''$ moulded and hollow grooved bottom bead, tongued for sill, $\frac{7}{8}'' \times \frac{7}{8}''$ quarter-round stop moulding, $\frac{3}{8}''$ parting beads, $6\frac{1}{2}'' \times \frac{1}{4}''$ back linings, $2'' \times \frac{1}{4}''$ division linings between weights, let through end of head of frame, with pin top above the head. The axle pulleys to be $1\frac{3}{4}''$ brass faced.

The sashes to be $2''$, ovolo-moulded and rebated, with $2\frac{1}{4}''$ stiles and top rails, $2''$ meeting rails with rebated joints, and $4\frac{1}{2}''$ bottom rails. The stiles of top sash to have moulded horns. All to be double hung with best flax lines and weights complete. Put No. 1 pair brass sash lifts to bottom sash, and No. 1 flush sash eye to top sash. Put approved patent sash fasteners.

Put $1\frac{1}{2}'' \times \frac{3}{4}''$ moulding around outside of frame to cover joint of frame with brickwork.

MATERIALS REQUIRED FOR CASED FRAMES AND SASHES. (Plates 102, 103, 104, 105.)

	Length.	Total Length.		Description.
	′ ″	3′ 9″		
1		3 9	run	$6\frac{1}{2}'' \times 3''$ sill, double sunk, weathered and throated, grooved for window board, water bar, and bottom bead.
2	5 6	11 0		Pulley stiles.
1		3 9		Head.
		14 9	run	$5\frac{1}{4}'' \times 1\frac{1}{4}''$ pulley stiles and head, grooved for parting bead, and tongued to linings.

MATERIALS REQUIRED FOR CASED FRAMES AND SASHES (PLATES 102, 103, 104, 105)—*Continued.*

	Length.		Total Length.			Description.
	′	″	′	″		
2	5	10	11	8		
1			3	1		
			14	9	run	$4\frac{1}{2}'' \times \frac{7}{8}''$ outside linings, grooved for pulley stiles and head.
2	5	10	11	8		
1			3	1		
			14	9	run	$3\frac{3}{4}'' \times \frac{7}{8}''$ inside linings, grooved for pulley stiles and head and inside linings.
2	5	9	11	6	,,	$6\frac{1}{2}'' \times \frac{1}{4}''$ back linings.
2	5	2	10	4	,,	$2'' \times \frac{1}{4}''$ division linings.
2	5	4	10	8		
1			3	1		
			13	9	run	$1\frac{1}{4}'' \times \frac{3}{8}''$ parting bead.
2	5	2	10	4		
1			3	1		
			13	5	run	$\frac{7}{8}'' \times \frac{7}{8}''$ quarter-round stop bead.
1			3	1		$3'' \times 1''$ moulded, hollow grooved and tongued bottom bead.
4						$1\frac{3}{4}''$ brass-faced axle pulleys.
4						Cast-iron sash weights.
6					yds.	Best flax sash line.
3						Fir blocks $4\frac{1}{2}'' \times 3'' \times 3''$.
4	3	0	12	0		
1			3	1		
			15	1	run	$2\frac{1}{4}'' \times 2''$ rebated and moulded sash stiles and head.
2	3	1	6	2	,,	$2\frac{1}{2}'' \times 2''$ rebated, moulded and grooved meeting rails.
1			3	1	,,	$4\frac{1}{2}'' \times 2''$ rebated and moulded bottom rail.

MATERIALS REQUIRED FOR CASED FRAMES AND SASHES (PLATES 102, 103, 104, 105)—*Continued.*

	Length.		Total Length.			Description.
	′	″	′	″		
2	3	1	6	2		
4	2	8	10	8		
			16	10	run	2″ × 1¼″ rebated and moulded sash bars.
1						Strong brass sash fastener.
1						Pair brass sash lifts.
1						Brass flush sash eye for top sash.
2	5	9	11	6		
1			3	4	run	1½″ × ¾″ moulding around outside of frame
			14	10		to cover joint with brickwork.

SPECIFICATION FOR CASED FRAMES AND SASHES WITH CIRCULAR AND SEGMENTAL HEADS.
(PLATES 106, 107, 108, 109, 110.)

THE windows to have $6\frac{1}{2}$″ × 3″ sunk, weathered and throated sills, grooved for water bar, bottom bead, and window board, $1\frac{1}{4}$″ pulley stiles grooved for parting bead, 4″ × $\frac{7}{8}$″ inside linings grooved for window linings, $4\frac{3}{4}$″ × 1″ outside linings, 3″ × 1″ bottom bead tongued to sill, 1″ × $\frac{3}{4}$″ stop beads, $\frac{3}{8}$″ parting beads, $6\frac{1}{2}$″ × $\frac{1}{4}$″ back linings, 2″ × $\frac{1}{4}$″ division linings between weights let through portion of head and pinned. The axle pulleys to be $1\frac{3}{4}$″ brass faced.

The sashes to be 2″, ovolo-moulded and rebated, with $2\frac{1}{4}$″ stiles and top rails, 2″ meeting rails with rebated joints, $4\frac{1}{2}$″ bottom rails. Top sashes to have moulded horns. Put No. 1 pair brass sash lifts to bottom sash, and No. 1 brass flush sash eye to top sash. Put approved patent brass sash fasteners. The sashes to be hung with best flax lines and cast-iron weights complete.

Put around outside of frames to cover joint of frame with brickwork $1\frac{1}{4}''$ quarter-round moulding.

CIRCULAR HEAD.

The head to be circular inside and out, and to be framed as detail out of solid, joints to be dowelled and fastened with hand-rail screws, one to each joint. The inside and outside linings to be cut circular and jointed as shown. The stop bead and parting bead to be worked circular out of solid. The head of sash to be worked circular out of solid in two segments and jointed as shown.

SEGMENTAL HEAD.

The head of frame to be segmental inside and out, and to be worked out of solid, and jointed to frame as shown on detail. The head of sash to be worked segmental as shown, also inside and outside linings and stop bead.

MATERIALS REQUIRED FOR CASED FRAME AND SASHES WITH CIRCULAR HEAD. (Plates 106, 107, 108, 109, 110.)

	Length.		Total Length.			Description.
	′	″	′	″		
1			3	6		$6\frac{1}{2}'' \times 3''$ sill, double sunk, weathered and throated, grooved for window board, water bar, and bottom bead.
2	5	6	11	0		$4\frac{3}{4}'' \times 1\frac{1}{4}''$ pulley stiles, grooved for parting bead.
2	1	7	3	2		
2	1	4	2	8		
			5	10		Head worked circular out of $4\frac{3}{4}'' \times 3''$.
2	5	7	11	2		$4'' \times \frac{7}{8}''$ inside linings, grooved for linings.
2	2	0	4	0		
1			1	10		
			5	10		Inside head linings worked circular out of $7'' \times \frac{7}{8}''$, and grooved for linings.

MATERIALS REQUIRED FOR CASED FRAME AND SASHES WITH CIRCULAR HEAD (PLATES 106, 107, 108, 109, 110)—*Continued.*

	Length.		Total Length.			Description.
	′	″	′	″		
2	5	6	11	0		$4\frac{3}{4}'' \times 1''$ outside linings.
2	2	0	4	0		
1			1	10		
			5	10		Outside head linings worked circular out of $8'' \times 1''$.
2	5	4	10	8		$6\frac{1}{2}'' \times \frac{1}{4}''$ back linings.
2	5	4	10	8		$2\frac{1}{2}'' \times \frac{1}{4}''$ division linings.
2	5	4	10	8		$1\frac{1}{4}'' \times \frac{3}{8}''$ parting bead.
2	2	2	4	4		Parting bead worked circular out of $6'' \times \frac{3}{8}''$.
2	5	2	10	4		$1'' \times \frac{3}{4}''$ stop bead.
2	2	2	4	4		Stop bead worked circular out of $6'' \times 1''$.
1			2	11		$3'' \times 1''$ bottom bead tongued to sill.
4						$1\frac{3}{4}''$ brass-faced axle pulleys.
7					yds.	Best flax sash line.
2	3	7	7	2		$2\frac{1}{4}'' \times 2''$ rebated and moulded sash stiles.
2	3	1	6	2		$2\frac{1}{4}'' \times 2''$ rebated and moulded sash stiles.
2	2	2	4	4		$2\frac{1}{4}'' \times 2''$ head worked circular out of $7'' \times 2''$ (as above described).
1						$5'' \times 2'' \times 1''$ oak dove-tail for joint of head.
2	2	11	5	10		$2\frac{1}{2}'' \times 2''$ rebated, moulded and grooved meeting rails.
1			2	11		$4\frac{1}{2}'' \times 2''$ bottom rail, rebated and moulded.
1						Strong brass sash fastener.
1					pair	Brass sash lifts.
1						Brass flush eye for top sash.

MATERIALS REQUIRED FOR CASED FRAME AND SASHES WITH SEGMENTAL HEAD. (PLATES 106, 107, 108, 109, 110.)

	Length.		Total Length.			Description.
	′	″	′	″		
1			3	6		$6\frac{1}{2}'' \times 3''$ sill, double sunk, weathered and throated, grooved for window board, water bar, and bottom bead.
2	5	6	11	0		$4\frac{3}{4}'' \times 1\frac{1}{4}''$ pulley stiles, grooved for parting bead.
1			3	6		Head worked circular out of $4\frac{3}{4}'' \times 4''$ and grooved for parting bead.
2	5	9	11	6		$4'' \times \frac{7}{8}''$ inside linings, grooved for parting bead.
1			2	11		Head lining worked circular out of $8'' \times \frac{7}{8}''$ and grooved for lining.
2	5	9	11	6		$4\frac{3}{4}'' \times 1''$ outside linings.
1			2	11		Head lining worked circular out of $8'' \times 1''$.
2	5	6	11	0		$6\frac{1}{2}'' \times \frac{1}{4}''$ back linings.
2	5	6	11	0		$2\frac{1}{2}'' \times \frac{1}{4}''$ division linings.
2	5	6	11	0		$1\frac{1}{4}'' \times \frac{3}{8}''$ parting bead.
1			2	11		Parting bead worked circular out of $4'' \times \frac{3}{8}''$.
2	5	3	10	6		$1'' \times \frac{3}{4}''$ stop bead.
1			2	11		Stop bead worked circular out of $4'' \times 1''$.
1			2	11		$3'' \times 1''$ bottom bead tongued to sill.
4						$1\frac{3}{4}''$ brass-faced axle pulleys.
6					yds.	Best flax sash line.
4	3	2	12	8		$2\frac{1}{4}'' \times 2''$ rebated and moulded sash stiles.
			2	11		Head worked circular out of $5'' \times 2''$ (as above described).
2	2	11	5	10		$2\frac{1}{2}'' \times 2''$ rebated, moulded and grooved meeting rails.
1			2	11		$4\frac{1}{2}'' \times 2''$ bottom rail, rebated and moulded.
1						Strong brass sash fastener.
1					pair	Brass sash lifts.
1						Brass flush eye for top sash.

SPECIFICATION OF CASED FRAME AND SASHES WITH FANLIGHT OVER. (PLATES 111, 112, 113.)

THE window to have $6\frac{1}{2}'' \times 3''$ sunk, weathered and throated sill, grooved for water bar, bottom bead, and window board, $1\frac{1}{4}''$ pulley stiles and head tongued for linings, $3\frac{3}{4}'' \times 1''$ inside linings grooved for pulley stiles and window linings, $5'' \times 1\frac{1}{4}''$ outside linings grooved for pulley stiles and back linings, $3\frac{1}{2}'' \times 1\frac{3}{8}''$ moulded bottom bead tongued for sill, $\frac{7}{8}'' \times \frac{7}{8}''$ quarter-round stop moulding, $\frac{3}{8}''$ parting beads.

The transom to be $5\frac{1}{2}'' \times 4''$ sunk, weathered, throated and moulded, and tenoned to pulley stiles.

Put $1\frac{1}{4}''$ quarter-round moulding fixed to outside of frame to cover joint of frame with brickwork.

The sashes to be $2''$, ovolo-moulded and rebated, with $2\frac{1}{4}''$ stiles, $2''$ rebated meeting rails, $2\frac{1}{4}''$ top rails and $4\frac{1}{2}''$ bottom rails, $1\frac{1}{4}''$ bars. The sliding sashes to be double hung on $2\frac{1}{4}''$ patent ball-bearing, brass-faced axle pulleys, with strong woven copper cords and weights complete. Provide strong brass sash fasteners, and fix with brass screws. Put to bottom sash 1 pair brass sash lifts, and to top sash No. 1 flush sash eye.

The fanlight to be $2''$, ovolo-moulded and rebated similar to sliding sashes, to be hung at top (opening outwards) with 1 pair $3\frac{1}{2}''$ strong brass butts and screws. Put Leggot's patent fanlight opener with cords complete.

The window board to be $9'' \times 1\frac{1}{2}''$ tongued to sill, and with rounded nosing with returned and mitred ends. Put $3'' \times 2''$ moulding under window board with returned and mitred ends.

Put around window $6'' \times \frac{7}{8}''$ linings tongued to frames, all to be tongued and grooved together.

The architraves to be $4'' \times 2''$, moulded and securely fixed to grounds.

The sashes to be glazed with best selected 21 oz. British sheet glass, properly bedded, sprigged, and front puttied.

MATERIALS REQUIRED FOR CASED FRAME AND SASHES WITH FANLIGHT OVER. (PLATES 111, 112, 113.)

	Length.		Total Length.			Description.
	′	″	′	″		
1			4	0	run	$6\frac{1}{2}$″ × 3″ sill, sunk, weathered and throated, grooved for window board, water bar, and bottom bead.
2	7	6	15	0		Pulley stiles.
1			4	0		Head.
			19	0	run	$5\frac{1}{2}$″ × $1\frac{1}{4}$″ pulley stiles, and head grooved for parting bead and tongued to linings.
1			3	6	,,	$5\frac{1}{2}$ × 4″ transom, rebated, weathered, throated, grooved and rounded.
2	7	10	15	8		
1			3	4		
			19	0	run	5″ × $1\frac{1}{4}$″ outside linings, grooved for pulley stiles, head, and back linings.
2	7	10	15	8		
1			3	4		
			19	0	run	$3\frac{3}{4}$″ × 1″ inside linings, grooved for pulley stiles, head, and window linings.
2	7	9	15	6	,,	6″ × $\frac{1}{4}$″ back linings.
2	5	3	10	6	,,	2″ × $\frac{1}{4}$″ division linings.
2	5	6	11	0		
2	1	6	3	0		
2	3	4	6	8		
			20	8	run	$1\frac{1}{4}$″ × $\frac{3}{8}$″ parting bead.
2	7	0	14	0		
1			3	4		
			17	4	run	$\frac{7}{8}$″ quarter-round stop moulding.
1			3	4	,,	$3\frac{1}{2}$″ × $1\frac{3}{8}$″ bottom bead, bevelled, tongued and moulded.

MATERIALS REQUIRED FOR CASED FRAME AND SASHES WITH FANLIGHT OVER (PLATES 111, 112, 113)—*Continued.*

	Length		Total Length.			Description.
	′	″	′	″		
2	7	8	15	4		
1			3	7		
			18	11		1¼″ quarter-round moulding fixed to outside of frame to cover joint of frame with brickwork.
4						2¼″ patent ball-bearing axle pulleys.
6					yds.	Woven copper sash cord.
4						Cast-iron sash weights.
4	3	0	12	0		
2	1	11	3	10		
2	3	4	6	8		
			22	6	run	2¼″ × 2″ rebated and moulded sash stiles and top rails.
1			3	4	,,	3″ × 2″ rebated and moulded bottom rail.
1			3	4	,,	4½″ × 2″ rebated and moulded bottom rail.
2	3	4	6	8	,,	2½″ × 2″ rebated, moulded and grooved meeting rails.
2	3	4	6	8		
4	2	8	10	8		
2	1	9	3	6		
			20	10	run	1¼″ × 2″ rebated and moulded sash bars.
1						Brass sash fastener.
1					pair	Brass sash lifts.
1						Brass flush sash eye.
1					pair	3½″ brass butts and screws.
1						Leggot's patent fanlight opener and cord complete.
1			4	9	run	9″ × 1½″ window board, tongued and nosed, and with mitred and returned ends.

MATERIALS REQUIRED FOR CASED FRAME AND SASHES WITH
FANLIGHT OVER (PLATES 111, 112, 113)—*Continued.*

	Length.		Total Length.			Description.
	′	″	′	″		
1			4	6	run	3″ × 2″ moulding under window board, with mitred and returned ends.
2	7	8	15	4		
			4	0		
			19	4	run	6½″ × 1″ linings tongued to frame.
2	8	0	16	0		
1			4	6		
			20	6	run	4″ × 2″ moulded architraves, with mitred angles.
12					13½″ × 11½″	panes 21 oz. best selected British sheet glass, bedded, sprigged, and front puttied.
3					15″ × 11½″	

SPECIFICATION OF BAY WINDOW.
(PLATES 114, 115.)

THE bay window to be constructed with $8\frac{1}{2}'' \times 3''$ sunk, weathered and throated sills, grooved for weather bar and window board. The sill to be halved and mitred at angles, and fastened together with stout screws. Pulley stiles and heads to be $1\frac{1}{4}''$ thick, grooved for parting bead, $\frac{7}{8}''$ outside linings, $1''$ inside linings, grooved where requisite for window linings, $\frac{1}{4}''$ back linings and $\frac{1}{4}''$ division linings between weights, $\frac{3}{4}''$ stop beads, $\frac{3}{8}''$ parting beads, $3'' \times 1\frac{1}{4}''$ bottom bead.

The linings at angles to have $3\frac{1}{2}''$ half-round moulding planted on to cover joint, inside and out. Put similar moulding at sides to cover joint, with brickwork outside and with plaster inside.

The sashes to be $2''$, ovolo-moulded and rebated for glass, with $2\frac{1}{4}''$ stiles and top rails, $4\frac{1}{2}''$ bottom rails and $2''$ meeting rails with rebated joints, to be hung on $2''$ brass-faced secret axle pullies, with strong woven flax cords and weights complete. Put approved brass sash fasteners. Put No. 2 sash lifts to each front bottom sash, and No. 1 each to bottom sashes of splays. The top sashes to be provided with brass flush eyes, No. 1, to each sash.

The window boards to be $1\frac{1}{2}''$ thick, tongued to frames, and with rounded nosing, with returned and mitred ends. The window linings to be $1''$ thick, tongued to frames, all to be tongued and grooved together, and securely fixed to grounds.

The sashes to be glazed with best selected 21 oz. British sheet glass, and to be properly bedded, sprigged, and front puttied.

MATERIALS REQUIRED FOR CASED BAY WINDOW FRAME WITH MULLION. (PLATES 114, 115.)

	Length.		Total Length.			Description.
	'	"	'	"		
2	4	2	8	4		
1			7	10		
			16	2	run	8½" × 3" sills, sunk, weathered, throated and grooved for water bar and window board.
2	3	0	6	0		
1	7	8	7	8		
8	7	0	56	0		
			69	8	run	4½" × 1¼" pulley, stiles and heads grooved for parting bead.
2	7	4	14	8		End linings.
2	2	1	4	2		Heads.
2	3	1	6	2		,,
			25	0	run	5½" × ⅞" outside linings.
4	7	4	29	4	,,	6" × ⅞" outside linings at angles.
1			7	4	,,	9¼" × ⅞" outside linings at mullion.
2	7	4	14	8		End linings.
2	2	1	4	2		Heads.
2	3	1	6	2		,,
			25	0	run	4" × 1" inside linings, grooved for window linings.
4	7	4	29	4	,,	3" × 1" inside linings at angles.
1			7	4	,,	7½" × 1" inside linings at mullion.
2	7	4	14	8	,,	6" × ¼" back linings.
1			6	10	,,	6" × ¼" division linings to mullion.
8	6	10	54	8	,,	2" × ¼" division linings between weights.
8	6	6	52	0		
2	2	1	4	2		
2	3	1	6	2		
			62	4	run	1" × ¾" stop bead.

CASED BAY WINDOW FRAME WITH MULLION

MATERIALS REQUIRED FOR CASED BAY WINDOW FRAME WITH MULLION (PLATES 114, 115)—*Continued.*

	Length.		Total Length.			Description.
	′	″	′	″		
2	2	1	4	2		
2	3	1	6	2		
			10	4	run	3″ × 1¼″ bevelled bottom bead.
8	6	10	54	8		
2	2	1	4	2		
2	3	1	6	2		
			65	0	run	1¼″ × ⅜″ parting bead.
9	7	2	64	6	,,	3½″ half-round moulding to cover joints with brickwork, plaster, and to angles of bay, inside and out.
16	3	9	96	0		Stiles.
2	2	1	4	2		Heads.
2	3	1	6	2		,,
			106	4	run	2¼″ × 2″ rebated and moulded sash stiles and heads.
4	2	1	8	4		
4	3	1	12	4		
			20	8	run	2½″ × 2″ rebated, moulded and grooved meeting rails.
2	2	1	4	2		
2	3	1	6	2		
			10	4	run	4½″ × 2″ rebated and moulded bottom rails.
16						Cast-iron sash weights.
23					yds.	Strong woven flax sash line.
16						2″ brass-faced secret axle pulleys.
4						Strong brass sash fasteners.
3					pairs	Brass sash lifts.
4						Brass sash eyes.
2	3	2	6	4		
1			7	4		
			13	8	run	9½″ × 1½″ window boards, tongued to sill, and with rounded nosing, with ends mitred and returned.

MATERIALS REQUIRED FOR CASED BAY WINDOW FRAME WITH
MULLION (PLATES 114, 115)—*Continued.*

	Length.	Total Length.		Description.
2	7′ 2″	14′ 4″	run	6″ × 1″ inside linings tongued to frame.
4	3′ 0″ × 2′ 8″	=	32′ 0″	
4	3′ 0″ × 1′ 8″	=	20′ 0″	
			52′ 0″	sup. 21 oz. best selected British sheet glass, properly bedded, sprigged, and front puttied.

SPECIFICATION FOR CASEMENTS AND FRAME.
(PLATE 116.)

THE frames to be 5″ × 4″, solid, rebated, rounded and grooved for linings. Sill 5″ × 4″, rebated, sunk, weathered, throated and rounded, grooved for water bar and window board. The transom to be 5″ × 4″, rebated, sunk, weathered, throated and rounded.

Sashes to be 2″, ovolo-moulded, with $2\frac{1}{4}$″ stiles and top rails, $4\frac{1}{2}$″ bottom rails, 3″ bottom rails to fanlight.

The bottom sashes to be side hung, fanlights to be hung at top, opening. outwards, all on $3\frac{1}{2}$″ strong brass butts and brass screws.

The bottom sashes to have strong approved brass casement fasteners, and 12″ strong brass stay-bars.

The fanlights to have strong approved brass fanlight openers and cords complete.

Put around outside of frames to cover joint $1\frac{1}{4}$″ quarter-round moulding.

Put around inside of frame 1″ linings tongued to frames, and $1\frac{1}{2}$″ window boards, with rounded nosing, with returned and mitred ends.

CASEMENTS AND FRAME

The architrave to be $2\frac{1}{2}'' \times 1''$ flat section, with edges slightly rounded.

The fanlights to have plain leaded lights glazed with 21 oz. best selected British sheet glass. The bottom sashes to be glazed with similar glass, all to be properly bedded, sprigged, and front puttied.

MATERIALS REQUIRED FOR CASEMENTS AND FRAME.
(PLATE 116.)

	Length.		Total Length.			Description.
	'	''	'	''		
4	6	2	24	8		
2	2	9	5	6		
			30	2	run	$5'' \times 4''$ rebated, rounded and grooved posts and heads.
2	2	9	5	6	,,	$5'' \times 4''$ double sunk, weathered and throated sills, grooved for water bar and window board, with rounded edge.
2	2	9	5	6	,,	$5'' \times 4''$ double sunk, rebated, rounded and throated transoms.
4	3	8	14	8		
4	2	1	8	4		
4	2	$2\frac{1}{2}$	8	10		
			31	10	run	$2\frac{1}{4}'' \times 2''$ ovolo-moulded and rebated sash stiles and top rails.
2	2	$2\frac{1}{2}$	4	5	,,	$3'' \times 2''$ ovolo-moulded and rebated bottom rails to fanlights.
2	2	$2\frac{1}{2}$	4	5	,,	$4\frac{1}{2}'' \times 2''$ ovolo-moulded and rebated bottom rails to sashes.
4					pairs	$3\frac{1}{2}''$ strong brass butts and screws.
2						Brass casement fasteners.
2						$12''$ brass stay-bars.
2						Brass fanlight openers and cords.
4	6	1	24	4		
2	2	10	5	8		
			30	0	run	$1\frac{1}{4}''$ quarter-round moulding.

MATERIALS REQUIRED FOR CASEMENTS AND FRAME
(PLATE 116)—*Continued.*

	Length.	Total Length.		Description.
4	6′ 1″	24′ 4″		
2	2 9	5 6		
		29 10	run	$2\frac{1}{2}″ \times 1″$ inside linings tongued to frames.
1		6 5	,,	$5\frac{1}{2}″ \times 1\frac{1}{2}″$ window board, tongued to frame, and with rounded nosing, with returned and mitred ends.
2	6 3	12 6		
1		6 1		
		18 7	run	$2\frac{1}{2}″ \times 1″$ flat architrave, with edges slightly rounded.
1		6 1	,,	$4\frac{1}{2}″ \times 1″$ flat architrave, with edges slightly rounded to mullion.
2	1′ 10″ × 1′ 7″		=	5′ 10″ sup. plain leaded lights glazed with best selected 21 oz. glass to fanlights.
2	3′ 1″ × 1′ 7″		=	9′ 10″ sup. best selected 21 oz. glass to sashes.

SPECIFICATION FOR ANGLE CASEMENT WINDOW. (PLATES 117, 118.)

THE frame to have $5″ \times 4\frac{1}{2}″$ rebated, throated and moulded head, $7″ \times 5″$ rebated, moulded, splayed and grooved wall-posts, $5″ \times 5″$ twice rebated and moulded angle-posts, $7″ \times 3\frac{1}{2}″$ rebated, sunk, weathered, throated and moulded transom, $7″ \times 4″$ rebated, sunk, weathered, throated and grooved sill.

The sashes to be $2″$, ovolo-moulded, $2\frac{1}{4}″$ stiles and top rails, $4″$ bottom rails, $3″$ bottom rails to fanlights. Bottom sashes to be side hung, fanlights hung at top, opening outwards, all on $3\frac{1}{2}″$ strong brass butts and screws. Bottom sashes to be provided with strong brass casement fasteners and 12″ strong brass casement stays. The sashes to be glazed with best selected 21 oz. British sheet glass, properly bedded, sprigged, and front puttied.

Put 4″ oak solid cut and moulded bracket, with end tailed and pinned into wall to form support for window, and resting on 9″ × 6″ × 7″ moulded York stone corbel.

The soffit of window to have 3″ × 2″ fir bearers nailed to sills, and with cross bearers framed into same, and ends resting on wall. The soffit framing to be 1½″ panelled, bead and flush.

Put to sides of frame 2¾″ part-round moulding, bedded in red-lead, and nailed to frame to cover joint with brickwork.

The roof to have 4″ × 2″ rafters, 5″ × 1½″ wall rafters and hip, 3″ × 1″ eaves board, 6″ × 3″ moulded fascia. Cover the roof with 1″ wrot, grooved and tongued boarding, and on this lay 6 lb. milled sheet lead turned up against wall and brought down over edge of fascia, and copper tacked 6″ apart to form drip, and properly dressed over roll. Put 1½″ wood roll to angle. The flashing to be of 5 lb. lead, stepped, lead wedged to joints, and pointed in cement mortar. Put 5 lb. lead tray over window 9″ wide and 12″ longer than opening width. Put 1¼″ quarter-round moulding nailed to frame under eaves board. Lath plaster float, and set to underside of rafters. Put 2¾″ part-round moulding, nailed to frame to cover joint of plaster with frame.

The window linings to be 1″, tongued to frame. Window board 1″ thick, with glued and cross-tongued joints, cut to shape, and properly fitted to frame, with 3″ × 1½″ rebated and rounded nosing fixed to front edge, with returned and mitred ends.

The panelling under window board to be 1½″, framed bead and flush. Put 1¼″ × ¾″ cove moulding under window board.

The architraves to be 4½″ × 2″, moulded and fixed to 3″ × ¾″ grounds. The head of architrave to be worked circular to follow line of segmental arch over opening.

MATERIALS FOR ANGLE CASEMENT WINDOW.
(Plates 117, 118.)

	Length.		Total Length.			Description.
	′	″	′	″		
2	3	8	7	4	run	$5'' \times 4\frac{1}{2}''$ rebated, moulded and throated head.
2	5	9	11	6	,,	$7'' \times 5''$ rebated, moulded, bevelled and grooved wall-posts.
1			5	9	,,	$5'' \times 5''$ twice rebated and moulded angle-post.
2	3	9	7	6	,,	$7'' \times 4''$ double sunk, weathered and throated sills.
2	3	9	7	6	,,	$7'' \times 3\frac{1}{2}''$ double sunk, rebated, moulded and throated transoms.
4	3	9	15	0		
4	1	7	6	4		
4	2	9	11	0		
			32	4	run	$2\frac{1}{4}'' \times 2''$ ovolo-moulded sash stiles and top rails.
2	2	9	5	6	,,	$3'' \times 2''$ ovolo-moulded sash stiles and bottom rails.
2	2	9	5	6	,,	$4\frac{1}{2}'' \times 2''$ ovolo-moulded sash stiles and bottom rails.
4					pairs	$3\frac{1}{2}''$ strong brass butts and screws.
2						Brass casement fasteners.
2						Brass casement stays.
2						Brass fanlight opener and cords.
2	$3' 2'' \times 2' 3''$				=	$14' 3''$.
2	$1' 2'' \times 2' 3''$				=	$5' 3''$.
						$19' 6''$ sup. 21 oz. best selected British sheet glass.
					No.1	Solid cut and moulded bracket out of oak, $2' 6''$ long, $1' 5''$ wide, $4''$ thick.
					,,	$9'' \times 6'' \times 7''$ moulded York stone corbel.

MATERIALS FOR ANGLE CASEMENT WINDOW (PLATES 117, 118)
—Continued.

	Length.		Total Length.			Description.
	'	"	'	"		
2	3	3	6	6		
2	1	3	2	6		
1			2	8		
			11	8	run	3″ × 2″ fir bearers under window board.
					No. 1	Piece 1½″ panelled bead and flush framing to soffit, triangular-shaped sides 4′ 9″ long nearest wall, and 3′ 4″ long on each side under sill = (11′ 0″ sup.).
2	5	6	11	0	run	2¾″ part-round moulding to sides of frame on outside.
3	3	2	9	6	,,	5″ × 1½″ wall rafters and hip.
4	1	9	7	0	,,	4″ × 2″ rafters.
2	3	10	7	8	.,	3′ × 1″ eaves board.
2	4	0	8	0	,,	1¼″ quarter-round moulding under eaves board.
2	4	6	9	0	,,	6″ × 3″ fascia moulding.
2/½	4′ × 2′ 6″				=	10′ sup. 1″ wrot, grooved and tongued-roof boarding.
			3	6	run	2″ wood roll for lead, end worked circular.
2/½	5′ 3″ × 3′				=	15′ 9″ sup. 6 lb. lead to roof.
			8	6	run	Copper nailing 6″ apart.
2	4′ 4″ × 6″				=	4′ 4″ sup. 5 lb. lead flashing.
						Lath plaster float and set under rafters.
2	3	4	6	8	run	2¾″ part-round cover moulding to joint of ceiling with frame.
2	5	3	10	6	,,	13″ × 1″ inside linings tongued to frame.
½	6′ 3″ × 3′ 3″				=	10′ 2″ sup. 1″ window board.
2	1	5	2	10		
2		10	1	8		
1			2	4		
			6	10	run	3″ × 1½″ nosing to front edge of window board, rebated and rounded, and with returned and mitred ends.

Materials for Angle Casement Window (Plates 117, 118)
—Continued.

	Length.	Total Length.		Description.
2	1′ 2″	2′ 4″		
2	8	1 4		
1		2 2		
		5 10	×	1′ 5″ = 8′ 4″ sup. 1½″ panelling framed bead and flush under window board.
		8 0	run	1¼″ × ¾″ cove moulding under edge of window board.
2	5 9	11 6	,,	4½″ × 2″ moulded architrave.
		5 2	,,	4½″ × 2″ moulded architrave worked circular to head.

SPECIFICATION FOR BAY WINDOW.
(Plates 119, 120, 121.)

The frame to have 5″ × 3″ wall-posts, 7″ × 4″ main mullions, 5″ × 4″ centre mullion, 5″ × 3½″ head. Sill to be 7″ × 4″, transom 7″ × 3½″, all to be rebated, moulded, throated and grooved as details. The sill to be 7″ × 4″, rebated, sunk, weathered, throated and grooved for window board and drip. Transom 7″ × 3½″, rebated, sunk, weathered, throated and moulded.

Sashes to be 2″, ovolo-moulded, with 2¼″ stiles and top rails, 4½″ bottom rails, 3″ bottom rails to fanlights. The two bottom sashes to front of bay to be side hung. The fanlights over to be hung at top, opening outwards, all on 3½″ strong brass butts and screws. Provide strong gun-metal casement fasteners, and 12″ gun-metal casement stays to bottom sashes. Fanlights to be fitted with gun-metal fanlight openers with cords complete.

The sashes to be glazed with ¼″ best selected polished British plate glass, bedded in wash-leather, sprigged, and front puttied.

BAY WINDOW

The flat over bay to have 7″ × 2″ joists tapered to fall to gutter, 7″ × 2″ trimmer spiked to wall, 4″ × 1″ eaves board, 5″ × 1″ fascia, 1½″ × 1″ rounded moulding under eaves gutter. Cover the flat with 5″ × 1″ grooved and tongued wrot boarding, and on this lay 6 lb. milled sheet lead turned up at wall, brought over into gutter, and properly dressed down. Provide 2″ wood rolls for lead. The flashings to be of 5 lb. lead, and stepped where shown on drawing.

Provide and fix to eaves 4″ × 3″ cast-iron moulded eaves gutter, with purpose-made returned and mitred angles over main mullions, and circular gutters, as details. The gutters to be fastened with galvanized bolts and screws.

The bearers for window board to be 3″ × 1¾″, resting on wall, and framed to top rail of cupboard. The window board to be 1½″ thick, tongued to sill, and with rounded nosing, with 1¼″ × ¾″ cove moulding under. The cupboards to be 1½″ framed and panelled. Frame to have 3″ stiles and muntins, 1¾″ top rail. Doors to be in three pairs, with 3″ stiles and top rails, 4½″ bottom rails. Shutting joints to be rebated and beaded. Put 1½″ × ½″ strip nailed to underside of bearers to form stop for doors. Doors to be hung with 3″ brass butts and screws, and fitted with oval pattern gun-metal turn buckles and 3″ brass bolts. Put ¾″ quarter-round moulding nailed to wall-posts on inside to cover joint of frame with plaster.

MATERIALS REQUIRED FOR BAY WINDOW.
(PLATES 119, 120, 121.)

	Length.	Total Length.		Description.
2	7′ 0″	14′ 0″	run	5″ × 3″ rebated, throated, moulded and grooved wall-posts.
2	7 0	14 0	,,	7″ × 4″ rebated, throated, moulded and grooved main mullions.

MATERIALS REQUIRED FOR BAY WINDOW (PLATES 119, 120, 121)
—*Continued.*

	Length.		Total Length.			Description.
	′	″	′	″		
1			7	0	run	5″ × 4″ twice rebated, throated and moulded centre mullion.
1			5	6	,,	5″ × 3½″ rebated, moulded and throated head.
2	2	9	5	6	,,	5″ × 3½″ rebated, moulded and throated head, worked circular, quadrant shaped, out of 11″ × 3½″.
1			6	0		7″ × 4″ double sunk, weathered, throated, moulded and grooved sill, with front edge rounded.
2	3	0	6	0	run	7″ × 4″ as above described, worked circular, quadrant shape, out of 13″ × 4″.
1			6	0	,,	7″ × 3½ double sunk, rebated, weathered, throated, grooved and moulded transom. .
2	3	0	6	0	,,	7″ × 3½″ as above described, worked circular, quadrant shape, out of 13″ × 3½″.
8	4	8	37	4		
8	1	11	15	4		
4	2	4	9	4		
			62	0	run	2¼″ × 2″ ovolo-moulded and rebated sash stiles and top rails.
4	2	5	9	8		2¼″ × 2″ as above described, worked circular, quadrant shape, out of 8″ × 2¼″.
2	2	4	4	8		3″ × 2″ ovolo-moulded and rebated bottom rails.
2	2	4	4	8		4½″ × 2″ ovolo-moulded and rebated bottom rails.
2	2	5	4	10		3″ × 2″ as above described, worked circular, quadrant shape, out of 8″ × 3″.
2	2	5	4	10		4½″ × 2″ as above described, worked circular, quadrant shape, out of 8″ × 4½″.

BAY WINDOW

	Length.	Total Length.		Description.
2	3' 11" × 1' 11"		=	15' 0"
2	1' 5" × 1' 11"		=	5' 6"
				20' 6" sup. best selected ¼" polished British plate glass, bedded in wash-leather, sprigged, and front puttied.
2	3' 11" × 2' 3"		=	17' 8"
2	1' 5" × 2' 3"		=	6' 5"
				24' 1" sup. as above described, only circular, measured on face 1' 9" radius.
4			pairs	3½" strong brass butts and screws.
2				Gun-metal casement stays.
2				,, ,, fasteners.
2				,, ,, openers.
1		9 0		
7	2 5	16 11		
		25 11	run	7" × 2" trimmer and joists to flat, joists tapered to fall.
1		6 2	,,	3" × 1" eaves board.
2	2 10	5 8	,,	3" × 1" eaves board, worked circular, quadrant shape, out of 11" × 1".
1		7 0	,,	5" × 1" fascia board.
2	3 0	6 0	,,	5" × 1" fascia board, worked circular, quadrant shape, out of 9" × 5".
1		7 0	,,	1½" × 1" rounded moulding under eaves gutter.
2	3 0			1½" × 1" rounded moulding, worked circular out of 9" × 1½".
	9' 6" × 2' 6"		=	23' 9" sup. 5" × 1" grooved and tongued boarding laid to flat.
3	2 6	7 6	run	2" × 1½" wood rolls for lead, with one end worked circular.

MATERIALS REQUIRED FOR BAY WINDOW (PLATES 119, 120, 121)
—Continued.

	Length.	Total Length.		Description.
	11′ 6″ × 2′ 10″	=		32′ 7″ sup. 6 lb. lead laid to flat.
	6′ 0″ × 6″	=		3′ 0″
2	3′ 0″ × 7″	=		3′ 6″
				6′ 6″ sup. 5 lb. lead flashing.
2	7′ 0″ × 7″	=		8′ 2″ sup. 5 lb. lead flashing stepped to sides of window.
	′ ″	6 9	run	4″ × 3″ cast-iron moulded eaves, gutter with returned and mitred ends cast on.
			No.2	Pieces cast-iron moulded eaves, circular, quadrant shape.
			No.2	Stopped ends to gutter.
			No.1	Outlet to gutter.
5	1 10	9 2	run	3″ × 2″ fir bearers under window board.
	8′ 2″ × 2′ 0″	=		16′ 4″ sup. 1½″ window board with rounded nosing.
		7 8	run	1¼″ × ¾″ cove moulding.
2	6 9	13 6	,,	¾″ quarter-round moulding to sides of wall-posts.
	7′ 4″ × 1′ 3½″	=		9′ 6″ sup. 1½″ framed and panelled cupboard under window board.
		8 0	run	1½″ × ½″ stop to cupboard.
6			pairs	3″ brass butts and screws.
3				3″ brass cupboard bolts.
3				Oval pattern gun-metal turn buckles.

SPECIFICATION FOR STAIRCASE WITH CLOSE STRINGS. (Plates 122, 123, 124, 125, 126, 127.)

The staircase to be constructed out of best selected pitch pine. Strings to be $11'' \times 2''$, housed for treads and risers. Treads $13'' \times 1\frac{1}{2}''$, with moulded nosings, and grooved to receive small moulding under. Risers $5'' \times 1''$. Newels $6'' \times 6''$, with sunk panels to bottom newel, others left plain, to have moulded caps with mahogany ball terminal. Put half-round mahogany drops to newels where shown. Handrail to be $4'' \times 3''$, mahogany, moulded to detail, the ends to be tenoned to newels, and housed into newels $\frac{3}{8}''$, and pinned. Balusters, alternately $1\frac{1}{4}''$ plain round and $3'' \times 1\frac{1}{4}''$ pierced. The stairs to be properly framed, housed, glued, blocked, screwed and bracketed together.

The wall strings to be grooved, and have small hollow worked on edge. Put $2\frac{3}{4}'' \times 1\frac{1}{4}''$ moulding tongued to string, and continue same up the stairs and around landings. Put $4'' \times 2''$ bevelled and moulded capping to outside string.

Form the two bottom steps, as shown, with bull-nosed ends, the risers to be veneered and properly glued and blocked to treads.

The landings to have $5'' \times 3''$ joists, to be properly trimmed, and ends of joists to be securely pinned into walls. Cover the landings with $1\frac{1}{2}''$ pitch pine boards, grooved, tongued, and glue-jointed together, and properly fitted to stairs.

The stairs, 1st flight, to have $4'' \times 3''$ fir carriage pieces splayed to floor and trimmers, and securely fixed. The 2nd and 3rd flights to be $3'' \times 2''$.

The spandril under outside string of 1st flight to be $1\frac{1}{2}''$, framed, panelled and moulded. Put $2\frac{1}{2}'' \times 1\frac{1}{2}''$ moulding to cover joint with spandril and string of stairs, moulding of similar section to be used on the outside strings throughout.

Put under the 1st landing $5'' \times 3''$ rebated wall-post and bead framed together and to newel to form jambs for door. The door to be 2″, five-panel, square framed and moulded, and hung with No. 1 pair 4″ brass butts, and fitted with 6″ two-bolt mortice lock and furniture.

The lining board to top landing to be 1″ thick, with 4″ × 1½″ nosing piece, and 3″ × 2″ grooved and rounded base rail for balusters. Execute circular work to landing as shown on drawing.

The soffite of stairs to 1st flight to be covered with ¾″ V-jointed best red matchboard. The soffites of 2nd and 3rd flights, also the ceiling of second landing, to be covered with ¾″ best selected pitch pine matchboard in narrow widths, secret nailed.

MATERIALS REQUIRED FOR STAIRCASE WITH CLOSE STRINGS. (PLATES 122, 123, 124, 125, 126, 127.)

	Length.		Total Length.			Description.
	′	″	′	″		
1			15	0		Wall string, 1st flight.
1			3	3		Wall string, 2nd flight.
1			5	6		Wall string, 3rd flight.
			23	9	run	11″ × 2″ wall strings, with hollow worked on top edge, grooved for moulding, and housed for treads and risers.
1			2	9	,,	8″ × 2″ short piece, tongued, grooved and glue-jointed to string at bottom to form ramp.
2	3	3	6	6	,,	8″ × 1¼″ skirting to landings same section as wall strings, ramped to intersect with strings of 1st and 2nd flights.
2	3	3	6	6	,,	11″ × 1¼″ skirting as before described, ramped to intersect with strings of 2nd and 3rd flights.

MATERIALS REQUIRED FOR STAIRCASE WITH CLOSE STRINGS
(PLATES 122, 123, 124, 125, 126, 127)—*Continued.*

	Length.		Total Length.			Description.
	′	″	′	″		
1			11	9	run	$2\frac{3}{4}'' \times 1\frac{1}{4}''$ moulding, tongued to string of 1st flight.
5	3	3	16	3		
1			2	9		
1			4	9		
			23	9	run	$2\frac{3}{4}'' \times 1\frac{1}{4}''$ moulding, tongued to strings and skirting, worked circular for ramps.
1			11	3		Outside string, 1st flight.
1			2	8		Outside string, 2nd flight.
1			4	6		Outside string, 3rd flight.
			18	5	run	$11'' \times 2''$ outside strings, housed for treads and risers, and tenoned to newels.
1			10	7		
1			1	7		
1			3	7		
			15	9	run	$4'' \times 2''$ capping to outside strings, grooved, bevelled and moulded.
1			10	7		
1			1	7		
1			3	7		
			15	9	run	$2\frac{1}{2}'' \times 1\frac{1}{4}''$ moulding, rebated and planted on bottom edge of outside strings.
1			3	3	,,	$10'' \times 1''$ rebated apron board.
1						$10'' \times 1''$ rebated apron board, worked circular, quadrant 1′ 10″ radius.
1			3	3	run	$4'' \times 1\frac{1}{2}''$ nosing, rounded and grooved for scotia.
1						$4'' \times 1\frac{1}{2}''$ nosing as above described, worked circular, quadrant 1′ 8½″ radius.
1			3	3		$1\frac{1}{4}'' \times \frac{3}{4}''$ scotia moulding.

MATERIALS REQUIRED FOR STAIRCASE WITH CLOSE STRINGS
(PLATES 122, 123, 124, 125, 126, 127)—*Continued.*

	Length.		Total Length.			Description.
	′	″	′	″		
1						$1\frac{1}{4}''\times\frac{3}{4}''$ scotia moulding, worked circular, quadrant 1′ $9\frac{1}{4}''$ radius.
1			3	3		$3''\times 2''$ dust rail, rounded on both edges and morticed for balusters.
1						$3''\times 2''$ dust rail as above described, worked circular, quadrant 1′ $9\frac{1}{4}''$ radius.
1			3	3		$2''\times 1''$ moulding, to cover joint of apron board and plaster.
1						$2''\times 1''$ moulding as above described, worked circular, quadrant 1′ $8''$ radius.
1			4	9		$6\times 6''$ bottom newel, sunk panelled and moulded on solid, morticed and housed for strings, treads, risers, handrail and capping.
4						$5''\times 1\frac{1}{2}''$ short pieces of moulding planted on newel, with returned and mitred ends.
4						$4''$ diameter $\frac{1}{4}''$ thick semicircular pieces planted on newel beneath mouldings.
1			11	3		$6''\times 6''$ newel, morticed and housed for strings, treads, risers, handrail and capping, and rebated for spandril.
1			5	0		$6''\times 6''$ newel ⎫ morticed for strings, and
1			4	6		,, ,, ⎭ housed as above described.
4						$8\frac{1}{2}''\times 8\frac{1}{2}''\times 2''$ moulded caps to newels.
4						Ball terminals to newels out of mahogany, $6''$ diameter, dowelled to caps.
2						Drops to newels out of mahogany, $6''$ diameter, dowelled to newels.
17	3	4	56	8	run	$13''\times 1\frac{1}{2}''$ treads, with rounded nosing and grooved for scotia.

MATERIALS REQUIRED FOR STAIRCASE WITH CLOSE STRINGS
(PLATES 122, 123, 124, 125, 126, 127)—*Continued.*

	Length.	Total Length.		Description.
	′ ″	′ ″		
1		3 6	run	$14\frac{1}{2}″ \times 1\frac{1}{2}″$ tread as above described, with quadrant-shaped end.
1		4 4		$14\frac{1}{2}″ \times 1\frac{1}{2}″$ tread as above described, with bull-nosed end.
1		1 6		$12″ \times 1\frac{1}{2}″$ short piece, grooved, tongued and jointed to above to form bull-nosed end.
3	3 2	9 6	run	$4″ \times 1\frac{1}{2}″$ nosings to landings, with rounded edge and grooved for scotia.
2	$3″\,6″ \times 3″\,6″ \times 1\frac{1}{2}″$		=	24′ 6″ sup. in landings, grooved, tongued and glue-jointed together.
14	3 4	46 8	run	$1\frac{1}{4}″ \times \frac{3}{4}″$ scotia moulding.
6	3 2	19 0	,,	,, ,, ,, ,,
2	2 8	5 4	,,	
		71 0	,,	,, ,, ,,
1		3 6		Scotia under 2nd step out of $10″ \times \frac{3}{4}″$, with quadrant-shaped end.
1		2 8		$3″ \times \frac{3}{4}″$ scotia under 1st step.
1		2 6		Scotia out of $10″ \times \frac{3}{4}″$, jointed to above to form bull-nosed end.
1		11 0		
1		2 0		
1		4 0		
1		3 6		
		20 6	run	$4″ \times 3″$ moulded mahogany handrail, grooved for balusters and tenoned to newels.
1				Piece as above described, worked circular, quadrant $1″ \times 9\frac{1}{4}″$ radius.
14	1 10	25 8		
7	2 5	16 11		
		42 7	run	$3″ \times 1\frac{1}{4}″$ balusters pierced to detail.

Materials required for Staircase with Close Strings
(Plates 122, 123, 124, 125, 126, 127)—*Continued.*

	Length.		Total Length.			Description.
	′	″	′	″		
16	1	9	28	0		
8	2	5	19	4		
			47	4		1¼″ diameter plain round balusters.
100						4′ × 2″ × 2″ blocks, glued to treads, risers and strings.
1			10	9		
1			6	8		
			17	5	run	5″ × 1½″ top rail and stile to spandril framing, grooved one edge for panels.
1			8	9		9″ × 1½″ bottom rail to spandril framing, grooved one edge for panels.
1			4	10		
1			4	0		
1			3	2		
1			2	4		
1			1	6		
			15	10	run	4½″ × 1½″ muntins to spandril framing, grooved both edges for panels.
1			5	3		
1			4	5		
1			3	7		
1			2	9		
1			1	11		
1			1	0		
			18	11	run	14″ × ½″ panels.
			5	2		
			4	7		
			4	4		
			3	9		
			3	6		
			2	10		
Carried Forward			24	2		

STAIRCASE WITH CLOSE STRINGS

Materials required for Staircase with Close Strings
(Plates 122, 123, 124, 125, 126, 127)—*Continued.*

	Length.	Total Length.		Description.
Brought Forward		24′ 2″		
		2 8		
		2 0		
		1 10		
		1 3		
		1 0		
5	1′ 4″	6 8		
5	1 · 1	5 5		
		1 6		
		1 9		
		48 3	run	2″ × ¾″ bed moulding to panels, mitred at angles.
1		7 0		5″ × 3″ rebated wall-post, to form doorway under 1st landing.
1		3 6		5″ × 3″ head to rebated wall-post, to form doorway under 1st landing.
2	6 10	13 8		
1		2 11		
		16 7	run	4½″ × 2″ stiles and top rail to door, grooved one edge for panels.
1		2 11	,,	9″ × 2″ bottom rail to door, grooved one edge for panels.
1		2 11	,,	9″ × 2″ lock rail, grooved both edges for panels.
1		2 11		
1		1 11		
1		2 6		
		7 4	run	4½″ × 2″ frieze rail and muntins, grooved both edges for panels.
2	1 8	3 4		
2	2 2	4 4		
1		2 2		
		9 10	run	12″ × ½″ panels.

235

MATERIALS REQUIRED FOR STAIRCASE WITH CLOSE STRINGS
(PLATES 122, 123, 124, 125, 126, 127)—*Continued.*

	Length.		Total Length.			Description.
	'	"	'	"		
10	1	0	10	0		
4	1	8	6	8		
6	2	2	13	0		
			29	8	run	2″ × ¾″ bed moulding to panels, mitred at angles.
1						pair 4″ brass butts and screws.
1						6″ two-bolt mortice lock and furniture.
3	13	0	39	0	run	4″ × 3″ fir carriage pieces to 1st flight.
3	2	9	8	3	,,	3″ × 2″ ,, ,, ,, ,, 2nd flight.
3	4	8	14	0	,,	3″ × 2″ ,, ,, ,, ,, 3rd flight.
3	4	0	12	0		
5	3	9	18	9		
			30	9	run	5″ × 3″ fir joist framed to landings.
3	1	3	3	9		4″ × 3″ short studs under 2nd step.
	3′ 4″ × 1′		=			3′ 4″.
	11′ 3″ × 3′ 4″		=			37′ 6″.
	3′ 0″ × 3′ 4″		=			10′ 0″.
						50′ 10″ sup. ¾″ best red matchboard in 4″ widths, secret nailed to soffites of stairs, 1st flight and 1st landing.
	3′ 4″ × 2′ 9″		=			9′ 2″.
	3′ 4″ × 3′ 4″		=			11′ 2″.
	4′ 6″ × 3′ 4″		=			15′ 0″.
						35′ 4″ sup. ¾″ best selected pitch pine matchboard in 4″ widths, secret nailed to soffites of stairs, 2nd and 3rd flights and 2nd landing.
			5	6	run	2′ × 1″ cove moulding to joint of string with matchboard.
			15	0	,,	2″ × 1½″ cove moulding at joint of matchboard with wall.

BUILDING CONSTRUCTION DRAWING

A CLASS-BOOK FOR THE ELEMENTARY STUDENT AND ARTISAN

BY

RICHARD B. EATON

LECTURER ON BUILDING CONSTRUCTION

Part VI

JOINERY DRAWINGS AND SPECIFICATIONS

30 PLATES

London

E. & F. N. SPON, Ltd., 57 HAYMARKET, S.W. 1

New York

SPON & CHAMBERLAIN, 120 LIBERTY STREET

1921

PREFACE

In continuation of Parts IV. and V., *Joinery Drawings*, already published, it has been my aim in Part VI. to place before the student a further set of useful and practical drawings which are not beyond the reach of the average student in Building Construction.

It is hoped these books will also be of service to the craftsman who is unable to attend the Building Construction Class.

The drawings and details generally are fully dimensioned, and show the joiner's work in its accustomed setting.

A specification for each set of drawings is given, and I find from correspondents and reviews of the previous parts that this idea is considered to be a good one. It certainly enables the student early in his career to learn how to work with specification in conjunction with plan.

R. B. E.

"Lakeside," Seldown, Poole.

SPECIFICATION OF SKIRTINGS, PICTURE AND CHAIR RAILS, AND ARCHITRAVES.

SKIRTINGS. (PLATE 128.)

THE skirtings throughout to be fixed to $2'' \times \frac{3}{4}''$ single splayed grounds, and to have vertical backing pieces placed $2'\ 0''$ apart, securely plugged to walls. Skirtings to be tongued and mitred (or scribed) at angles, and scribed to floor.

PICTURE RAILS AND CHAIR RAILS. (PLATE 128.)

The picture and chair rails to be fixed to $2'' \times \frac{3}{4}''$ double splayed grounds securely plugged to walls; angles to be mitred.

ARCHITRAVES. (PLATE 129.)

Put around doors and windows $5'' \times 1\frac{1}{2}''$ moulded architraves, mitred at angles, and housed for skirting, fixed to $2'' \times \frac{3}{4}''$ single splayed grounds securely plugged to walls.

PLATE 128.

Sections of Picture Rails, Chair Rails & Skirtings.

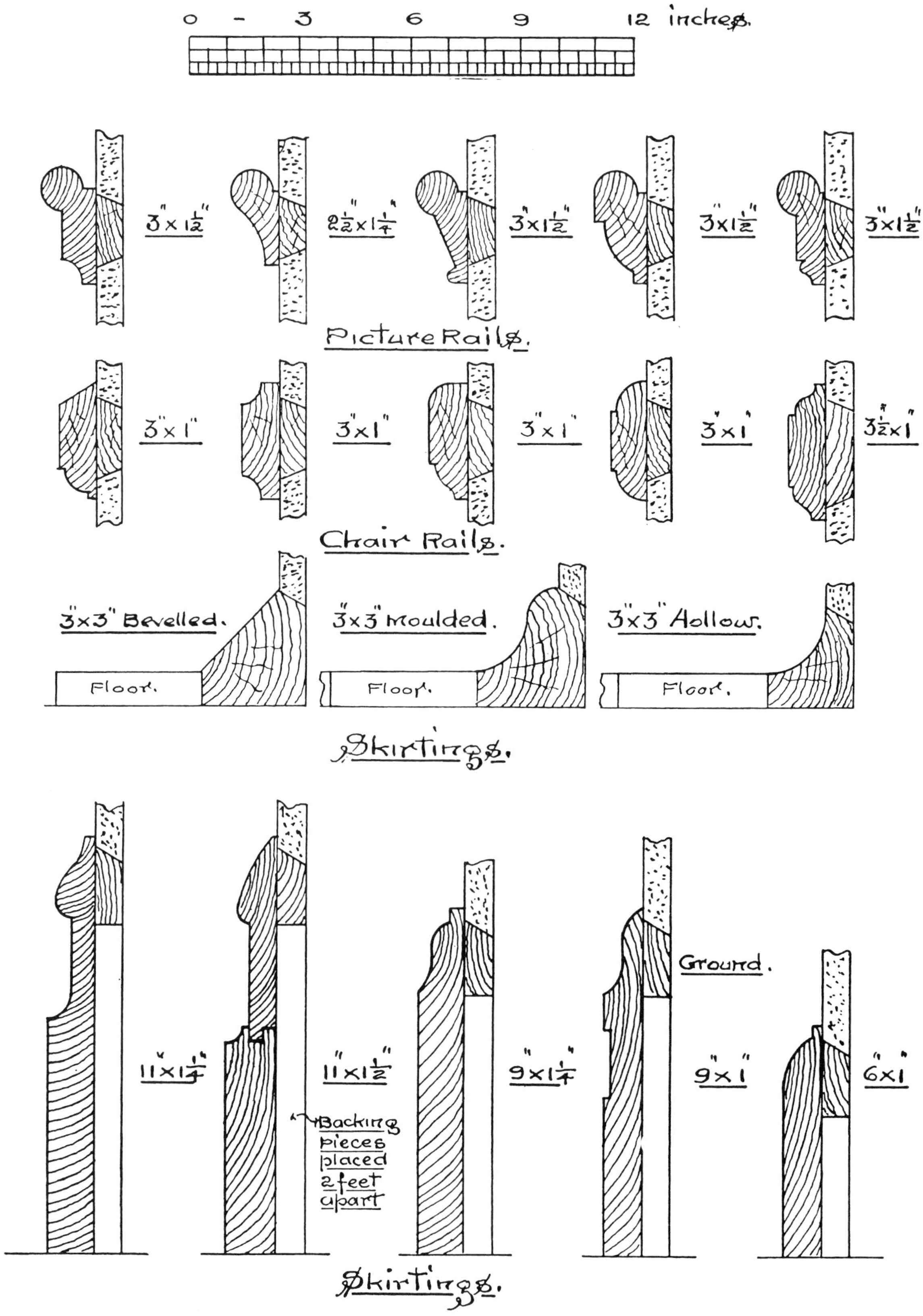

0 — 3   6   9   12 inches.

3"×1½"   **2½"×1¼"**   **3"×1½"**   **3"×1½"**   **3"×1½"**

Picture Rails.

3"×1"   **3"×1"**   **3"×1"**   **3"×1"**   **3½"×1"**

Chair Rails.

3"×3" Bevelled.   **3"×3" Moulded.**   **3"×3" Hollow.**

Floor.   Floor.   Floor.

Skirtings.

11"×1¼"   **11"×1½"**   **9"×1¼"**   **9"×1"**   Ground.   **6"×1"**

Backing pieces placed 2 feet apart

Skirtings.

PLATE **129.**

Architrave Mouldings, 1" Scale.

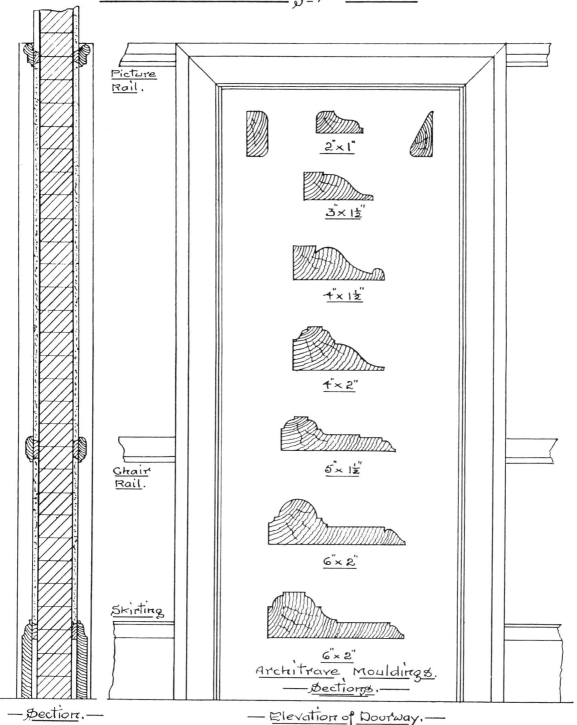

Picture
Rail.

Chair
Rail.

Skirting

2"×1"

3"×1½"

4"×1½"

4"×2"

5"×1½"

6"×2"

6"×2"
Architrave Mouldings.
—Sections.—

—Section.—

— Elevation of Doorway. —

Plan of Doorway showing
Linings, Architraves & Grounds.

SPECIFICATION OF CASEMENT FRAME WITH PIVOT HUNG SASHES.

(PLATE 130.)

THE frame to be 4″ × 3″, with rebated, bevelled and throated sill and head, sill to be grooved for window board and water bar. Fix to posts of frames 1″ × 1″ ovolo-moulded stops, carefully cut to allow sash to open freely. The sash to be 2″ ovolo-moulded, rebated for glass and hung on patent sash centres. Put brass sash fastener and opening cord, and fix small brass cleat hook.

PLATE 130.

Pivot Hung Casement.   1½" Scale

Inches.
12 - 9 - 6 - 3 - 0   1 Foot.

Section.

Specification.
Frame.
4½"x3" Head
& Sill.
4½"x2½ Jambs.

Casement.
2" Ovolo Moulded.
2" Stiles &
Top Rail.
3½"Bottom Rail.
1"x1" Stop
Mouldings.

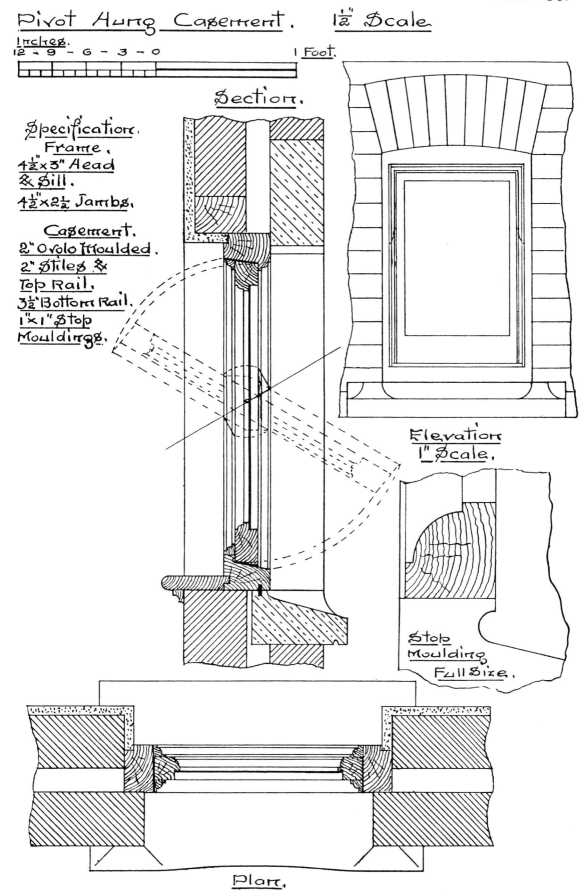

Elevation
1" Scale.

Stop
Moulding
Full Size.

Plan.

SPECIFICATION OF SKYLIGHT.
(PLATES 131–133.)

THE skylight to have $9\frac{1}{2}'' \times 1\frac{1}{2}''$ frame tongued and grooved at angles. The top edge to be tongued to skylight. Put to cover joint of ceiling $2'' \times 1''$ hollow-moulded architrave mitred at angles.

The sash to be $2''$ thick, with $7'' \times 2''$ stiles and top rail, $7'' \times 1\frac{1}{4}''$ bottom rail, and one $2'' \times 2''$ bar, all rebated for glass and chamfered on inside. The sash to be grooved to fit over frame; allowance to be made for lead flashings in the grooves; the underside of sashes to be grooved for drip.

The leadwork to be executed with 5 lb. milled sheet lead throughout. The gutter at top of skylight to have welted top edge under slates. All leadwork to be to the widths shown, and dressed over tongue of frame and copper nailed. The lead soakers to be of 3 lb. lead, one to each slate, and nailed to frame with one copper nail to each. Put No. 3, 7 lb. lead tacks to keep lead apron in position.

The skylight to be glazed with Hartley's rolled $\frac{1}{8}''$ plate glass, properly bedded in and front puttied.

PLATE 131.

Skylight for Roof Covered with Slate. 1" Scale.

Specification. Frame 10"x1½", Skylight, 7"x2" Stiles and Top Rail, 7"x1¼" Bottom Rail, 2" Bar, 2"x¾" Cover Strip Mitred around Frame on Inside.

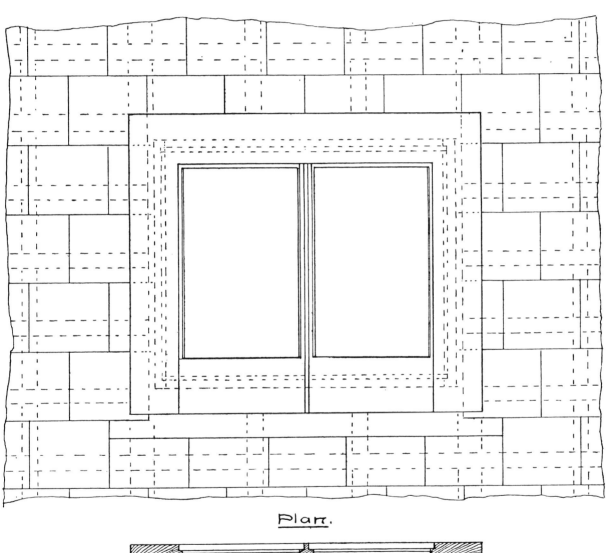

Plan.

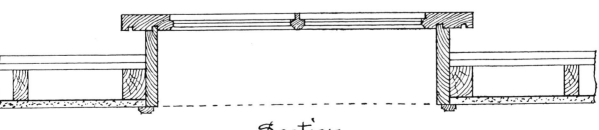

Section.

245

PLATE **132.**

Details of Skylight. 3" Scale.

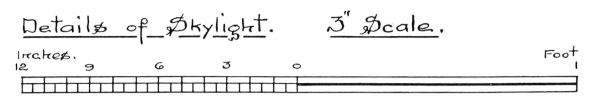

Inches.
12   9   6   3   0   Foot
1

Roof Boarded, Felted,
and Battened, Slate covering.
5lb Lead Gutter.

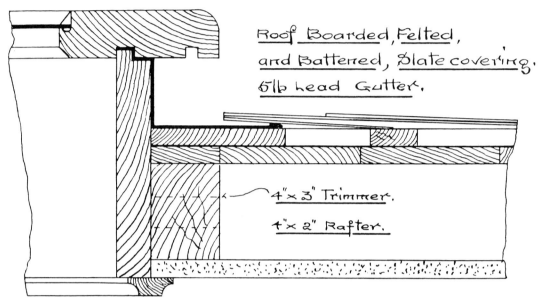

4"× 3" Trimmer.

4"× 2" Rafter.

Section thro Top Rail of Skylight.

5lb Lead Apron.

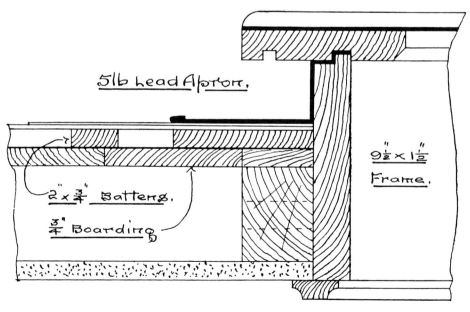

$9\frac{1}{2}$"× $1\frac{1}{2}$"
Frame.

2"× $\frac{3}{4}$" Battens.

$\frac{3}{4}$" Boarding.

Section thro Bottom Rail of Skylight.

PLATE 133.

Details of Skylight.   1½" & 3" Scales.

Inches
12 - 9 - 6 - 3 - 0   1   2 Feet.

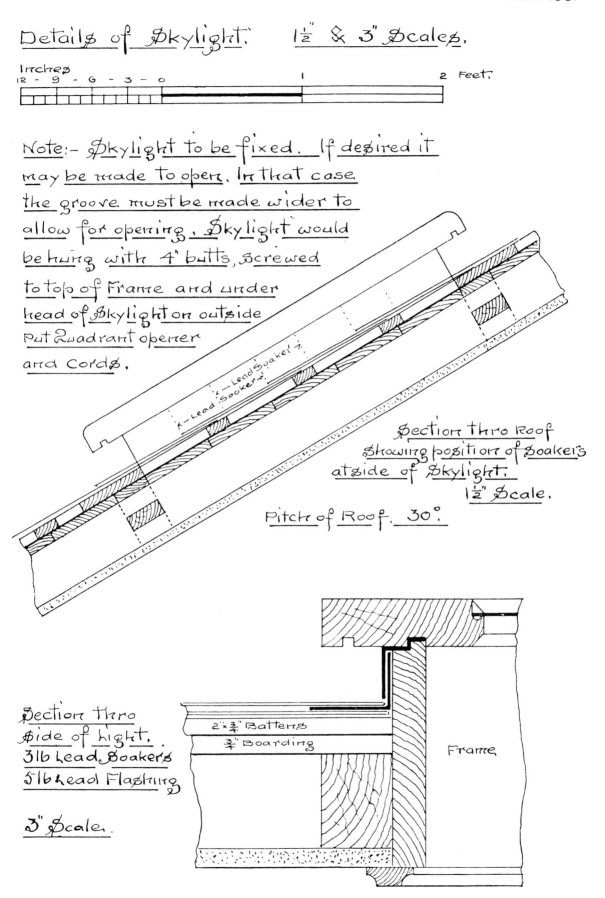

Note:- Skylight to be fixed.   If desired it
may be made to open. In that case
the groove must be made wider to
allow for opening. Skylight would
be hung with 4" butts, screwed
to top of Frame and under
head of Skylight on outside
Put Quadrant opener
and Cords.

Lead Soaker.
Lead Soaker.

Section thro Roof
Showing position of Soakers
at side of Skylight.
1½" Scale.

Pitch of Roof. 30°.

Section thro
Side of light.
3 lb Lead Soakers
5 lb Lead Flashing

3" Scale.

2 × ¾" Battens
¾" Boarding

Frame

SPECIFICATION OF LANTERN LIGHT WITH FLAT TOP.

(Plate 134.)

The lantern light to be framed with $5\frac{1}{2}'' \times 3\frac{1}{2}''$ double rebated, throated and grooved sill, $4'' \times 4''$ corner posts, $4'' \times 3''$ mullions and head, all rebated and chamfered. Sashes to be $2''$ ovolo-moulded and rebated for glass. Two sashes to be hung at top with $3''$ brass butts opening outwards. Put strong brass openers and cords. Put to carry top No. 4, $3'' \times 2''$ chamfered joists tenoned to frame. Cover top with $1''$ **V**-jointed matchboard, the outer edge to overhang frame $1\frac{1}{2}''$ and rounded for lead. Provide and fix No. 2, $2'' \times 1\frac{1}{2}''$ wood rolls for lead.

Lay 6 lb. milled sheet lead to top properly dressed over rolls, the edges to be dressed over nosing brought down $2''$ and nailed to frame with copper nails $3''$ apart. Sashes to be glazed with 21 oz. best British sheet glass.

Provide and fix to cover trimmer joists, $1\frac{1}{2}''$ square-framed and panelled casing, with $2'' \times \frac{3}{4}''$ half-round moulding to cover joint of frame with panelling.

PLATE **134.**

Lantern Light, with Flat Top. $\frac{3}{4}''$ Scale.

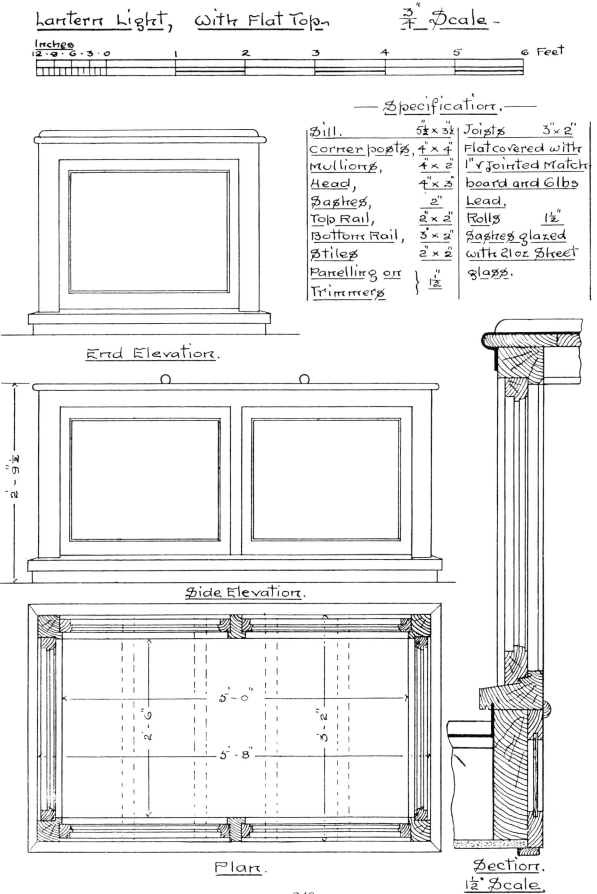

End Elevation.

Side Elevation.

Plan.

Section.
1½" Scale.

— Specification. —

Sill.	5½" × 3½"	Joists	3" × 2"
Corner posts,	4" × 4"	Flat covered with	
Mullions,	4" × 2"	1" v Jointed Match	
Head,	4" × 3"	board and 6lbs	
Sashes,	2"	Lead.	
Top Rail,	2" × 2"	Rolls	1½"
Bottom Rail,	3" × 2"	Sashes glazed	
Stiles	2" × 2"	with 21oz Sheet	
Panelling or	} 1½"	glass.	
Trimmers			

2′-6½″

5′-0″

2′-6″

3′-2″

5′-8″

LANTERN LIGHT

SPECIFICATION OF LANTERN LIGHT.
(PLATES 135–136.)

THE lantern light to be framed with $6'' \times 3\frac{1}{2}''$ rebated, throated and grooved sills, $4'' \times 3''$ frames and mullions, all rebated, chamfered and weather grooved. The ends to be $2\frac{1}{2}''$ thick, each framed in one piece with top rail tongued to roof lights, to have $11''$ bottom rail, $3\frac{1}{2}'' \times 3\frac{1}{2}''$ top rail, $7''$ stiles, and $2''$ bars, all rebated and ovolo-moulded. The roof lights to be $2\frac{1}{2}''$ thick, properly framed together, with $6'' \times 2\frac{1}{2}''$ stiles and top rails, $6'' \times 1\frac{1}{2}''$ bottom rails, $2''$ bars, all rebated and ovolo-moulded, the roof lights to be grooved to fit over frame and ends. The ends and sides to have slip tongued and grooved joint. The bars to have $2'' \times 1\frac{1}{2}''$ grooved and rounded cover strips. The side sashes to be $2''$ ovolo-moulded, and rebated with $1''$ bars. Put $3\frac{1}{2}''$ wood roll to ridge. The tie rods to be of wrought iron $\frac{1}{2}''$ diameter, bolted at each end to head of frame.

One sash on each side to be hung at top with $3''$ butts, opening outwards. Put proper brass openers and cords complete.

Put $1''$ lining board on trimmer with bevelled bottom edge and quadrant moulding to cover joint at ridge. The joint of frame with plaster to be covered with $3'' \times 1''$ moulded strips properly mitred at angles.

The joints throughout to be painted with good red-lead paint before fixing.

Cover the ridge roll with 6 lb. lead properly dressed over rolls and down to glass. The aprons to be 6 lb. lead, carried up under sill and turned up 1″ on inside of sill. Put No. 8, 7 lb. lead tacks No. 4 to each apron. Flashings to ends to be 5 lb. lead, soakers 4 lb. lead, one to each slate and nailed to frame with one copper nail to each.

The side and end sashes to be glazed with 21 oz. best British sheet glass properly bedded, sprigged and back puttied. The roof lights to be glazed with Hartley's roll $\frac{1}{8}$″ plate. The cover strips to bars, etc., to be bedded in white lead, and fastened with brass screws.

PLATE 135.

Lantern Light. ½" Scale.

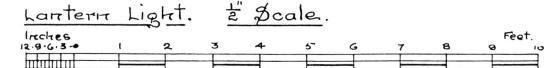

Roof Lights, 2½" thick, 2" bars, 6" Stiles, 6" × 3¼" Top rails, 6" × 1¾" Bottom Rails, 2" × 1½" Covers to bars, 2¾" Ridge Roll, Vertical lights, 6" × 3½" Sills, 4" × 3" Frames, 3" Mullions, 2" Sashes, 1" Bars, Ends, 2½" thick, tongued to Roof.

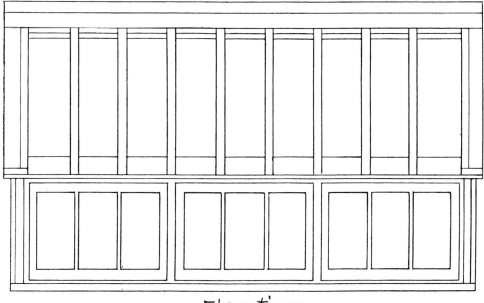

— Elevation. —

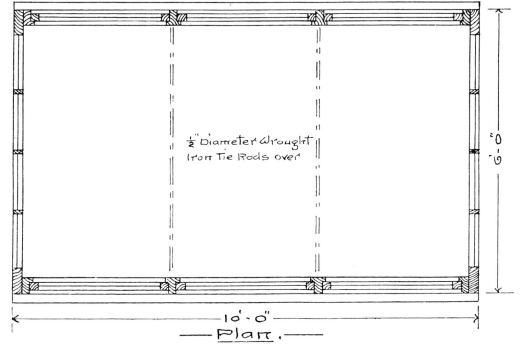

½" Diameter Wrought Iron Tie Rods over

6'·0"

10'·0"

— Plan. —

PLATE 136.

Lantern Light, — Section ¾" Scale, Details 1½" Scale.

Inches
12 9 6 3 0   1   2   3
Feet

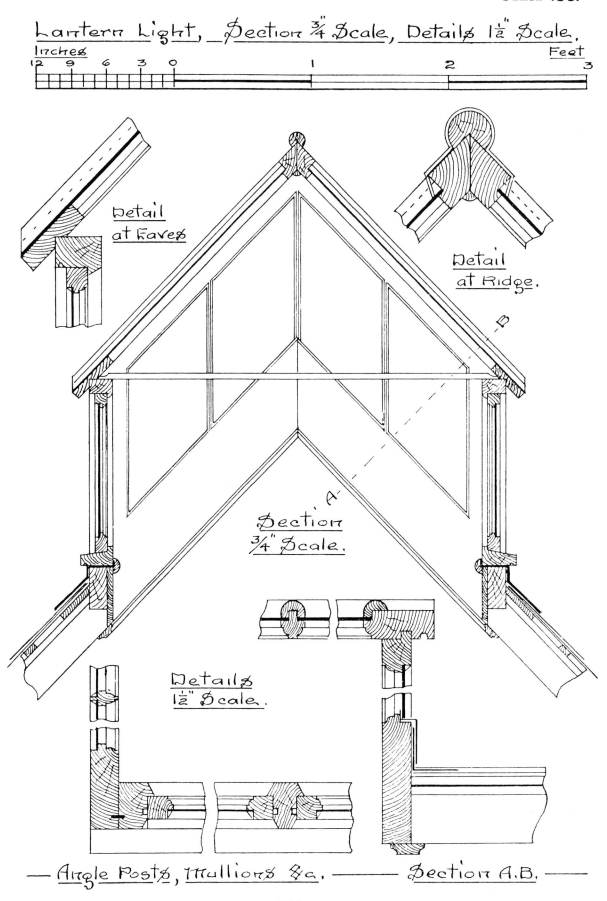

Detail
at Eaves

Detail
at Ridge.

Section
¾" Scale.

Details
1½" Scale.

— Angle Posts, Mullions &c. ——— Section A.B. ———

SPECIFICATION OF OCTAGONAL LANTERN LIGHT.

(PLATES 137–138.)

THE lantern light to be framed octagonal, with $6\frac{1}{2}'' \times 3''$ sunk, weathered and throated sills, hollow grooved for drip. The angles of sills to be halved and screwed together, $4\frac{1}{2}'' \times 3''$ rebated and throated head with hollow on inside edge, $5\frac{1}{2}'' \times 4''$ angle posts rebated and hollow grooved. Sashes to be $2''$ ovolo-moulded and rebated for glass. Put $1\frac{1}{2}'' \times 1''$ bottom bead. Two sashes to be hung at top, with $3''$ brass butts opening outwards, and fitted with brass fanlight openers and cords complete.

Roof lights to be $2\frac{1}{2}''$ thick, framed in eight sections, with $2'' \times 1\frac{3}{4}''$ hollow grooved stiles, with hollow worked on bottom edge, the stiles to be bevelled and grooved for galvanised iron tongue. Bottom rails to be $7'' \times 1\frac{1}{2}''$, with hollow worked on edge. Put to cover joints of lights chamfered and bevelled capping out of $4'' \times 1\frac{1}{4}''$.

The whole to be properly fitted and framed, the joints throughout to be painted with good red-lead paint before putting together.

The side sashes to be glazed with 21 oz. best British sheet glass, and roof lights with Hartley's roll $\frac{1}{8}''$ plate.

Put 5 lb. lead cover piece at top, cut to shape, and dressed down to glass, and fastened to boarding with soldered dot and brass screw. Apron under sill to be 6 lb. lead turned up 1″ on inside of sill and 3″ over curb. Put 3″ × 1¼″ moulding to cover joint of sill with curb.

PLATE **137.**

Octagonal Lantern Light. ¾" Scale.

Inches.
12 - 9 - 6 - 3 - 0   1   2   3   4   5   6 Feet.

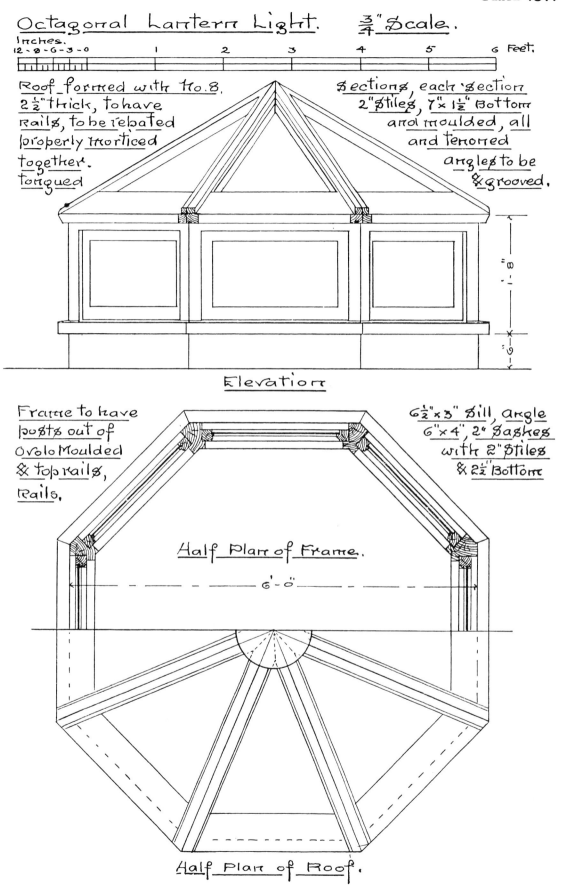

Roof formed with No.8. Sections, each section
2½" thick, to have 2" stiles, 7"× 1½" Bottom
rails, to be rebated and moulded, all
properly morticed and tenoned
together. angles to be
tongued & grooved.

Elevation

Frame to have 6½"×3" Sill, angle
posts out of 6"× 4", 2" Sashes
Ovolo Moulded with 2" Stiles
& top rails, & 2½" Bottom
Rails.

Half Plan of Frame.

6'- 0"

Half Plan of Roof.

PLATE 138.

Details of Octagonal Lantern Light.

Inches.
12   9   6   3   0   Foot. 1

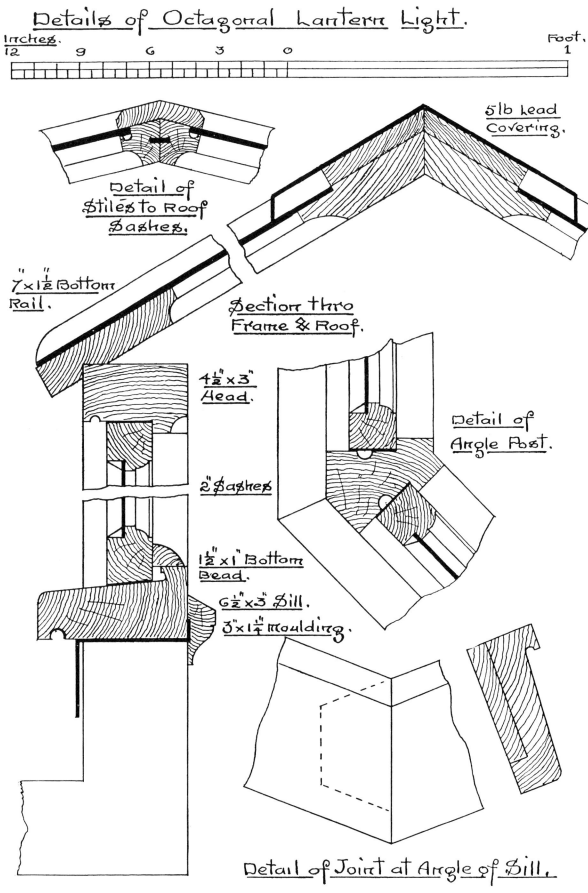

Detail of
Stiles to Roof
Sashes.

5 lb Lead
Covering.

7"×1½" Bottom
Rail.

Section thro
Frame & Roof.

4½"×3"
Head.

2" Sashes

Detail of
Angle Post.

1½"×1" Bottom
Bead.

6½"×3" Sill.
3"×1¼" Moulding.

Detail of Joint at Angle of Sill.

SPECIFICATION OF PANELLING TO DINING ROOM.

(PLATES 139–144.)

THE panelling to be $1\frac{1}{4}''$ square framed, stiles, top, frieze and bottom rails to show $3''$ on face, extra width to be allowed on stiles and bottom rails at angles and skirting as requisite. Panels to be $\frac{7}{16}''$ thick. Put $9'' \times 1''$ moulded skirting grooved and mitred at angles. Dado moulding $2\frac{1}{2}'' \times 1\frac{1}{4}''$. Frieze moulding $3\frac{1}{4}'' \times 1\frac{3}{4}''$. Cornice moulding worked hollow out of $7'' \times 1\frac{3}{4}''$. The beads at edges of cornice to be $1\frac{1}{4}'' \times \frac{1}{2}''$. Put above frieze moulding $3'' \times 1''$ plain vertical strips securely plugged to walls. The panelling throughout to be fixed on $2'' \times \frac{3}{4}''$ grounds plugged to walls. Put $2'' \times 1\frac{1}{2}''$ vertical blocking pieces below lower ground, flush with face of panelling to form base on which to fix the skirting.

The panelling to be tongued and grooved at all angles, mouldings and skirtings mitred or scribed together as the case may be. The cornice to be fixed to angle bracket pieces, $1\frac{1}{2}''$ thick, spaced two feet apart.

The doorway to have $7\frac{1}{2}'' \times 2''$ solid rebated linings, with $1\frac{1}{4}''$ architraves $5''$ wide tapered to $4''$; head to be $6'' \times 1\frac{1}{4}''$ with $5'' \times 1\frac{3}{4}''$ moulding on top with returned and mitred ends and scribed to frieze moulding. Put $\frac{5}{8}'' \times \frac{1}{4}''$ fillet across head.

The door to be $2''$, framed in six panels, the framing ovolo-moulded on solid. Hang door with $4''$ brass butts, and fit $6''$, 2 bolt mortice lock and gun-metal furniture.

The chimney-piece to be constructed with 4″ × 4″ solid posts, the tops finished with moulded caps out of 6″ × 1½″. The panelling to be 1½″ thick sunk into posts ½″, skirting and chair rail to be scribed into posts. The shelf to be 8″ wide, with rounded corners. The bottom rail of panelling to have moulded edge, and with small moulding planted on as detail.

The ceiling to be panelled as shown on drawing, with 3″ × 1″ plain strips nailed on face of plaster.

PLATE 139.

Plan of Panelling to Dining Room.

Scale $\frac{3''}{8}$ = One Foot.

Inches.

12·9·6·3·0   1   2   3   4   5   6   7   8   9   10   11   12   13   Feet. 14

Dotted lines denote plan of Ceiling.

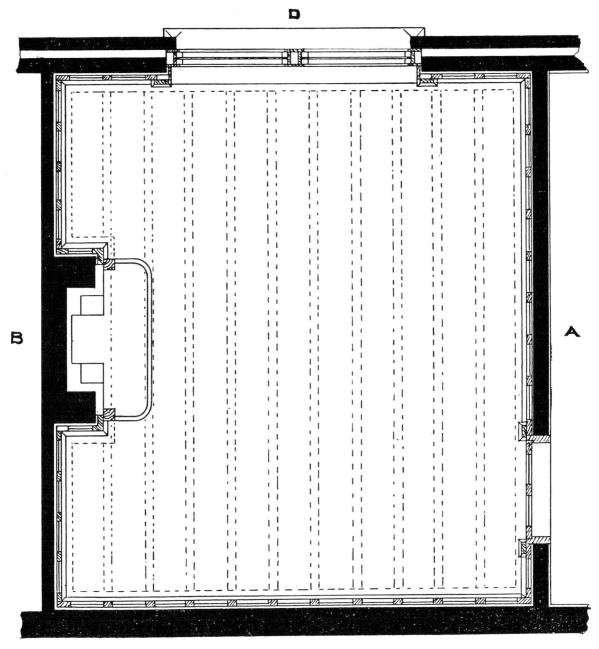

Plan

C

PLATE **140.**

Panelling to Dining Room.   ½" Scale.

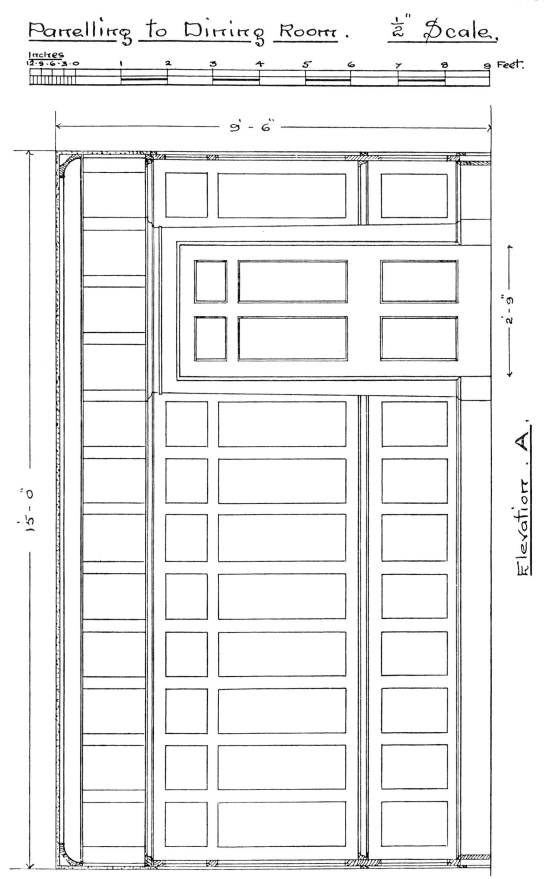

Elevation . A .

PLATE 141.

Panelling to Dining Room. $\frac{1}{2}$" Scale.

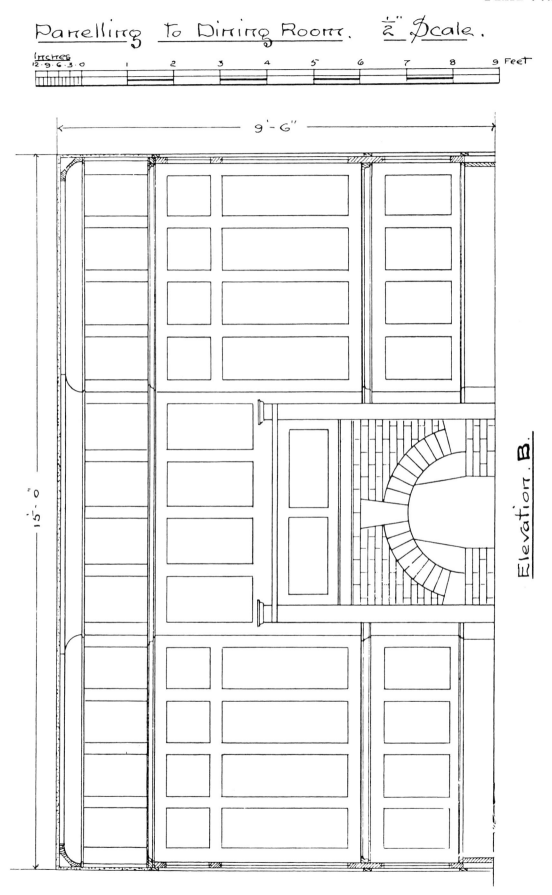

Elevation. B.

PLATE **142**.

Panelling to Dining Room   ½" Scale.

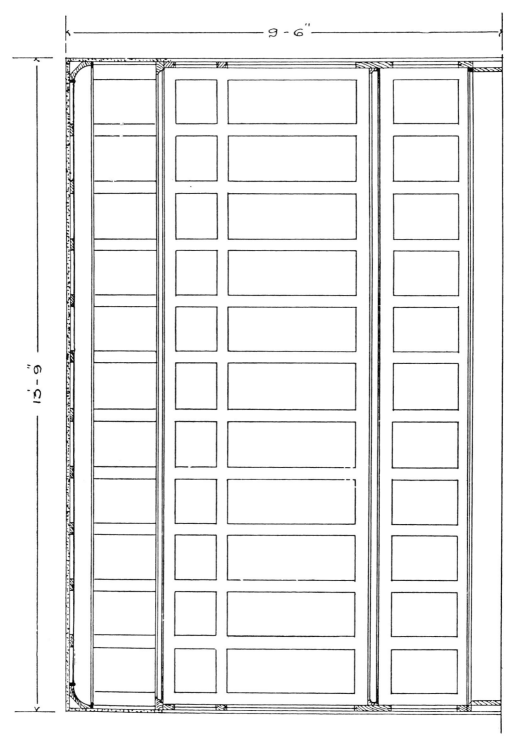

Elevation, **C**.

PLATE **143.**

Panelling to Dining Room.   ½" Scale

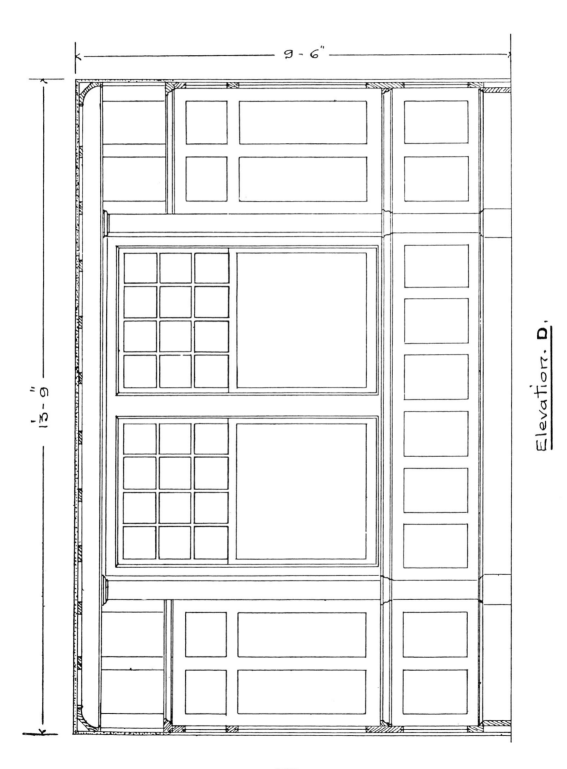

9 - 6"

13 - 9"

Elevation. D.

PLATE **144.**

Details of Panelling to Dining Room.

Scale 1½" = One Foot.

Inches
12 - 9 - 6 - 3 - 0   1   2   Feet.
                                                                                3.

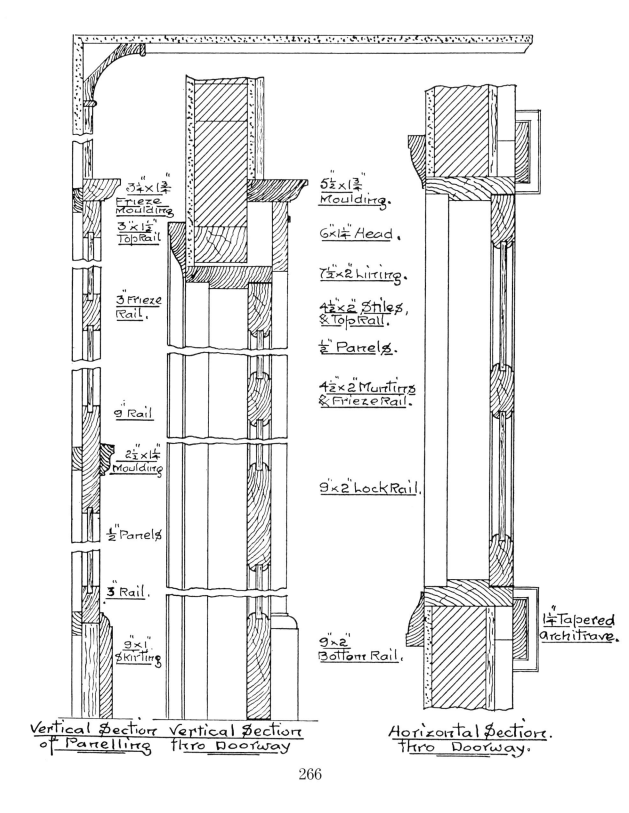

3¼"×1¾"
Frieze
Moulding

3"×1½"
Top Rail

3" Frieze
Rail.

9" Rail

2½"×1¼"
Moulding

½" Panels

3" Rail.

9"×1"
Skirting

5½"×1¾"
Moulding.

6"×1¾" Head.

7½"×2" Lining.

4½"×2" Stiles,
& Top Rail.

½" Panels.

4½"×2" Muntins
& Frieze Rail.

9"×2" Lock Rail.

9"×2"
Bottom Rail.

1¼" Tapered
Architrave.

Vertical Section
of Panelling

Vertical Section
thro Doorway

Horizontal Section.
thro Doorway.

SPECIFICATION OF KITCHEN DRESSER.
(PLATE 145.)

THE kitchen dresser to be constructed with 1″ tops and ends, ½″ **V**-jointed matchboard back, and 1¼″ framed front, with three 1¼″ framed and panelled doors hung with 3″ steel butts and fitted with 1¼″ brass turn buckles. The three drawers to have 1″ fronts, ½″ sides and backs, ⅜″ bottoms, all properly dovetailed, grooved, and blocked together. Fix proper rebated runners for drawers. Put 1½″ brass knob to each drawer.

Each cupboard to be fitted with two 1″ shelves. The bottom to be ¾″ thick, with ¾″ chamfered plinth mitred at angles.

Shelves to dresser to be 1″ housed into 1″ sides and bevel grooved for plate rest, 2″ × 1″ head, 1¼″ cornice moulding mitred at angles, ½″ **V**-jointed matchboard back and 1″ top. Portion of shelves to be provided with cupboard, with 1¼″ framed door and 21 oz. clear glass panel. Door to be hung with 2½″ steel butts and fitted with brass turn buckle.

PLATE 145.

Kitchen Dresser.

Scale ¾" = One Foot.

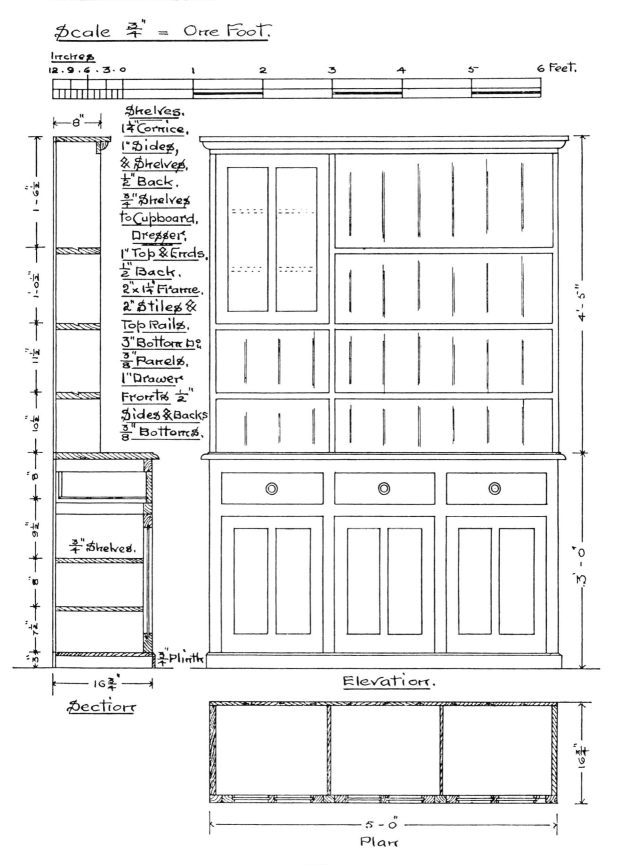

Inches
12.9.6.3.0 · 1 · 2 · 3 · 4 · 5 · 6 Feet.

Shelves.
1¼"Cornice.
1"Sides,
& Shelves.
½" Back.
¾"Shelves
to Cupboard.
Dresser.
1" Top & Ends.
½" Back.
2"×1¼"Frame.
2" Stiles &
Top Rails.
3"Bottom D⁰.
⅜" Panels.
1"Drawer
Fronts ½"
Sides & Backs
⅜" Bottoms.

¾"Shelves.

¾"Plinth

8"

1'-6½"   1'-0½"   1'-1½"   10½"   8"   9½"   8"   7½"   3"

16¾"

Section

4'-5"

3'-0"

Elevation.

5'-0"

16¾"

Plan

SPECIFICATION OF KITCHEN DRESSER WITH GLAZED DOORS.

(PLATE 146.)

THE dresser to have $1''$ top, $1''$ ends, $\frac{1}{2}''$ V-jointed matchboard back, $1\frac{1}{2}''$ frame to front, provided with two $1\frac{1}{2}''$ framed and panelled doors hung to framing, with $3''$ steel butts, and fitted with $1\frac{1}{4}''$ brass turn buckles. Put drawers over open space, with $\frac{7}{8}''$ fronts, $\frac{1}{2}''$ sides and backs, and $\frac{3}{8}''$ bottoms, all properly dovetailed, grooved, and blocked together. Put proper rebated runners for drawers. The drawers to have brass sunk drawer-pulls. Divisions to cupboards to be $\frac{3}{4}''$ thick.

Shelves above dresser to have $1''$ sides bottoms and $\frac{7}{8}''$ shelves, $\frac{1}{2}''$ V-jointed matchboard back. Nail $\frac{3}{8}''$ bead on shelves for plate rest. Put $1\frac{1}{4}''$ framed doors rebated for glass and provided with loose fixing beads. Centre joint of doors to be rebated and beaded. Hang doors to $1\frac{1}{4}''$ frame, with $3''$ steel butts. Put $3''$ brass barrel bolt and $1\frac{1}{4}''$ brass turn buckle to doors.

The cornice moulding to be $1\frac{1}{2}'' \times 1\frac{1}{4}''$, mitred at angles and returned across ends.

Glaze doors with best selected 21 oz. British sheet glass.

PLATE 146.

Kitchen Dresser Top portion with Glazed Doors.

Scale 1" = One Foot.

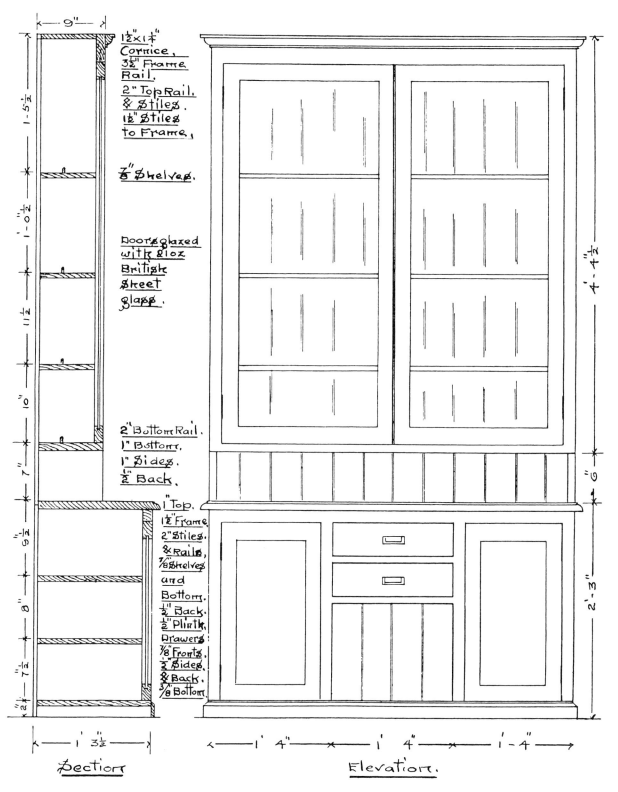

1½"×1¾" Cornice, 3½" Frame Rail. 2" Top Rail. & Stiles. 1½" Stiles to Frame.

⅞" Shelves.

Doors glazed with 21oz British Sheet glass.

2" Bottom Rail. 1" Bottom. 1" Sides. ½" Back.

1" Top. 1½" Frame. 2" Stiles. & Rails, ⅞" Shelves and Bottom. ½" Back. ½" Plinth. Drawers ⅞" Fronts, ½" Sides & Back. ⅜" Bottom.

Section

Elevation.

SPECIFICATION OF BOOKCASE AND SIDEBOARD.

(PLATES 147-148.)

PROVIDE and fix in recess at side of fireplace a sideboard having $1\frac{1}{4}''$ framed front, with $1\frac{1}{4}''$ framed and panelled doors, ovolo-moulded on solid, six panels to each door, hung folding, with $3''$ brass butts, and fitted with $3''$ brass bolt and $3''$ brass cut cupboard lock.

The top to be $1\frac{1}{4}''$ thick, with moulded front edge returned at one end to chimney breast. Put $1''$ shelf full depth of cupboard on $2'' \times 1''$ chamfered cleats plugged to walls. Provide and fix similar cleats under ends of top.

The bookcase to have $1''$ sides grooved for four $1''$ shelves and bottom. Shelves to rest on $1'' \times \frac{1}{2}''$ movable cleats with two dowels to each cleat, the sides to be holed in two rows $3''$ apart vertically to receive cleats. Put $2\frac{1}{2}'' \times 2''$ cornice moulding. Provide three cut and shaped brackets under bookcase $1''$ thick. Doors to be $1\frac{1}{4}''$ thick rebated for glass, with $1''$ horizontal bars, and provided with loose fixing beads. Hang doors to frame with $3''$ brass butts, three to each door. Put $3''$ brass barrel bolt and $3''$ brass cut cupboard lock to doors.

The doors to be glazed with 26 oz. best British sheet glass.

PLATE **147.**

Bookcase & Sideboard, Fixture for Small House.
Scale ¾" = One Foot.

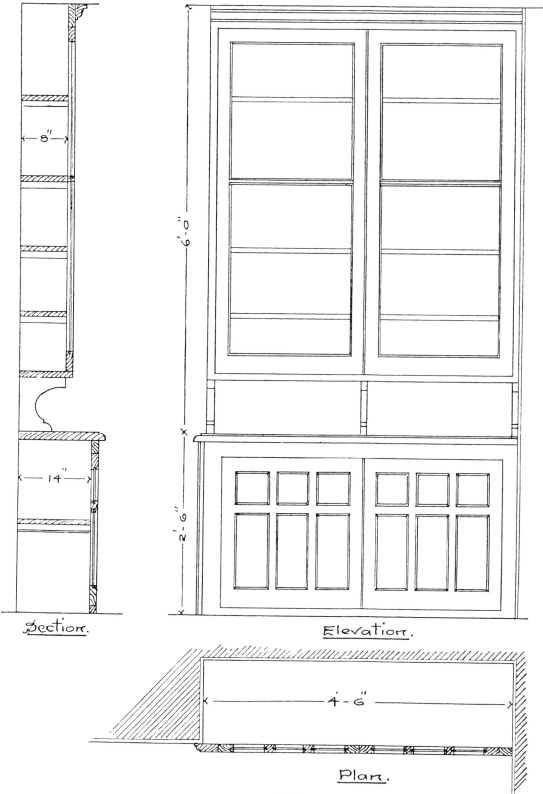

Section.

Elevation.

Plan.

8"

6'-0"

2'-6"

14"

4'-6"

PLATE **148.**

Bookcase & Sideboard, Fixture for Small House.

Details, Scale Half Full Size.

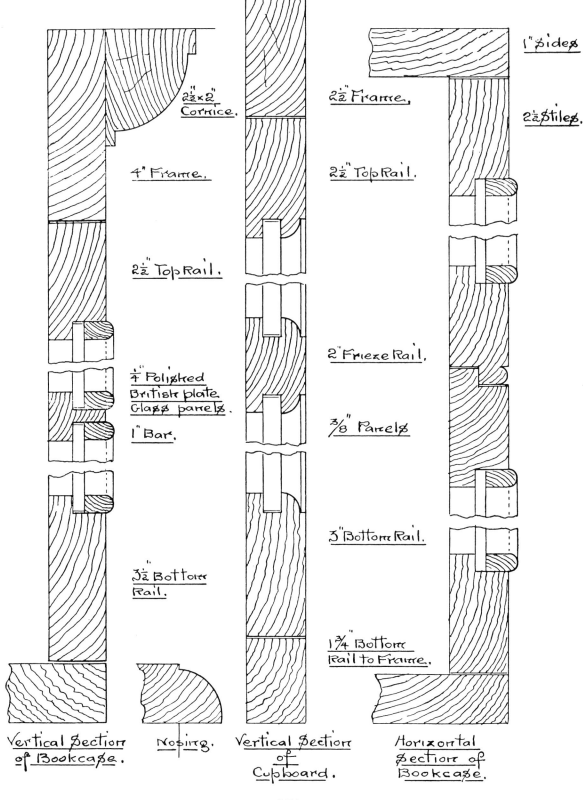

2½"×2" Cornice.

4" Frame.

2½" Top Rail.

¼" Polished British plate Glass panels.

1" Bar.

3½" Bottom Rail.

2½" Frame.

2½" Top Rail.

2" Frieze Rail.

⅜" Panels

3" Bottom Rail.

1¾" Bottom Rail to Frame.

1" Sides

2½" Stiles.

Vertical Section of Bookcase.

Nosing.

Vertical Section of Cupboard.

Horizontal Section of Bookcase.

274

SPECIFICATION OF SIDEBOARD WITH CUPBOARD OVER.

(PLATES 149–151.)

PROVIDE and fix in recess by the side of fireplace a sideboard with $\frac{3}{4}''$ back, ends and divisions, $1\frac{1}{4}''$ shaped top with moulded front edge and scotia moulding under. The front to be recessed, with $1\frac{1}{4}''$ framed and panelled doors moulded on solid, doors hung to frame with $3''$ brass butts and fitted with $3''$ brass cut cupboard locks. Put one shelf in each cupboard tongued into ends. The recessed portion to have one open shelf $1''$ thick, with drawer over, with $1''$ front, $\frac{1}{2}''$ sides and back, and $\frac{3}{8}''$ bottom, all properly dovetailed, grooved, and blocked together. The drawer to be provided with brass sunk pull.

The cupboard over to be constructed with $\frac{3}{4}''$ ends holed for shelf pins in two rows $3''$ apart. Put four movable shelves $1''$ thick and $1''$ top. Provide sixteen movable pins $\frac{1}{2}''$ diameter, with mushroom tops. Front to be $1\frac{1}{4}''$ thick, fitted with $1\frac{1}{4}''$ framed and rebated doors with loose fixing beads for glass. Hang doors to frame with $3''$ brass butts, three butts to each door. Put $3''$ brass bolt and $3''$ brass cut cupboard lock to doors.

The cornice moulding to be $2'' \times 2''$. Put small beaded moulding across head.

The doors to be glazed with leaded lights in diamond squares.

Put one saddle bar to each door.

The space above sideboard between brackets to have polished silvered plate glass panels, with quarter round moulding mitred at angles, to keep glass in position.

Plate 149.

SideBoard with Cupboard over, Fixture

Scale ¾" = One Foot.

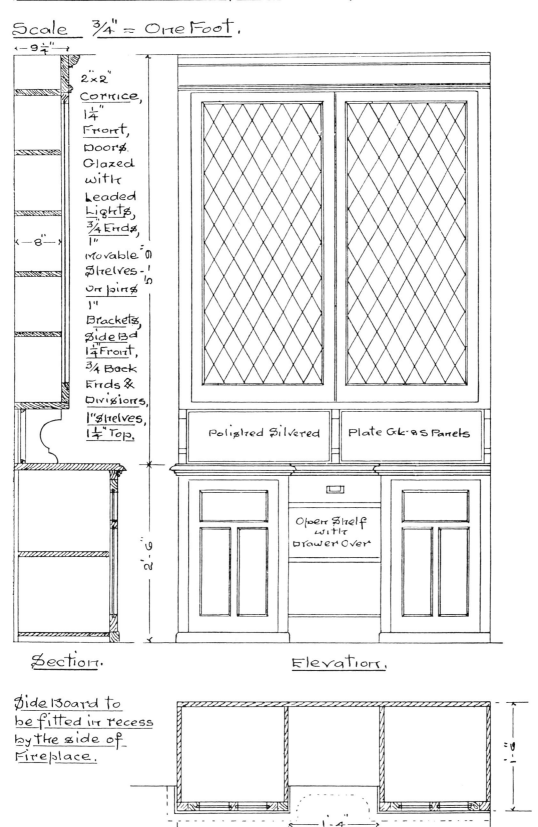

2"×2" Cornice, 1¼" Front, Doors. Glazed with Leaded Lights, ¾ Ends, 1" Movable Shelves - on pins 1" Brackets, Side Bd 1¼" Front, ¾ Back Ends & Divisions, 1" Shelves, 1¼" Top.

Polished Silvered

Plate Gk-ss Panels

Open Shelf with Drawer Over

Section.

Elevation.

Side Board to be fitted in recess by the side of Fireplace.

1'-7"

1'-4"

Plan.

1'-7"

277

Plate **150.**

Side Board with Cupboard over, Fixture.
Details,   Scale 3" = One Foot.

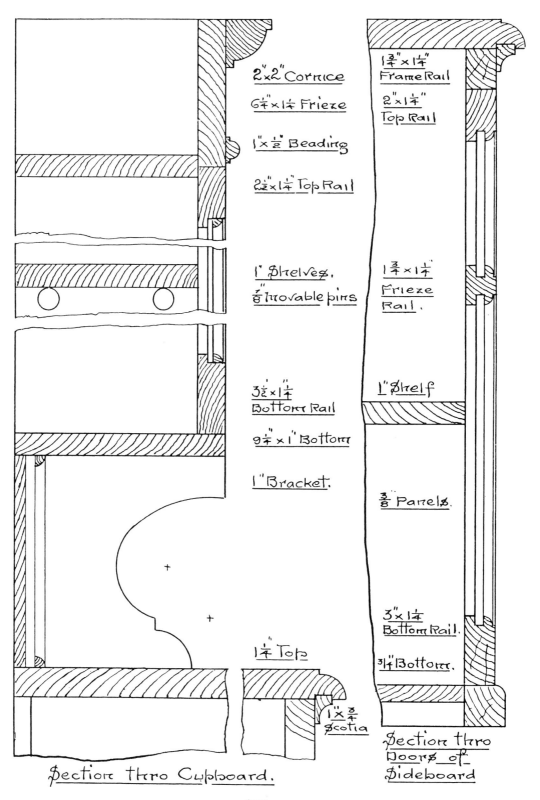

2"x2" Cornice

6¼"x1¼" Frieze

1"x½" Beading

2½"x1¼" Top Rail

1" Shelves.
⅞" movable pins

3½"x1¼" Bottom Rail

9¼"x1" Bottom

1" Bracket.

1¼" Top

1"x¾" Scotia

1¾"x1¼" Frame Rail

2"x1¼" Top Rail

1¾"x1¼" Frieze Rail.

1" Shelf

⅜" Panels.

3"x1¼" Bottom Rail.

3¼" Bottom.

Section thro Cupboard.

Section thro Doors of Sideboard

PLATE **151.**

Sideboard with Cupboard over, Fixture.

Details   Scale 1½" = One Foot.

Full Size Details of Framing
1. Sideboard.
2. Cupboard

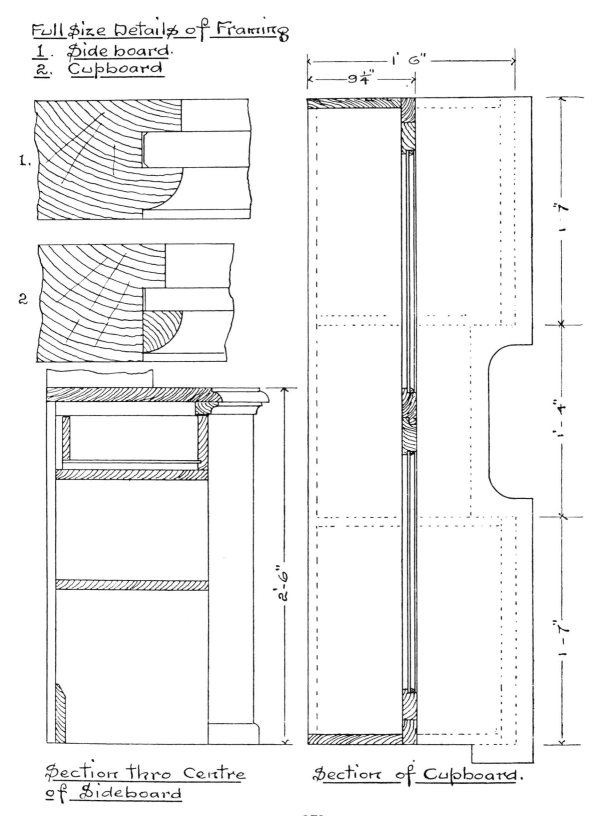

1' 6"

9¼"

1' 7"

1' 4"

2'-6"

1' 7"

Section thro Centre
of Sideboard

Section of Cupboard.

SPECIFICATION OF PORCH TO ENTRANCE.

(PLATES 152–154.)

THE framing to porch to have 4″ × 2″ wall-posts and mullions, 4″ × 4″ corner-posts, 4″ × 2½″ head, to have ½″ beaded stops nailed on to form rebate. Sills and transoms 6″ × 3″, rebated, beaded, weathered, and throated. Sashes to be 2″, ovolo-moulded, and rebated for glass; bottom sashes to have one horizontal bar, and glazed with 21 oz. best British sheet glass; the fanlights and gable over door to be glazed with tinted cathedral glass. The gable sash over door to be ovolo-moulded and rebated with bars as detail, the bottom rail to have moulded edge. Door to be 2″, framed and panelled, top portion prepared for glass, and glazed with 21 oz. best British sheet glass. Hang door with 4″ brass butts, and put 6″ two-bolt mortice lock and gun-metal furniture.

One bottom sash on each side to be side hung on 3″ brass butts and fitted with 12″ brass casement stays and fasteners complete. One fanlight on each side, also fanlight over door, to be hung at top opening outwards on 3″ brass butts, and fitted with brass openers and cords complete.

Put framed and shaped brackets under ends of plate as detail.

Rafters to be 4″ × 2″, rebated, moulded, and hollow grooved, with 2″ × 1½″ grooved and rounded capping. Ridge 7½″ × 1½″ rebated and moulded. Barge rafters 6″ × 2″, rebated, hollow grooved, and moulded, with rebated and double rounded capping and quarter-round moulding nailed on face of barge rafter.

Ridge roll $2\frac{1}{2}''$, bevel rebated. Put $9'' \times \frac{7}{8}''$ board at eaves, the rafters to be cut to receive these boards. The boards at ridge to be $5'' \times 1\frac{1}{4}''$, mitred at ridge.

Put $4''$ half-round cast-iron gutter at eaves on proper gutter brackets screwed to feet of rafters.

Cover the ridge with 5 lb. lead properly dressed over rolls and down to glass. Put 5 lb. lead stepped flashings on wall, wedged into joints of brickwork, and dressed over rafters on to glass

The roof to be glazed with Hartley's roll $\frac{1}{8}''$ plate. The caps over rafters to be bedded in white lead and screwed to rafters with brass screws.

The whole of the joints of frame and roof to be painted with good red-lead paint before being fixed.

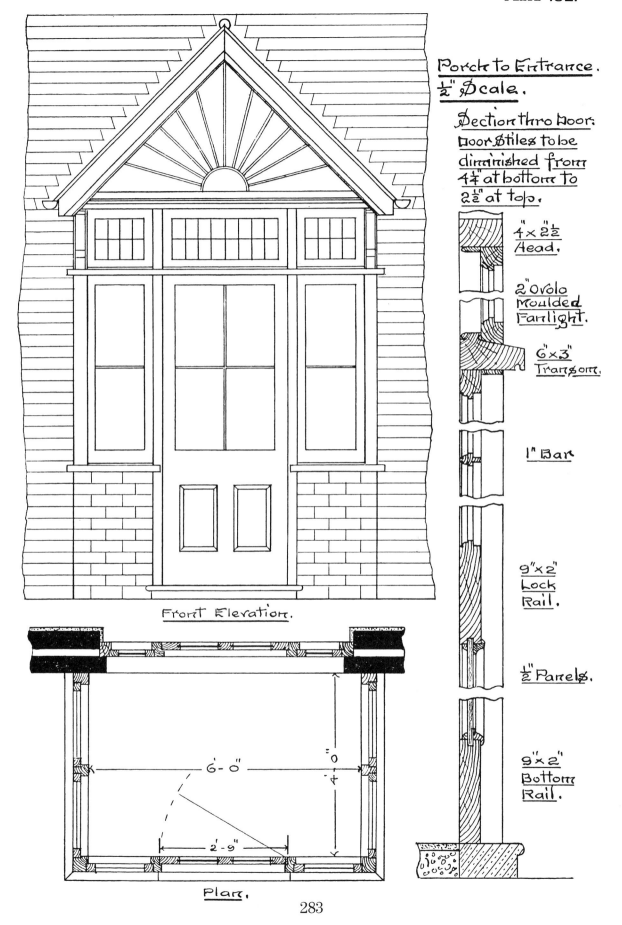

PLATE 152.

Porch to Entrance.
½" Scale.

Section thro Door.
Door Stiles to be
diminished from
4¼ at bottom to
2½ at top.

4"×2½
Head.

2" Ovolo
Moulded
Fanlight.

6"×3"
Transom.

1" Bar

9"×2"
Lock
Rail.

½" Panels.

9"×2"
Bottom
Rail.

Front Elevation.

6-0"

4'-0"

2'-9"

Plan.

283

Plate 153.

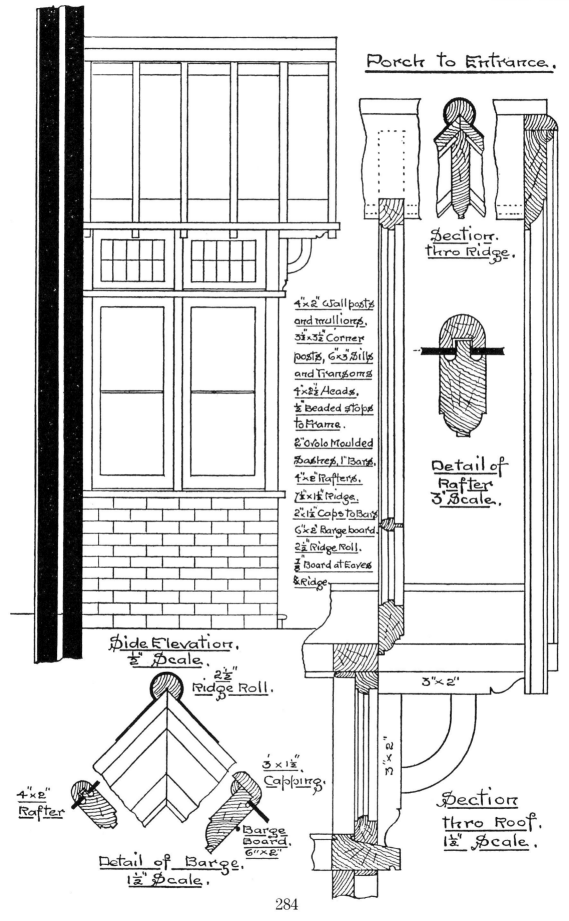

Porch to Entrance.

Section thro Ridge.

Detail of Rafter 3" Scale.

4"x2" Wall posts and mullions. 3½"x3½" Corner posts, 6"x3" Sills and Transoms 4"x2½" Heads. ½" Beaded stops to Frame. 2" Ovolo Moulded Sashes, 1" Bars. 4"x2" Rafters. 7½"x1½" Ridge. 2"x1½" Caps to Bars 6"x2" Barge board. 2½" Ridge Roll. ⅞" Board at Eaves & Ridge.

Side Elevation, ½" Scale.

2½" Ridge Roll.

3"x1½" Capping.

4"x2" Rafter

Barge Board, 6"x2"

Detail of Barge. 1½" Scale.

3"x2"

3"x2"

Section thro Roof. 1½" Scale.

PLATE **154.**

Details of Porch to Entrance.

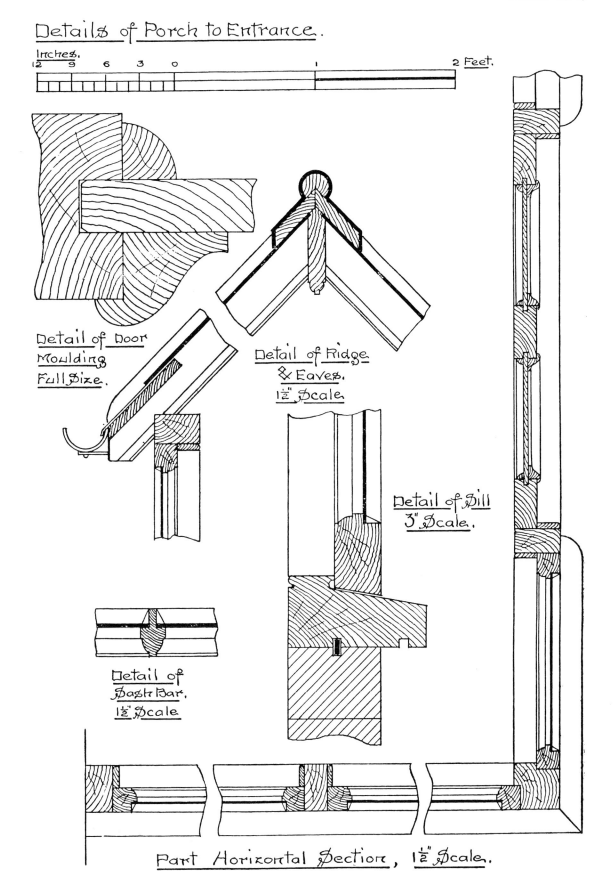

Detail of Door
Moulding
Full Size.

Detail of Ridge
& Eaves.
1½" Scale.

Detail of Sill
3" Scale.

Detail of
Sash Bar.
1½" Scale

Part Horizontal Section, 1½" Scale.

SPECIFICATION OF HOOD OVER FRONT DOOR.

(PLATE 155.)

FORM hood over front door with $3'' \times 2''$ bearers, with ends cut and pinned into wall, $5'' \times 1\frac{1}{2}''$ chamfered fascia mitred at angles, with $3'' \times 3''$ ovolo-moulding planted on face. Cover the top with $1''$ wrot, grooved and tongued flooring firred to falls as drawing. Lay 5 lb. lead covering dressed down over edges and copper nailed $3''$ apart, the back edge to be turned up $3''$ against wall. Put 5 lb. cover flashing wedged into joint of brickwork.

Put $1\frac{1}{4}''$ framed and panelled soffit moulded on solid, and screwed to underside of bearers.

The brackets to be cut, framed, shaped, and moulded to detail out of oak, with $6'' \times 4''$ tapered wall piece, $4'' \times 4''$ head with moulded ends, and $3'' \times 3''$ curved bracket pieces.

PLATE 155.

Hood over Front Door. $\frac{3}{4}$" Scale.

Inches.
12 . 9 . 6 . 3 . 0   1   2   3   4   5   6   Feet. 7

Detail of Bracket.

Specification.
Bearers, 3"x 2"
Fascia, 5"x 1½"
Moulding 3"x 3"
1" Boarded Top
Covered with
5 lb lead.
1½ Framed, panelled,
& moulded Soffit.
Brackets 4" thick
Framed out of Oak.

Elevation.

Section thro Fascia.
3" Scale.

SPECIFICATION OF HOOD OVER FRONT DOOR.

(PLATE 156.)

THE bearers to be 3″ × 2″, with ends cut and pinned into wall; 6″ × 2″ fascia mitred at angles, with 3″ × 3″ moulding planted on face. Top to be covered with 1″ wrot, grooved and tongued flooring firred to falls; on this lay 5 lb. lead turned up against wall 3″ and down over edges, and copper nailed 3″ apart. Put 4 lb. lead cover flashing wedged into joint of brickwork. Put framed, panelled, and solid moulded soffit in six panels. The soffit to be fastened to underside of bearers with screws.

The brackets to be 4″ thick out of oak, cut, shaped, and worked to detail, and dowelled to corbel stones.

The corbel stones to be 8″ × 7½″ × 6″, with moulded front and sides returned back to face line of brickwork.

The joints of woodwork to be painted with red-lead paint before fixing.

PLATE 156.

Hood over Front Door. $\frac{3}{4}''$ Scale

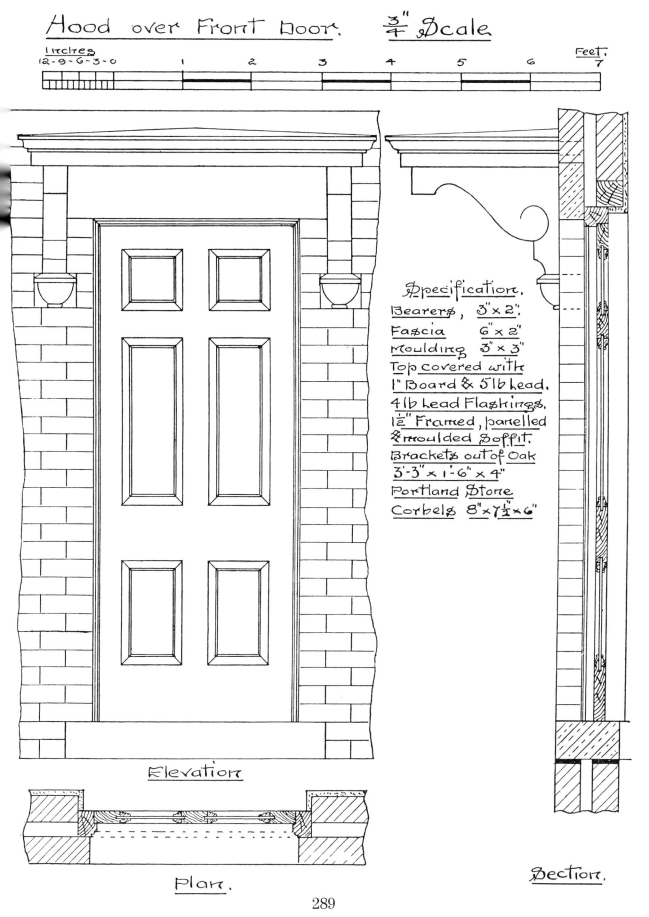

Inches
12-9-6-3-0   1   2   3   4   5   6   Feet. 7

Specification.
Bearers, 3" x 2".
Fascia   6" x 2"
Moulding   3" x 3"
Top covered with
1" Board & 5 lb lead.
4 lb lead Flashings.
1½" Framed, panelled
& moulded Soffit.
Brackets out of Oak
3'-3" x 1'-6" x 4"
Portland Stone
Corbels 8" x 7½" x 6"

Elevation

Plan.

Section.

SPECIFICATION OF HOOD OVER FRONT DOOR WITH CURVED TOP.

(PLATE 157.)

PROVIDE and fix over front door, hood as drawing, with $5'' \times 3\frac{1}{2}''$ moulded fascia mitred at angles, and with curved piece in front. The bearers to be $4'' \times 2''$ curved. Cover the top with $1''$ wrot, grooved and tongued flooring in narrow widths, and on this lay 5 lb. lead turned up against wall face $3''$ and down over edge of fascia, and copper nailed $3''$ apart. Put 5 lb. lead cover flashing properly wedged into joint of brickwork.

The soffit of hood to be covered with $\frac{3}{4}''$ V-jointed match-board in narrow widths.

The brackets to have $4'' \times 2\frac{1}{2}''$ wall pieces, $4'' \times 2\frac{1}{2}''$ heads with ends cut and pinned into wall, and $4'' \times 3\frac{1}{2}''$ curved bracket pieces. Put $1\frac{1}{2}'' \times 1\frac{1}{2}''$ vertical bars. The brackets to be properly framed and pinned together. All joints to be painted with good red-lead paint before putting together.

PLATE **157.**

Hood over Front Door. Curved Top. $\frac{3}{4}$" Scale.

Inches
12·9·6·3·0   1   2   3   4   5   6   Feet. 7

Moulded Fascia 5"x3½" Curved bearers 4"x2" 1" Boarded Top covered
with 5lb Lead, ¾" Matchboard Soffit. Brackets:- 4"x2½" Plate & Wall
piece, 4"x3½" Curved
Bracket piece, 1½" Bars.

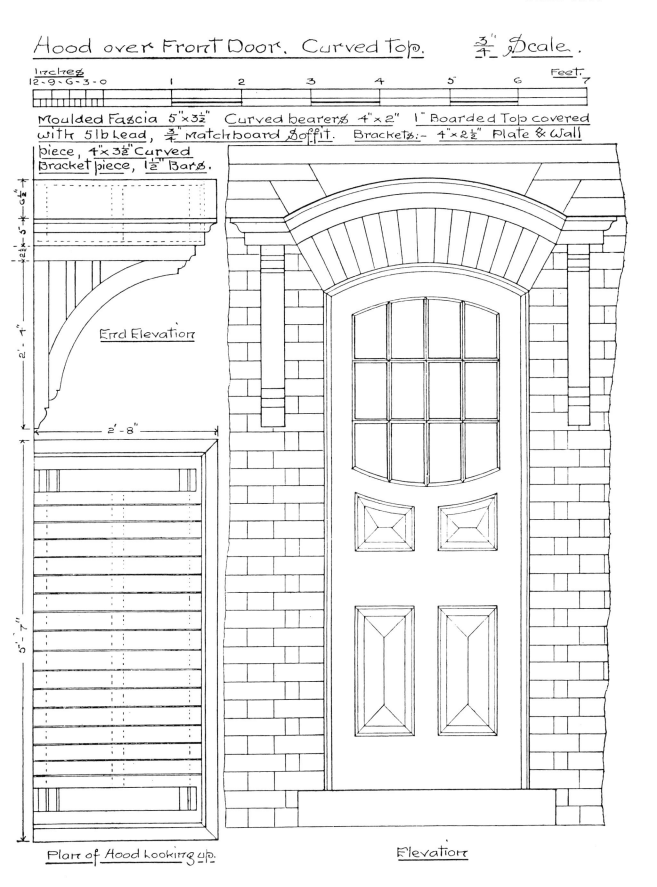

End Elevation

2' - 8"

2' - 4"

5' - 7"

Plan of Hood Looking up.

Elevation

BUILDING CONSTRUCTION DRAWING.   By Richard B. Eaton.
(Messrs. E. & F. N. Spon, Ltd.   *Price 3s. 6d. net.*)

This manual consists of Part VI of a series. It contains joinery drawings and specifications, being intended for the use of the elementary student and the artisan. There are 30 plates illustrating such fittings as skylights, panelling, dressers, and the like. The book is well adapted to its purpose and should give a good idea of the methods of framing and fixing joinery.

Jan. 6, 1921

Municipal Engineering and The Sanitary Record

Building Construction Drawing : A Class Book for the Elementary Student and Artisan. By RICHARD B. EATON, Lecturer on Building Construction. Part 6, *Joinery Drawings and Specifications.* 30 plates. Price 3s. 6d. (3s. 9d. post free). E. and F. N. Spon. 74 pp. 4to.

THIS is the sixth of the series of practical drawings with specifications for the use of students in building construction compiled by Mr. Eaton. Amongst the drawings with specifications are those of skirtings and picture and chair rails, architraves, casement frames with pivot-hung sashes, skylights, lantern light with flat and octagonal tops, kitchen dressers, bookcase and sideboard, sideboard with cupboard over, entrance porch, and hoods over front door. The drawings are clear and fully detailed, whilst the accompanying specifications are practical and to be commended.

JANUARY 28, 1921

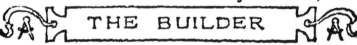

THE BUILDER

Building Construction Drawing. Part VI. By RICHARD B. EATON. London : E. & F. N. Spon, Ltd. Price, 3s. 6d. net.

PART VI of this series of books, which is of use to apprentices and students, consists, like the others, of large-scale detail drawings, each provided with a specification. The method in which this and the illustrations are presented is practically in the same form actually employed by the contractor during the erection of buildings. The salient features of Part VI, which treats of joinery, include interior fittings for small houses, skirtings, picture and chair rails, architraves, mouldings, panelling, kitchen dressers, bookcases, and sideboards. Exterior work is represented by pivot-hung sashes, skylights, porches, and hoods to front doors.

THE ARCHITECTS' JOURNAL
Book Notice
Training the Artisan.

One of the most popular topics for conversation arising out of the building trade dilution controversy is that concerning the various methods of training apprentices, and remarkably different opinions are often expressed as to the time required to produce a skilled artisan or mechanic. No matter what opinions are held, it is clear, for obvious reasons, that working from the specification, either alone or in conjunction with the $\frac{1}{8}$ scale or detail drawings, should form the essential part of instruction. Perhaps the chief difficulties immediately confronting the apprentice are those connected with " reading " the various drawings, and understanding the almost legal formality of the specification clauses. To visualise the work in plan, elevation, and section is an "art " only in many cases to be laboriously acquired. To-day, however, the apprentice is fortunate in having within his reach the very practical class-books of Mr. Richard B. Eaton, from which valuable assistance may be obtained. Part VI., just published, consists, like the others, of large-scale detail drawings, each provided with a specification, the method in which they are presented coinciding with that actually employed during the erection of buildings. The first three parts of these books deal with general construction, and the last three with joinery generally, the salient features of Part VI. embracing interior fittings for small houses, skirtings, picture and chair rails, architraves, mouldings, panelling, kitchen dressers, bookcases, and sideboards. Exterior work is represented by pivot-hung sashes, skylights, porches, and hoods to front doors.

Building Construction Drawing. Part VI.
By Richard B. Eaton. E. & F. N. Spon, Ltd.
Price 3/6 net.

ESTATE CLERKS OF WORKS

BUILDING CONSTRUCTION DRAWING.

This is a new work by Mr. Richard B. Eaton, a member of this SOCIETY. It was said on one occasion in the JOURNAL that there appears to be no defined limit to the occupation of an estate clerk of works, and a case in kind in evidence of this is that Mr. Eaton fills the position also of Lecturer on Building Construction at the Poole School of Art and Technology.

His book contains twenty-six plates of details of constructional work in connection with brick-work and carpentry, accompanied with brief specifications. It is a useful book, and should be of assistance in setting out workshop details and working drawings, for which it is primarily intended. It is of greater value to the student than to clerks of works of long experience. In this respect the author says its object is to provide the student in building construction and others connected with the building trades with drawings which will help them to acquire a knowledge of drawing and the simpler forms of building construction.

It is published by E. and F. N. Spon, Ltd., 57, Haymarket, London, and the price is 1s. 6d.

From "The Surveyor" Jan 16ᵗʰ 1920

Building Construction Drawing, Parts 4 & 5. By Richard. B. Eaton. 5s nett each. London: E & F. Spon Ltd.

These two parts of a class book on building construction are intended chiefly for the elementary student and artisan, but will be found very useful by many architects and engineers. The arrangement differs from other text books on building construction, as, in addition to providing some fifty plates of joinery details, a specification and measured bill is provided for each door or window illustrated. The drawings are clearly drawn to a fairly large scale, and the specifications and measured bills give these books a more practical and more useful character than books of this class usually possess. They will be found extremely useful in most drawing offices, and especially where, as in the case of surveyors to the smaller councils, architectural design and quantity surveying are not a usual part of their ordinary routine work.

The Librarian. June 1921.

BUILDING CONSTRUCTION DRAWING : A Class-Book for the Elementary Student and Artisan. By R. B. Eaton. Part VI.—Joinery Drawings and Specifications. 30 plates. Spon, Ltd., London, 1921, 3/6.
Parts I., II. and III. of this well-known series deals with general construction. Parts IV. and V. are concerned with joinery generally. The completed work is one of greatest usefulness to everyone concerned with buildings and their construction.

TIMBER IMPORTS AND CONVERSION METHODS.

A COMPARISON.

By RICHARD B. EATON.

On looking back over the past thirty-five years one is struck with the difference in the sizes of the timber imported and the methods employed for converting it into joinery.

Having lived in a seaport town where the timber imports are very large, I have been able to note the changes that have come with the years. My first recollection of a timber ship was a barque laden with balk timber having sealed ports near the bow and stern for unloading. On arrival at the dock side these ports were unsealed and the timber passed through and floated away to the timber ponds. There were many timber ponds in our harbour in those days—to-day there is only one. The ships now for the most part are steamers and come into port very heavily laden, the timber being piled high above the deck, the deck cargo being mostly 4in. by 2in. or small sized timber. The size of timber imported to-day varies from a lath to a balk; in the old days it was only large sized timber. I can well remember the first shipment of 4in. by 2in. being discharged on our quay, its importation causing quite a revolution in the building trade. The advantage of that particular size of timber is difficult to estimate; to estimate the benefit of 4in. by 2in., and other scantlings, you have only to examine an old roof from the inside and compare it with an ordinary modern roof. In the old form of roof you find the purlins and rafters cut from round sticks not sufficiently large to cut die square, the latter notched down to the purlins, and in many cases the rafters not strong enough to carry the weight of the roof, especially if it is tiled. In the modern roof every timber is cut die square and thereby a good fit is ensured, all things being equal. In the case of flooring many of the old floors were laid with very wide boards. I have seen them from 18in. to 24in. in width. These were not brought to a thickness throughout, but simply rebated down to a thickness at the edge to form a gauge, then traversed across the board where the joists occurred, usually with an adze. Sawn plasterers' laths were unknown in the old days, now the trouble is to get a riven lath. Personally I prefer the riven lath, and I think most practical men will agree that better work is obtained by using them.

Many other species of timber are imported to-day. The fancy woods that have been introduced in modern times lend themselves to the production of good joinery, and so there has been a marked improvement in the appearance of the interiors of modern buildings.

If you wanted a wide board thirty years ago, American pine was about the only wood you could get; now there are many wide timbers imported, such as Kauri, Oregon, and Columbian pine, Sequoia, American whitewood, etc. Mahogany imports have also undergone a change; thirty years ago it was rare to get a soft mahogany since only Spanish or Honduras was obtainable; now we get a kind of mahogany which I have heard lightly spoken of as having grown between a mahogany and a pine tree, and not being quite sure which it wanted to become, turned out half and half, poor stuff at the best, and requiring a lot of the polisher's art to get a good mahogany face. The good old English oak has formidable rivals in Austrian and American, and very excellent joinery has been produced from each. The advance made in the production of labour-saving machinery is responsible for the change in the size of timber imported to-day.

In making a comparison of the methods employed in the conversion of timber into joinery, I can well remember the time when doors were made throughout by hand, and when mouldings and skirtings were worked by hand, the mouldings being struck with a plane provided with a hole in the end for the insertion of an iron bar to permit two men using the plane, the front man being called the donkey. Architrave mouldings were made by using a base board of, say, 4in. by ½in. with a returned bead on edge, then a 2in. moulding worked and planted on, in this way forming a sunk moulding. Skirting boards and weather boards were also prepared by hand and the apprentice in those days had to go through the mill in using the plane and saw, and his muscles too. Joinery throughout was hand-made, and some very fine examples are extant, which prove that many of the craftsmen of the old days were good men. To-day the young joiners are in many cases only fitters up, following on after the machine.

Compare the man sitting on a dozen door stiles punching the mortices through by hand, with an up-to-date steam morticing machine, or a man with a rip saw cutting tenons with a steam tenoning machine, or the joiner with his routers and scrapes on a piece of circular moulding, with a vertical spindle machine. Surely the new type of joiner has a gentleman's life, from the hard work point of view, to what the old joiners had, and about double the pay for his job. The first planing machine I can recollect was an attachment for use on a circular saw bench. It was in the form of a disc about 3ft. in diameter with four sets of gouge irons and four sets of plane irons all fixed radiating from the centre; it was a most dangerous thing to use and very noisy, and was far from being efficient. The sawyer's work has undergone a radical change. As a boy I have watched with interest the sawyers in a pit sawing through a long log of timber, and making a good straight job of it too. Now we have circular saws and frame saws, with every appliance to ensure a straight and even cut. The work of the attendants on either type of machine is reduced to a minimum by the attachments provided with them. The march of science and the brains of the inventor have done much to improve the conditions of the apprentice, artizan, and employer, the work is lighter all round, and in many cases is turned out better than a good deal that was used on new buildings half a century since.

NEW BOOKS.

"BUILDING CONSTRUCTION DRAWING." PartI II. By Richard B Eaton. (E. and F. Spon, Limited; price 3s. net).

This is a class book for the student and artisan, consisting of detailed scale drawings of many examples of the work commonly met with in ordinary building practice. Included among them are plans, elevations, and sections of a small villa residence, and a short specification for these drawings is added. For the rest, letterpress is dispensed with, the drawings, with the notes and dimensions upon them, being self-explanatory. One of the plates is here reproduced as an example of the useful style of drawing adopted. It has been slightly reduced for convenience of printing in our pages, and consequently the scale indication does not apply. We have often had inquiries from students and others for drawings of precisely this character, and we have no doubt that the work will be widely appreciated.

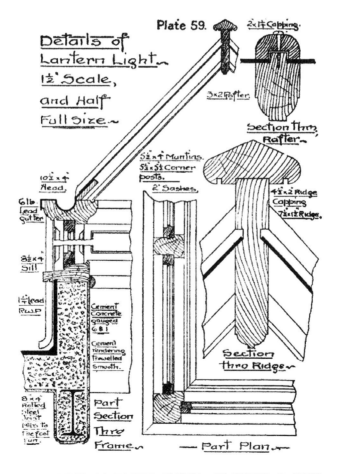

FROM "BUILDING CONSTRUCTION DRAWING."—BY RICHARD B. EATON.

NEW~BOOKS

Publishers are invited to send for review books dealing with Architecture, Building, and Craft subjects.

" BUILDING CONSTRUCTION DRAWING," Part II., by Richard B. Eaton. (E. and F. N. Spon, Ltd. Price 1s. 6d. net.)

This is primarily a set of drawings—a little more advanced than those in Part I. of this work, which we reviewed on its appearance, yet still comparatively simple. The aim is to teach the student of building construction by giving him examples of every-day work to study and draw. Each drawing is accompanied by a specification, which gives all the explanation the student needs. The practical and useful character of the drawings can best be judged from an example. We have, therefore, reproduced on a slightly smaller scale Mr. Eaton's drawing of a dormer window with curved top. The dimensions are given in the accompanying specification, and are not, therefore, marked on the drawings, and it should be observed that the scale indication applies to the drawing as given in Mr. Eaton's book, not as here reproduced.

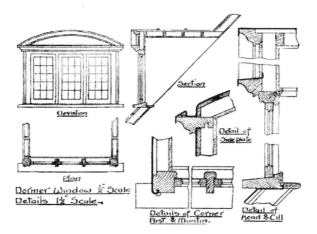

FROM "BUILDING CONSTRUCTION DRAWING," PART II.—BY RICHARD B. EATON.

LONDON COUNTY COUNCIL.

Letters should be addressed.
THE EDUCATION OFFICER.
EDUCATION OFFICES.
VICTORIA EMBANKMENT, W.C
They should shew the complete
postal address and designation
of the writer, and should, as far as
possible relate to one subject only

PLEASE QUOTE AT THE HEAD
OF ANY REPLY

EDUCATION OFFICES.

VICTORIA EMBANKMENT. W.C.

7 - MAY 1915

Sir,

    I have to inform you that the Committee concerned have decided to add the undermentioned book**s** to the requisition list named:-

Requisition list of books suggested for use in evening institutes -

Building Construction Drawing - Parts I and II, R.B.Eaton, 1s.6d. net, each part, 3s. net complete.

    I am, Sir,

        Your obedient Servant,

R. Blair

        Education Officer

    The resignation of Mr. R. B. Eaton, assistant in the Borough Engineer's department, consequent upon his reaching the age for superannuation, having been reported, it was resolved that a superannuation allowance, under the provisions of the Local Government and other Officers' Superannuation Act, 1922, be paid to him, calculated at the rate of one sixtieth of his salary in respect of each year of his service.—The Mayor paid tribute to an old and valued servant, and on his motion, seconded by Mr. G. W. Green, it was agreed the Clerk should send on behalf of the Council a letter expressive of their thanks to Mr. Eaton for his valued services for 23 years.

TECHNICAL SCHOOLS AND APPRENTICESHIP.

By R. B. Eaton.

Referring to the article on " After Effects of the War " in the February number in so far as it refers to Technical Schools and apprenticeship, I was apprenticed to a builder, served my full time, and have for the last twenty years been a teacher in connection with the building trades in Technical Schools.

I am of opinion that apprenticeship is necessary, but the system that has obtained for many years is out of date and wants quite a different arrangement. I am convinced, however, that with many employers, in the provinces at any rate, the apprentice is carefully taught his trade if he shows a desire to learn it, and as a result is given good work to practise on, and the apprentice who shows no inclination in this direction is often neglected. The difficulty at the present time is to get students to attend the classes and to keep them interested in the subjects taught, owing to the attractions of a different nature which did not exist in my young days, but are now found in every direction. It does happen occasionally that the teachers assume a higher plane and consider themselves far above their pupils in many ways : this is to be condemned. They should be, or have been, practical men, and know how to do work themselves as well as profess to teach others how to do it.

I have found one reason for the slackness of attendance to be the apathy shown by some employers. Another is that the technical questions set artisan students and apprentices are often of a nature that would require a high school education to solve. I remember one given out many years since where some of the students had left an elementary school only about two years and had served two years of an apprenticeship, as follows :—" What are the component parts of granite? " I sometimes wonder who originates these puzzles and if they have any practical knowledge in connection therewith. The examinations for technical teachers, too, are often absurd. I have known clever, intelligent joiners outclassed by elementary school teachers for carpentry and joinery who had read themselves up by means of books, but who possessed insufficient knowledge of how to join two pieces of wood together.

If we are to keep our place among the nations we must give more time to technical education and scientific teaching. We have ample proof that the Germans have practised these for many years, and we can now see the result and our own remissness in this direction.